Gerald Lamont Thomas

African American Preaching

The Contribution
of Dr. Gardner C. Taylor

PETER LANG
New York • Washington, D.C./Baltimore • Bern
Frankfurt am Main • Berlin • Brussels • Vienna • Oxford

Library of Congress Cataloging-in-Publication Data

Thomas, Gerald Lamont.
African American preaching: the contribution
of Dr. Gardner C. Taylor / Gerald Lamont Thomas.
p. cm. — (Martin Luther King, Jr. memorial studies in religion,
culture, and social development; v. 7)
Includes bibliographical references.
1. African American preaching. 2. Taylor,
Gardner C. I. Title. II. Series.
BV4241.5.T46   251'.0092—dc21   2003011135
ISBN 0–8204–3127–3 (Hardcover)
ISBN 0-8204-7412-6 (Paperback)
ISSN 1052–181X

Bibliographic information published by **Die Deutsche Bibliothek**.
Die Deutsche Bibliothek lists this publication in the "Deutsche
Nationalbibliografie"; detailed bibliographic data is available
on the Internet at http://dnb.ddb.de/.

© 2004 Peter Lang Publishing, Inc., New York
275 Seventh Avenue, 28th Floor, New York, NY 10001
www.peterlangusa.com

To the honor and memory of my
Mom and Dad, Janie and Eddie Thomas,
two loving, devoted and wonderful parents,
who taught me to trust in Jesus,
be grateful for every blessing,
and help those who are unable
to help themselves.

CONTENTS

FOREWORD

I am greatly pleased at the appearance of this volume, but not alone for the obvious reasons of pride and pleasure at seeing one's work seeming to merit scrutiny. The preaching art is such a difficult, but fulfilling, undertaking that much is to be learned from those who have served the proclamation of the gospel. One adds quickly that what may be learned is substantially enhanced by seeing the mistakes of the subject under study. Such a method may be described as a kind of homiletical via negativa, or getting at what is, or ought to be, by seeing what ought not to be, to borrow from eastern orthodoxy. In that sense, if in no other, this book may be greatly helpful.

After sixty, and more, years of attempting to preach the gospel, the conviction grows that more is left unuttered than can ever be expressed, even inadequately. This volume will reveal that Gerald Lamont Thomas has astutely examined one journeyman's efforts with rare skill and insight. His analysis will, hopefully, help many to see what to seek, and maybe of greater importance, what to avoid in pursuit of the high calling of preaching the Gospel of Jesus Christ.

Dr. Gardner C. Taylor

ACKNOWLEDGMENTS

I wish to acknowledge, with gratitude, those individuals who have been chosen by God to assist me along my spiritual and ministerial journey with their prayers, friendship and guidance. Of exceptional significance for this manuscript has been the faithful commitment of my dear comrades in the struggle, Charlotte and Lallie Banks, proprietors of LC Technologies, Inc.

I am indebted to those pastors who have guided me in the faith and kept my hope alive in the midst of trials, doubts, and failures: the late R. M. Jones and the wonderful people of the Price Memorial A.M.E. Zion Church of Youngstown, Ohio, where I was born into the church; the late Dr. E. V. Hill and the dedicated members of the Mt. Zion Missionary Baptist Church of Los Angeles, California, who licensed me to preach the Gospel of Jesus Christ; Dr. A. Russell Awkard and the loving parishioners of the New Zion Baptist Church of Louisville, Kentucky, who nurtured me during my theological training at Southern Seminary; Dr. Morris W. Lee and the kind, considerate members of the Third Baptist Church of Youngstown, Ohio, who ordained me into the pastoral ministry and supported me during my entire ten year seminary career. I am grateful to the Concord Baptist Church of Christ, Brooklyn, New York, for the prodigious insights of Rev. Charles L. Gill, a former Associate Minister, and the Pastor, Dr. Gary Simpson

I acknowledge, with deep gratitude, the four congregations who called me to serve as their pastoral leader and helped me to preach on Sunday mornings. They are the Pilgrim Baptist Church of Midway, Kentucky, the Burnett Avenue Baptist Church of Louisville, Kentucky, the Metropolitan Baptist Church of Philadelphia, Pennsylvania and the Shiloh Baptist Church of Plainfield, New Jersey.

I thank God for words of encouragement during some "tough times" from my true friends and brothers, Rev. L. B. Jones, II, Dr. J. Wendell Mapson, II, Rev. G. Lind Taylor, and Rev. Walter Thompson. I am also grateful to Dr. Manfred Brauch, the former president of the Eastern Baptist Theological Seminary in Wynnewood, Pennsylvania for extending the opportunity to share my gifts with the many students who endured my preaching classes for the ten years of my professorship. Much love and appreciations to Dr. Leah G. Fitchue, Dr. J. Deotis Roberts, Dr. Horace O. Russell, and Dr. James Earl Massey for their guidance, exhortation, and nurturing spirits.

I must also thank, with all my heart, my sister, Carolyn Jean Mitchell, for her wisdom and confidence in her little brother, and my three children, Seth, Camille and Keenan, who serve as a constant reminder that their sacrifices in assisting me to "get the work done" will never be forgotten.

To the one who said, "If you're going to preach, then you must be prepared to do it." Thank you.

I owe recognition to Dr. Mozella Mitchell, former president of the Society for the Study of Black Religion, for making this publication possible in the series, "Martin Luther King, Jr., Memorial Studies in Religion, Culture and Social Development." Praise God for you!

Special appreciations to Dr. Paul Debusman, former Reference Librarian of the James P. Boyce Library at Southern Seminary, for his knowledge, support, and patience during my thesis research.

Most of all, I want to acknowledge the kindness and generosity of one of this world's most prolific preachers, Dr. Gardner C. Taylor, who opened his heart, mind and soul to me during this study of his life and preaching ministry. You are a gracious man, filled with wit and humor, but also replete with genius and brilliance. Thank you for the many late night vignettes and introducing me to those saints, gone but not forgotten, who assisted me in learning more about Gardner, for the blessed privilege of meeting and sharing with your "in house grammarian," and finally, the opportunity to examine your artistic gift of preaching the Gospel of Jesus Christ.

Plainfield, New Jersey
December 2003

CHAPTER ONE

Introduction

The purpose of this book is to analyze the preaching ministry of Dr. Gardner Calvin Taylor, Senior Pastor Emeritus of the Concord Baptist Church of Christ in Brooklyn, New York.[1] This analysis will be governed by rhetorical criticism in the appraisal of the preacher's homiletical theory and practice. Within this stated purpose are several implications. Any exposition on preaching is based on the assumption that preaching is of such vital importance that Christianity thrives from it. This point is especially true within the African American church because preaching provides a presence of eschatological hope and spiritual healing against the evils of life—past, present, and future.

A commentary on preaching also implies that there is a need for studying a particular preacher's sermons and concepts related to the art and craft of preaching. With respect to Gardner Taylor, this is certainly the case. Although literature does not reflect a thesis or written work concerning Taylor, his preaching and lecturing have continued to flourish for over sixty years. He is in demand both internationally and nationally having preached on five continents. As a testament of his originality, *Time Magazine* honored him as "The Dean of the nation's black preachers."[2] In recognition of Taylor's esteem among all preachers, not only African Americans, *Ebony Magazine* asserted that he is "one of the greatest preachers in American history."[3]

African American preachers have been and persist to be a contributing phenomena within American history. In recent years scholars have paid increasing attention to African American preaching as an important source of African American culture.[4] As a conduit of the oral tradition of the African American community, the preaching event is unmatched in its historical role as a primary mediator for the African American community. Preaching is a prophetic voice, challenging issues of liberation, justice, love, and equality according to the Word of God.

Contemporary preaching theorists David Buttrick and Fred Craddock both have acknowledged the influence of the African American preaching event upon their personal development and methodology in the discipline.[5] Throughout the history of African American preaching, gifted persons such as Richard Allen,

Frederick Douglas, John Jasper, Sojourner Truth, Henry Highland Garnett, Amanda Berry Smith, Henry McNeil Turner, J. C. Austin, Sr., C. A. Tindley, C. T. Walker, L. K. Williams, Adam Clayton Powell, Jr., Manual Scott, Sr., C. L. Franklin, Sandy Ray, Ida B. Robinson, J. H. Jackson, Otis Moss, E. V. Hill, Caesar A. W. Clark, Samuel D. Proctor, Martin Luther King, Jr., Prathia Hall Wynn, John Hurst Adams, James Forbes, Joseph E. Lowery, Ernestine Cleveland Reems, Jesse Jackson, William A. Jones, and countless others have left indelible imprints upon the rhetorical art of proclamation.

Another perspective on the final implication of expositions on preaching is that they are a "nurturing rather than an investigative endeavor."[6] The usual pattern of sermon study categorizes the characteristics of sermons rather than analyzing the methodology involved within sermon development.[7] Whereas the initial description of research seeks to convey the end of the product, the second type desires to investigate the means of the product. The focus of this effort will be to study and analyze Gardner Taylor's homiletical theory and rhetorical practice in relation to the African American preaching tradition.

In an attempt to analyze the discipline of homiletics to include the genius and contributions of one such as Taylor, the objective is to document and gain insight into his life, ministry, and preaching experiences. The goal is not to assist ministers in becoming clones of Taylor's discipline or practice. The purpose of this book is to present the significance of the African American preaching tradition in homiletics, as realized through the rhetorical gifts of Taylor.

Background of the Study

The primary thrust of this study is rooted in my personal growth and development within the African American church. Since the earliest days of my youth at the Price Memorial African Methodist Episcopal Zion Church in Youngstown, Ohio, I have been fond of preaching and preachers. This appreciation became increasingly evident upon becoming a member of the Mount Zion Missionary Baptist Church, Los Angeles, California in 1978. The late minister, Dr. E. V. Hill, demonstrated specific characteristics of the black preaching tradition. He evoked the use of call and response dialogue, rhythmic vocal toning, and a spiritual celebration that I vividly recalled and experienced during the primary stages of my faith development in Youngstown. It was under his tutelage that I acknowledged my calling into the gospel ministry. The exposure to talented preachers and preaching received at Mt. Zion continued to nurture my interest in studying the theory and practice of homiletics.

As a Ph.D. student, I sought to study "black preaching" through the eyes and ears of a credible African American scholar. Although it became a part of my spiritual development, the opportunity to study formally the background and composition of black preaching did not occur at the Master of Divinity level. I recall reading two books in my formative years related to the field by Dr. Henry H. Mitchell, a Visiting Professor of homiletics at the Interdenominational Theological Center in Atlanta, Georgia. They were *Black Preaching* and *The Recovery of Preaching*.[8] Since Southern Seminary requires two university courses, I studied under Dr. Mitchell at United Theological Seminary in Dayton, Ohio. There he served as an Adjunct Professor in the doctoral program. I enrolled in a second course, "Black Theology," which was offered at the Pittsburgh Theological Seminary and taught by another prominent African American scholar, Dr. J. Deotis Roberts. He is the former Distinguished Professor of Philosophy at Eastern Baptist Theological Seminary in Philadelphia, Pennsylvania.

I had the occasion to meet Dr. Mitchell in August, 1989, during which time we designed a course entitled: "African American Spirituality in Contemporary Homiletics." The objective of the course was to read and study works relating to the origins and developments of "old-time Negro preaching" and "black preaching" in comparison with current and modern trends in homiletics.[9] This study formally introduced me, through the nature and function of African American preaching, to an undiscovered and most vital heritage. Two works in particular, *Say Amen Brother!* by William Pipes and *I Got the Word in Me and I Can Sing It, You Know* by Gerald L. Davis, provided the basis for further study in this area.[10]

While pursuing a thesis topic for my dissertation which would further create an opportunity for in-depth research, Dr. Mitchell suggested the investigation of several African American ministers in different geographical regions who had experienced extremely successful pastorates. The idea, while valid, was shelved because of time constraints and the difficulties it would present with respect to securing necessary data. Instead, I opted for the thorough study of one minister of national renown, one who had proven himself over an extended period of time. This approach provided an opportunity to research, analyze, and critique a minister in relation to his contribution to the field of homiletics.

Immediately, the eminent preacher/scholar, Dr. Gardner Taylor, Sr. Pastor of the Concord Baptist Church of Christ, came to mind. His credentials met all of the criteria for this type of study and research. He had been a successful pastor of one of the largest Baptist churches in America, a past president of the Progressive National Baptist Convention, and finally a denominational leader throughout both the Baptist World Alliance and the World Council of Churches.

It was in May of 1990, coincidentally, that Gardner Taylor came to Louisville to preach the commencement address of Simmons Bible College at Shiloh Baptist Church. I was extended the opportunity to meet him at the airport. This made a perfect opportunity to discuss the idea of studying his rhetorical practice and homiletical theory. Upon sharing the idea with Taylor, he consented and agreed to assist me by providing sermon tapes and manuscripts of his pulpit ministry, a list of individuals—colleagues and parishioners—to interview who were familiar with his preaching development, and the names of former students whom he taught at the seminary level. He also consented to be a resource person throughout the project.

Dr. Taylor has lectured and preached extensively throughout the United States and the world. Efforts were made to obtain lecture tapes from seminaries, divinity schools, colleges and seminaries in which he had participated from around the country. In March of 1991, I visited Dr. Taylor in Brooklyn, New York and received copies of audio sermons taped at the Concord Baptist Church of Christ. Interviews were also scheduled and recorded with former parishioners in Ohio, Louisiana, and New York, relatives, former students, and colleagues. He has written three books. They include the 1976 Lyman Beecher Lectures: *How Shall They Preach*, *The Scarlet Thread*, and *Chariots Aflame*.[11] Further, he has also contributed sermons and articles to various periodicals and publications. Samples of his sermons were taken from both printed materials and video tapes.

Methodology

Research for this book began by examining African American preaching with regard to its origins, functions, developments, and practicality in the experience of both church and society. Chapters two and three of the study are intended as a broad survey and constructive overview of African American preaching since Africans arrived in America as slaves and indentured servants. Primary and secondary sources on preaching in regard to African American culture and tradition will also be considered. A working knowledge of the historical developments of African American preaching was necessary to examine Taylor's pulpit work.

Following the historical overview, the study moves towards an examination of Taylor's background, early influences, education and ministerial growth as they related to his development as a preacher of the Gospel in chapter four. Only biographical information pertinent to his growth as a minister is considered. This chapter will give direct attention to his preaching in relation to his career as a pastor, seminary professor, lecturer, and denominational leader.

After the life and ministry of the Louisiana native is examined, his theory and practice of preaching—as indicated by accessible materials, especially his lectures and writings—becomes the focus of concern in chapter five. The rhetorical elements of Taylor's sermonic discourse will be evaluated using rhetorical criticism from the artistic canon perspective. This approach offers the standards and qualities necessary to understand, critique, and improve sermonic discourse through rhetorical theory. The basis of the artistic canon was first derived from Aristotle's proof "of being constructed systematically and by our own skill."[12] The standards of judgment and criteria related to the artistic canon included: 1) The canons of criticism—how does the preacher apply invention, arrangement, style, memory, and delivery towards the sermon discourse?[13] 2) Speech training and experience—what were the influences of his parents and early home life upon the preacher's views, skills, and motivation? To what extent has he studied the efforts of other preachers and sermons in particular? Is he a natural or trained preacher or both?[14] 3) General reading and study habits—how well informed is the preacher? Does he acquire and digest general information? and 4) Methods of sermonic preparation[15]—how does the preacher collect materials for a given sermon? What steps does he follow in digesting and analyzing the problem? What steps does the preacher take in preparing a sermon manuscript? And what efforts does he make to check the accuracy of the facts and the soundness of his analysis? Following the study of Gardner Taylor's sermon preparation methodology, an evaluation of ten sermons covering forty years of his preaching will be analyzed using the above methods.

The conclusion endeavors to review, evaluate, and capsulize the key characteristics and contributions of Gardner Taylor's preaching. In this chapter the critic asks such questions as the following: How did the preacher apply the Gospel to those who heard him? Did the preacher's general attitudes toward the world around him suggest a realistic view of the topic? Why did Taylor take the given approach on the subject? What were some of the historical or social factors affecting his views and how have they been altered over time? Here the task will consist of looking at Taylor's preaching from a pastoral theological context. The final section also considers implications for further study as it relates to the historical African American pulpit and contemporary homiletics.

CHAPTER TWO

An Overview of African American Preaching and Preachers Part I

The historical developments of African American preaching and its origins are an ongoing pursuit in American Christianity. Since Africans arrived on these colonial shores around the year 1619, there has been a perpetual investigation into their religious beliefs and practice. In order to gain a proper perspective of African American preaching, its preachers and traditional religious background, it is imperative that one investigate the foundational roots of civilization.[16]

African Traditional Religions and their Beliefs

Africans brought to America via the slave trade had an extensive fundamental faith for centuries prior to hearing the American religion and doctrines of its Eurocentric founders. Henry Mitchell, in his book, *Black Belief*, writes:

> For many years African religions have been studied ethnographically, first by European missionary-scholars who learned the native language, and later by African scholars who themselves went out with tape recorders and notebooks to penetrate the curtain of exclusivity and idiosyncrasy that surrounds a people of oral rather than written traditions. The result has been to open up the possibility of an African theology that is something more than a blackenization of the canons of Rome, Geneva, and Canterbury.[17]

Mitchell's thesis relies heavily upon African American religion being a direct translation of African beliefs as an adaptation to the needs of people and a product of the genius of both African American preaching and people. John S. Mbiti, a Christian African Theologian describes some of the early approaches and attitudes toward African religion:

> It was believed that Africans borrowed many of its beliefs, characteristics and foods from outside. All types of theories developed to explain how various religious traits reached Africans from the Middle East or Europe. There is evidence that Africa has always had contact with the outside world, but these contacts were based upon a 'give-and-take process.' Africa has exported ideas, cultures, and civilization to outsiders.[18]

Many European scholars use pejorative terms for African religions such as "primitive," "heathen," "savage," "animism" or "pagan," referring to African authenticity and resistance as European superiority.[19] The late Charles B. Copher, Professor Emeritus of Old Testament at The Interdenominational Theological Center, in Atlanta, Georgia states that "African traditional beliefs and practices have been significant resources in forming the Biblical heritage of the Judeo-Christian tradition."[20]

The majority of slaves came to America from the West Coast of Africa, primarily Ghana. In their tribal lifestyle, religion was intimately associated with every detail of life including personal, social, and political aspects. According to Stephen S. Farrow, "from birth to burial, and even beyond, the personal experiences of the African are regulated and controlled by his religion."[21] African traditional religion gravitates towards a cultural milieu shaped by generations of ancestral belief patterns. J. D. Y. Peel, through his study of the Aladura movement among the Yorubas, asserts:

> Culture is a society's characteristic way of life with special emphasis on its values, and much attention is paid to what cultural symbols are employed by the religious movement.[22]

Moreover, M. E. Spiro believes that "religion is an institution which is an attribute to social groups, comprising a component part of their cultural heritage."[23] Besides being an attribute of social groups, religion also is regarded as one of the several culturally constituted belief systems. These arrangements imply a belief in the supernatural expression of both animate and abstract forces. Nevertheless, the connection between culture and religion is expressed in the comments of Merrick Posnansky, who further explains:

> Religion for many societies is one of the most basic aspects of culture which may affect all the other facets of social life, though it is arguable as to which facets influence which. Hence, religious systems include objects of ritual use because of its common cultural heritage. This allows for ritual objects to be seen as a culturally patterned symbolic action.[24]

Some missionary-scholars have raised questions as to whether the African traditional religions are authentic channels of God's saving activity. Patrick Kalilombe, an African missionary argues this question with matters of personal interest. He writes:

> Are the African traditional religions salvific? Were these traditional religious systems and practices effective means whereby in the past, their adherents in Africa were able to seek

the deity and, by feeling their way toward him, succeed in finding him [who] is not far from any of us? Are these religions still authentic channels of God's saving activity so that the practitioner of these traditional religions are saved through them and not in spite of them?[25]

The answers to these critical issues concerning the legitimacy and value of African traditional religions have not been major concerns for the dominant cultural constituency. The African has always held the conviction that God was ever present among their people, just as God had been with all other peoples, culture and religious tendencies of the world.[26] Kalilombe continues the argument by declaring:

> The African Bible reader will thus not fear to state that the religious systems of his or her ancestors were not just tolerated by God. They were the results of the efforts of our cultures wherein the Spirit of God was an active agent. And therefore, there would be no fear in them to assert that, as long as these religions were the serious teachings of our culture for the deity, they are to be respected as the normal divinely-given means for salvation, put by God in His will for the salvation of all the peoples.[27]

According to Mitchell, there are three basic characteristics of African traditional religions because they have neither founders nor reformers:

> The religions simply flow out of the life of the people; the focus on communal experiences of life as celebration; the obligation to serve human needs by religious ideas of community as family.[28]

Monotheism—A Supreme Being

The tribes of West Africa have different names for God, but they conceive that "God is a personal Being, who made the heavens and the earth, created humanity, and the only fixed idea regarding their God is that God made everything."[29] The African belief is centered upon God looking down with indifference upon all cruelty, its sorrow, and its sin in the world. In his book, *African Religions and Philosophy*, John Mbiti makes two principal contentions about African religions. He asserts:

> One is that religion is the total experience which engulfs an individual's entire being. One claims that the African lived in a religious innocence which meant that all of their activities were imbued with religious meaning and significance. Religion was, there, the "whole system of being" for each African. Secondly, all of these societies without a single exception, people have a notion of God as the Supreme Being, and this is the most minimal and fundamental idea about God, found in all African societies.[30]

Westerners observed a variety of other divinities and spiritual beings, the identification of physical worship sites, and the deification of ancestors, tribal, and national heroes. However, it is Mbiti's contention that "in each case such beings are understood by the African to be created by the one Supreme God, and they cannot be perceived apart from the creation."[31]

The African Traditional Religions were central to the very daily existence of the people and focused on the one Supreme God and the varieties of ways in which that God manifested sovereignly in life. Charles Shelby Rooks confirmed Eurocentric oversight comprehending African Traditional Religions when he proposes:

> In Africa, as well as in other parts of the world, native religion has nearly been written about by white Christian missionaries who were not intellectually equipped to understand religious phenomenology and who allowed their Christian and Western biases to color completely their observations.[32]

To hold such bias attitudes towards African religions is to miss the fact that some are extremely rich and complex. These earlier theories are inadequate for the treatment of African Traditional Religions and the "High God" of these religions is likewise a phenomenon to demand further study.

The Egyptians

Some historians view Egypt, the cradle of civilization, as having a triune conceptualization of God. In *Foundations of African Thought*, the contemporary African scholar, Chukwenyere Kamalu, explicates:

> For the Egyptians there was one, immaterial and unknowable God who was, however, also personalized and whose myriad aspects were symbolized by a company of lesser gods, each of which was limited in the sense of symbolizing just one aspect of God's nature or of nature itself. Thus African religion was monotheistic and at the same time also symbolically pantheistic and polytheistic. The monotheism of Egypt, i.e. the Egyptian belief in and worship of one almighty God, predates the Pharaoh, Akhenaton, who lived about 1400 B. C.[33]

In Egyptian religion, the monotheistic idea is described in ancient texts which declare that "God is one and alone and none other existeth with Him . . . thou One, thou only One whose arms are many . . . thou One, thou only One who has no second . . . thou are the only One."[34] Thus African Traditional Religion can almost be referred to as a 'pure monotheism which manifested itself externally by a symbolic polytheism.' Kamalu also argues that it is not a pure monotheism in the sense that it also has a pantheistic aspect depicting God as nature as opposed to being separated from nature.[35] The complimentary perception among the African triune belief validates that God is of a Universal Being or Force and at the same time both immanent and transcendent.

The Dinka

The Dinka religion was formed in the swamps of the central Nile River basin located in the Southern Sudan. Though their territory boundaries are extended over several miles of land, they are still considered one single people. Godfrey Lienhardt insists "all Dinka assert that Divinity is One, *Nhialic ee Tok*."[36] The word *Nhialic* is meaningful in configuration as a Being, a personal Supreme Being, even, and sometimes as a "kind" of being and activity. *Nhialic*, Divinity, has no plural; it is at once both singular and plural in intention. Furthermore, he states:

> The implications of this affirmation are not that their *Nhialic* is the same Divinity as that which different people know under different names. The Divinity the Nuer call "Kwoth," the Muslims "Allah," the Christians "God," and so on. Powers are distinct from each other, though of most of them the Dinka may say simply, *ee Nhialic*, it is Divinity.[37]

Elsewhere in Dinkaland, there are other free-divinities with common names which are active only where their specific names are known and where effects in human life can be associated to them. According to Lienhardt, "the Dinka nation had a wonderful faith in the Supreme Being's power to help and deliver in all times of trouble in answer to their chief's prayers."[38] It was the roots of such a faith which sustained, protected and delivered African people during the degradation of slavery in America.

The Yoruba

The proverbs of the Yoruba tribes, which are numerous, often refer to *Olorun*, the God of greatness and majesty, in such a way as to show supremacy and excellence. Through his intense study of their tribal customs, Stephen Farrow has concluded the following concerning the Yoruba religious beliefs:

> The worship of the Yoruba people showed a belief in four spiritual beings of various types: 1) a Supreme Deity *Olorun*; 2) a large class of lesser gods, or *Orishas* (over 600 total); 3) the Spirits of the Dead (ancestor worship); and a supreme Spirit of Evil, *Eshu*, i.e., the "Devil." *Olorun* is regarded by pagans, Muslims and Christians alike as the one Supreme Eternal

> Being, and that this is not due to Muslim or Christian influences is evident from the fact that such was the pagan belief before either of the latter religions came into the country.[39]

Such is the testimony of witnesses who shared in the experience of West African tribes. The feeling of awe and reverence ascribes the high and holy mark the people hold of *Olorun*. The reason that He is not directly worshiped is that He is regarded as too exalted for humanity to approach with the familiarity that is shown to the lesser gods. The respect of a Supreme Deity is further elaborated by Farrow, who concludes:

> He is constantly spoken of in daily life, and that the salutations of the pagan Yorubas show trust in His preserving care and beneficent goodness. Faith in His justice to execute judgment after death may be inferred from the fact that only prayer is offered to God in cases of deepest distress, the ejaculation is uttered, "*Olorun shanu*," i.e., "God have mercy!" The Yoruba belief in *Olorun* has existed for untold generations and long before the first introduction of Christianity into the Yoruba country in 1838.[40]

One might resolve that the African belief in a universal God of the oppressed was also readily prevalent among the early slaves, who consciously believed in a better afterlife with their God. This rationalized hope has become the primary faith principle among the African American religious culture.

The Roots of African American Christianity
1619 to 1740

The African slave trade was one of the most devastating acts against humanity known in history. The late C. Eric Lincoln, the noted African American sociologist records the initial transaction of the holocaust:

> During the summer of 1619, twenty Africans held captive aboard a Dutch frigate were turned over to the English colonist at Jamestown, Virginia in exchange for provisions for the ship's crew. This event marked the beginning of the black experience with English America and American Christianity.[41]

The enslavement of these innocent people from their homeland became a major source of monetary revenue for foreign and local investors. Over the next two hundred and forty years, twelve million Africans would be captured for the middle passage voyage to become slaves in America.

As the new arrivals struggled to retain elements of their West African religions, they also struggled to understand the religion of their masters. Africans were pilgrims in America not because they intentionally sought a "New Jerusalem," but rather the confusion of this new land forced them to seek a spiritual meaning under their circumstances. Edward Smith maintains:

> As part of their spiritual quest, blacks sought to retain the religion of their native lands. Although differences existed, the people of West Africa shared a number of common religious beliefs, especially in a Supreme God as well as lesser gods. By meshing West African religious traditions with Euro-American Christianity, Afro-Americans were gradually able to create a new religious tradition—an Afro-American Christian faith.[42]

While the African slaves preserved portions of their traditional religions, by the process of transformation, they came to accept the Christian God and the church as the American counterpart of their Supreme God and practice. John Boles supports this reality by stating:

> No institution played a more significant role in acculturizing Africans to America than did the church. There were numerous attempts on behalf of slave masters to eradicate all traces of African background and teach slaves Christian precepts that were beneficial to the slaveowner; obedience and honesty became the prime tenets of the gospel taught by masters.[43]

Because religion held a primary reference point in the life of the African, the slaveowners used it to influence the thinking and living of their captives.

Religion was blatantly subversive of the institution of slavery. It offered to the slave the clearest glimpse of ones own worth and made manifest the value of striving to overcome the temptations and frustrations of this world.[44] Some white colonists considered Africans as creatures from another species who had no God given rights to baptism, let alone the sacraments. Lincoln writes:

> These reasons and others were main obstacles to the conversion of these poor people which held them to be "too dull" to be instructed, or "without souls," or otherwise incapable of Christian responsibility.[45]

Despite the slavemaster's fear and negligence towards introducing slaves to Christianity because of what they might learn, slaves still were baptized during the seventeenth century.

Eventually, church activity received white approval, for it was widely believed that religion sustained rather than threatened slavery. It was the Puritan cleric, Cotton Mather, who assisted both the slaves and the slaveowners on this pivotal issue. Smith further asserts:

In 1693, Cotton Mather responded to the request of a group of Massachusetts slaves seeking to form their own separate meetings under white guidance by drawing up *Rules for the Society of Negroes*. This is the earliest recorded account of a group of blacks organizing for religious meetings. Mather's continued interest in the propagation of the gospel among blacks is best summarized in his treatise entitled *The Negro Christianized*, published in 1701.[46]

A Charleston minister firmly supported this idea of sharing the gospel and maintaining complete control of the slaves, when he declared:

> . . . the Gospel is our mightiest safeguard, for it governs in secret as well as in public; it cultivates conscience, and thus establishes a more vigilant watch over individual conduct than the police. The best servants I know are those who have the most religious intelligence and piety. Those among them who are most intimately acquainted with the Bible understand best the relation between themselves and their masters, are best contented with it.[47]

However, a brighter day was on the horizon for the African slaves whereas they would persevere by integrating their new found faith with the ancestral rituals and customs from home.

The First Great Awakening

The First Great Awakening occurred between 1740 and 1790 in New England and spread to the West and the South. During this period of spiritual revival, large numbers of African slaves became Christians and the African American Church emerged. The most noted evangelist was George Whitefield, an Anglican cleric, who in 1738 inaugurated his preaching ministry among the colonies and slave states. As Whitefield became acquainted with America, his perceptions caused him to write *A Letter to the Inhabitants of Maryland, Virginia, North and South Carolina Concerning Their Negroes*.[48] Published throughout the colonies, this letter quickly became known to America and focused public attention on the treatment of slaves like nothing else before.

Other preachers were hesitant to share the gospel with a people of an obscure heritage, but not Whitefield. Arnold Dallimore writes:

> Whitefield's gifts—his ability to simplify Divine truth and to present the narratives of the Scriptures and the message of the Gospel with vivid clarity—rendered him particularly suitable to such a ministry. In turn, the Negroes found an unusual interest in his preaching, and many of them testified that God used it in bringing His grace to their hearts.[49]

From Boston to Charleston, Africans heard something in the modulated voice of Whitefield which stimulated their tribal roots and moved them closer to becoming instruments for "tellin de story." The African heard words that one could readily identify and understand. As the Bible narratives were told in a vivid, dramatic manner, the slaves quickly identified with the characters and seemed to be living their wondrous events over again.[50] Dallimore concludes by stating:

> Moreover, he heard a message to lighten his burden and ennoble his life, even the life of a slave, and as he returned to his toil he soothed his sorrows in its truths. Amidst the monotony of his labour he repeated over and over some phrase he had heard from the preacher's lips, until the repetition became rhythmic and his natively musical soul spontaneously linked it with melody. The words, the music, the song, remained with him; he sang it again, he added to it, others heard and joined their voices, and the whole was repeated day after day, till it became something permanent with them, a part and parcel of their lives.[51]

Whitefield's style of delivery and sermon content was intuitively retained by African slaves, who could later mimic the preacher word for word.

The First Great Awakening crossed denominational boundaries and created new religious worship communities, many biracial in membership. In his book, *Why Sit Here Until We Die?*, L. V. Stennis contends:

> The Baptist and Methodist preachers who lacked the education of the Established Church appealed to the poor, the ignorant and the outcast in ways that they could respond to. Their fiery message of salvation gave many blacks the hope and the escape they needed from their earthly woes. The preachers also placed an emphasis upon feeling as a sign of conversion. This feeling found a ready response in black slaves who were repressed in so many ways.[52]

Because both denominations deemphasized an educated clergy, and stressed a religion of the heart rather than of the mind, "Black converts were able to incorporate elements of West African religions into the Baptist and Methodist camp meeting tradition."[53] As slaves were permitted participation in the camp meetings of these all white churches, they eventually became involved as exhorters which inaugurated the calling of the African American preacher. Slave planters discovered substantial benefits could be reaped from turning the "unpredictable heathens" into Christians for the welfare of the slave master. Lincoln conveys:

> The chief obstacle was to insure that the version of the faith available to the slaves was always consistent with the critical objectives of slavery. Often the slaveholder or his wife assumed the responsibility of teaching and catechizing those slaves in attendance at the "Big House." Only selected passages were read from the Bible explaining God's will

regarding the slaves and their moral obligations. As time passed some of the most effective plantation preachers were slaves who learned enough approved scripture and doctrine from the white preachers and adapted it to their own interpretative style and delivery to develop large followings among the slaves and often among the whites as well.[54]

Over and over slave narratives tell of slave preachers speaking under the watchful eye of plantation owners, along with white preachers who minimized the grander themes of the Bible. With mechanical regularity they pronounced the importance of servants obeying their mistress and master.

The Emergence of the African American Church
1740 to 1800

The Great Awakening, along with the need for free religious expression, led to the creation of separate churches for the private worship practices of slaves. Here, the slave community could openly hear their preacher express spiritual convictions concerning slavery, the Bible, and hell-bound owners and overseers. Lincoln continues to report:

> This "Invisible Church" met deep in the woods and swamps, as far as possible from the suspicious eyes of the master or his overseer. There in the security of the wilderness, the black slave worshipers assembled around a large iron pot, inverted wash tubs, or wet blankets to capture the fervent praying, singing, and preaching which marked the style of the "Invisible Church." In the "Invisible Church" there were no "masters" and no "mistresses," and God ordained no special punishment or subservience for black people. The "Invisible Church" drew its membership primarily from the field slaves who were less accommodated than other slaves to the white man's way of life and less susceptible to his spiritual reasoning. Above all, the "Invisible Church" proved under the most adverse circumstances possible the slave capacity for responsible self-determination.[55]

It was quite often the very first station on the Underground Railroad providing protection, direction, and encouragement for slaves who elected to run away to the North.

The second half of the eighteenth century also brought religious reform untold throughout the colonies and orthodoxy was in serious decline in America. The established church pastors, usually men of considerable theological training, were particularly irritated at the spectacle of black slaves in the role of preachers. The few African slaves who believed God called them with spiritual orders were deterred by popular disapproval. Lincoln further elaborates on this development:

> One minister complained that "the very servants and slaves pretend to extraordinary inspiration, and under the veil thereof . . . run rambling about to utter enthusiastic

nonsense." Another divine was even more outraged to discover that "Negroes [had] even taken upon themselves the business of preaching."[56]

Hence, the issue of preaching was commonly perceived as a disgraceful undertaking, inappropriate and beyond the capabilities of slaves. The prevailing conviction was that "preaching was for mighty few white folks and no niggers a' tall, and if that dictum did not originate with the established clergy, it received from them a very fervent, Amen!"[57] Lincoln argues the above by acknowledging a critical fact:

> The black preacher represents one of the most remarkable developments in the history of Christianity in the West. Barred by law and custom from even the rudiments of literacy, shut out from professional associations with other religious leaders who might have lessened somewhat the awesome burden of his ministry by their fellowship and moral support, the black preacher, except for his God was on his own.[58]

John Blassingame unhesitatingly refutes the complete negation of slave preachers by describing opportunities afforded them among white congregations. He states that "an especially well-trained black noted for his piety, conservatism, obsequiousness, and preaching skill was occasionally permitted to preach to white congregations."[59] Since most whites had conversion experiences in conjunction with their slaves in camp meetings and had prayed together with them, they saw no major contradictions in listening to sermons from these bondsmen. Blassingame writes:

> Whites accepted slave ministers in their congregations because the blacks were remarkably well trained, (some of them read Greek, Latin, and Hebrew) or famous for their oratorical skills. The black preachers in white pulpits compromised; they either ignored the evils of slavery, preached submission to their brothers and sisters in bonds, or defended the peculiar institution.[60]

Based upon their understanding, in beginning and shaping a new church in America, slave preachers accepted the ridicule and risk along with the challenge and chance to be relevant. While whites debated the proper procedures for establishing separate congregations for slaves, Africans continued organizing their religious life as best they could. The immediate needs were deep, for slavery had stripped them of any meaningful pattern of life beyond that of the master and their bondage. Wade asserts:

> Deprived of nostalgia for the past and unable to discover any real meaning in the present, the blacks sought relief and consolation in a distant time. In the church, with their own kind, amid songs of redemption, and the promises of Paradise, a life-line could be thrown into the future. While whites saw the worship "a mockery of religion" or "a delusive

clothing of Christian forms and phrases," it added to the vague superstition of the African. But these observations missed the significance of the religious life for the Negroes. What seemed a burlesque was in fact a reverent, emotional experience. The clapping, chanting, shouting, and sometimes dancing, the fervent response to the minister's preaching, all expressed a longing that had no other sanctioned outlet.[61]

Under the camouflage of urban hideaways and camp meetings during the day and singing at night in slave cabins or secluded forest gatherings, the restrictive religion of whites blended with the free spirit of Africa to create a cover for the slave preacher.

This faith, according to Holes, was a genuine black folk religion that ministered to slaves in their peculiar unfree status in the land of the free.[62] Hence, the African American Church was born out of the desire to discover meaning and secure control in relation to the spiritual and communal lives of the oppressed. The earliest churches in the South evolved from plantation congregations at Lunenburg, Virginia (1756), Silver Bluff, South Carolina (1773), and Williamsburg, Virginia (1776). Edward Smith records the development of the two prominent African Methodist denominations during this period:

> Black independence was further exercised when Richard Allen led a group of blacks from the Saint George's Methodist Church, Philadelphia in 1792 after they were mistreated during prayer. In June of 1794, the Saint Thomas Episcopal Church, was formed, with Absolom Jones a comrade of Allen, as its first pastor. Although Allen desired separation from Saint George's, he wished to maintain the Methodist form of worship. Therefore he and a small group of blacks organized Mother Bethel Church in August 1794, establishing the African Methodist Episcopal denomination. Resisting restrictions at the John Street Church in New York, James Varrick, Peter Williams, Sr. and William Miller and others formed the Mother Zion Church in New York which birthed the African Methodist Episcopal Zion denomination.[63]

By the end of the eighteenth century, the first fledgling African American churches had emerged in both the North and South. However, only a few were totally independent from white supervision. Although blacks were willing to accept this temporary guardianship, for many churches in the North, full independence would come during the period of 1800 to 1860.

Oral Tradition

The ability of a preacher to provoke reflection on factors of significance to a congregation were clearly dependent upon his or her skills in identifying universal concerns among members of the Church. One instructional method sustaining the slave preacher in accomplishing this goal was the oral tradition. Henry H. Mitchell's classic work, *The Recovery of Preaching*, suggests:

> The primacy of the oral tradition is a call to the recovery of a living transgenerational, oral religious tradition, rather than a stereotypical promotion of bibliolatry. The oral processes have survived amazingly well in such places as West Africa. And the Black Church in America has been built not on the literacy denied slaves and their dependents, but on the African cultural bias for massive memory, lively renditions, "readings" and supportive situational sharing whether in ceremony or simple conversation. The process of oral tradition proposed here is actually the early church's method.[64]

Oral tradition simply defined is "culture that is transmitted from one generation to the next by word of mouth rather than through written accounts."[65] The term refers to a folk society without a written language. Oral tradition, known also as folklore, is the catalyst for establishing the culture of a people, therefore it is neither just words nor just stories. John S. Pobee claims:

> Oral tradition and folklore are broadly synonymous, whatever qualifications we might want to make. In the history of the world, folklore has been a unifying and nationalism-raising factor, especially when used by oppressed people struggling for their political and cultural identity against foreign rule. With such a role folklore becomes a most relevant background for what a church does for the selfhood of a people.[66]

For the early slave preacher, this method of preaching, founded upon culture and condition, originated in and consisted of messages from one slave to another. The antebellum slave preacher drew upon every available intuitive resource to fulfill "the charge to keep I have, and a God to glorify."

Rooted in West Africa and fragmented by slavery, the black oral tradition encompasses an elaborate system of music, dance, folklore, and oratory in which the black preacher reigns supreme.[67] However, the most formidable characteristic of the trait is the gift of learning through the vehicles of memory and delivery. In Africa, tales which taught a moral, either implicitly or explicitly, were widely used for didactic purposes during and long after slavery.[68] Ella Mitchell, the former Adjunct Professor of Preaching at The United Theological Seminary in Dayton, Ohio warrants:

> The oral process is a legitimate system of teaching and learning, not just a naive pattern that happens to have good memory as a by-product. The slave style of rearing children in "enforced intimacy" addressing the issues of life were more caught than formally taught. Training for coping the tragic mistreatment was thus handed down most effectively with no formal instruction, but lots of casual oral communication. Casual conversation became the power of an oral tradition to nourish identity and determination.[69]

Though illiterate, the African slave preacher possessed the innate and astounding ability to repeat long and complicated messages verbatim after one hearing. According to Herbert Klem, "memory is a highly developed skill among Yoruba religious professionals, but the tendency prevails throughout this culture and virtually all other cultures of West Africa."[70] Levine concludes by stating:

> Slave versions of history, like all slave tales, were enhanced by the manner of their delivery. The oral inventiveness of good storytellers, who appear to have been relatively common in slave black culture was a source of delight and stimulation to their audiences. Their narratives were interlarded with chants, mimicry, rhymes, and songs. In addition, slave storytellers would frequently supplement the rhythm and meter of their voices by utilizing their bodily rhythms to act out parts of their stories.[71]

The authority of the oral tradition lies in the fact that values are maintained and more normative, while the conceptualizations directly transcend to everyday lifestyle and its needs.

Characteristics of Early African American Slave Preachers

The African slaves were forced to accept the religion of the white slaveowners. This form of American Christianity supposedly taught them their place in this life and promised improvement in the next one. However, the slave preacher overcame the hardships of leading an exilic constituency by believing otherwise and became the primary mediator for the entire slave community. Albert J. Raboteau's book, *Slave Religion,* winner of both the National Religious Book Award and The African Roots Award of the International African Institute provides the testimony of a former slave. He reports, "As one former slave put it 'Back there they were harder on preachers than they were on anybody else. They thought preachers were ruining the colored people.'"[72] Despite the negative views of overseers, the slave preacher under any and all situations, became a catalyst for the community. W. E. B. DuBois, the famous black scholar, further contends:

> The black religious fervor in America is a continuation of their African heritage. The transplanted African priest became an important person in plantation life from the beginning, serving as interpreter of the supernatural, the comforter of those who were in sorrow, and the resentment of the people so far from their homeland.[73]

Presiding over slave baptisms, funerals and weddings, the slave preacher offered care and hope to people who lived in a harsh and unfriendly world. For this reason alone, both preacher and church became a symbol of socialization and rejuvenation of the slave community. The slave preacher, especially those who could spell, read and interpret the Bible, became an immediate hazard for some slavemasters. Licensed or unlicensed, with or without permission, the preacher held prayer meetings, preached and ministered under very difficult situations.[74] They also feared the independence which separate churches implied. Milton C. Sernett states:

> Contemporary evidence indicates that the black preacher was often both despised and feared by white Southerners. The bad character of the slave preachers was a frequent subject of general conversation. The manager of a large plantation in Mississippi believed such preachers merely used their religion as a cloak for habits of special depravity and they were the most deceitful and dishonest slaves on the plantation. An Episcopalian bishop from Minnesota was informed by a Florida planter that many times these black preachers are great rascals.[75]

The religious underground for the invisible church was led by slave preachers whose prime credentials was a "call" from God and whose principal learning was common sense, i.e., mother wit. The mere originality of their preaching emerged from the ability to adapt experiences to the existing needs and circumstances of the people. They had been endowed with a bona fide spirituality to transpose the subservient message of the white preachers and missionaries into one of hope, freedom, and equality.

The slave preacher possessed unique oratorical skills and was the master of the vivid phrase, folk poetry, and pictorial discourse. Being the true shepherd of the slave community, the preachers' sermons were noted with powerful imagination. Blassingame states that "in his sermons the slaves often saw the invisible hand of God working for their earthly freedom."[76] Hampered by illiteracy, the slave preacher employed imagery and a dramatic delivery that aroused excitement in the hearers as the key methods of communicating deliverance to the church.

Gifted with an enormous capacity to memorize words, phrases and forms, a white traveler observed that "they acquire a curious sort of poetic talent and a habit is obtained of rhapsodizing and exciting furious emotions . . ."[77] A most thorough and descriptive analysis of a slave preacher by a white missionary supports this view. Rabateau reports:

> Attempting to analyze the preaching of Uncle Robert a slave in Beaufort, North Carolina, a white missionary noted, "In his sermons there is often a clearness of statement, an earnestness of address, a sublimity and splendor of imagery, together with a deep pathos, which gives his public address great power." As a result, "many who want to despise the Negro, want to hear Uncle Robert when it is announced that he is to preach."[78]

Those who heard the slave preachers were amazed at how well they could proclaim the gospel with such authority, power, and eloquence. A. M. French, writing of the "Colored Ambassadors" at Port Royal, suggests factors for such compelling characteristics:

> . . . colored and mostly slaves, but of deep spiritual experience, sound sense, and capacity to state Scripture facts, experience, narratives, and doctrines, far better than most, who feed upon commentaries. True, the most of them could not read, still, some of them line hymns from memory with great accuracy and fervor, and repeat Scripture most appropriately and correctly. Their teaching shows clearly that it is God in the soul that makes the religious teacher. One is amazed at their correctness and power. They say: "God tell me 'you go teach da people what I tell you' I shall prosper you; I teach you in de heart."[79]

The slave preacher brought a belief, borrowed a message and begat a faith which became the voice of an isolated people. Another white missionary observed:

> When a black man was in the pulpit, there is a wonderful sympathy between the speaker and the audience, described as rude eloquence and genuine oratory, the sermons of black preachers excited the emotions. They were orations in which exposition was not attempted. Description, exhortation, appeal formed the warp and woof. The whole being expressive of . . . all Negro experiences, trials, comforts, and assurances.[80]

The slave preacher's allusions to earthly trials and heavenly rewards were punctuated with gestures and groans authentically designed to move the audience and engage their attention.

The ability to make the ear an eye lies heavily within the folk language of the slave preacher. Henry Mitchell contends for language/identity as the goal of preaching through a natural, relational, tongue. The following is an example of his analogy:

> The goal is the recovery or retention of nuances and subtleties of sound, significance, and frame of reference, signals of all sorts that the real teacher or preacher affirms who he/she was and is.[81]

This style of religious loquacity appears to have been detected in the sing-song style of conventional emotionalism. Newbell N. Puckett adds another cogent comment:

> To win the attention of folk unskilled in literary pursuits the ear must be appealed to not only by tonal devices of rhythm, clamor, and sudden shifts in sound intensity, and with "ahs" to break off and vocally italicize specific phrases, but the sermon itself must be well spiced with vivid imagery and illustrations from the familiar.[82]

Hence, the style, content and significance of the slave preacher and the unique components comprising the folk sermon have survived within the art of African American preaching. Equipped with an inherent talent to hold a Bible in their hands as if to be reading from it, the slave preacher made the Scriptures live in the hearts of their listeners.

Bruce Rosenberg has studied the oral traditions and the formulaic quality of the early folk sermon in *The Art of the American Folk Preacher*. He writes:

> I have described the delivery of the sermons without any manuscript and usually without notes of any kind except, perhaps, a Bible. However, most preachers do prefer to have some time to think about their sermons, though sometimes sermons are given extemporaneously without any immediate preparation. The sermons are hortatory, yet what is most important is that the language of the preachers is heavily formulaic, and that their sermons are composed by using language that is largely formulaic.[83]

The sermons of the slave preacher rested upon biblical language. They took the stories, characters, and images from both the Old and New Testaments which imparted the preaching, singing, and praying of the slave community. According to Rabateau, "the style of the folk sermon was built on a formulaic structure based on phrases, verses, and whole passages the preacher knew by heart."[84] The intuitive spirit of the preacher fortified by a rhythmic ear clearly marked the creative characteristics of this style. He elaborates even further into this method:

> Characterized by repetitions, parallelisms, dramatic use of voice and gestures and a whole range of oratorical devices, the sermon began with normal conversational prose, then built to a rhythmic cadence, regularly marked by exclamation of the congregation and climaxed in a tonal chant accompanied by shouting, singing, and ecstatic behavior. The preacher, who needed considerable skill to master this art, acknowledged not his own craft, but, rather the power of the spirit which struck him and "set him on fire." The dynamic pattern of call and response between the preacher and people was vital to the progression of the sermons, unless the spirit aroused the congregation to move and shout, the sermon was essentially unsuccessful.[85]

Such was a portrait of the early African American preacher, illiterate and illogical, however intuitive and imaginative. William Pipes believes:

> For him [the African American preacher] classical standards of rhetoric did not exist; his speeches were imaginative, emotional, and filled with imagery; word pictures became the keys to the mind of the Negro audience.[86]

The core of the sermon content came from experiences drawn upon life. Therefore, the messages were beyond abstract, cognitive thoughts from books, instead they were concrete, constructive, and highly visible with creative folk poetry and picturesque words.

Harry Hoosier

The best-known early African American evangelist was Harry Hoosier, surnamed Black Harry, who accompanied the Methodist Bishop Francis Asbury between 1784 and 1810. Lincoln writes:

> Black Harry's acclaim as a preacher was so great, it is said that wherever they journeyed, people flocked to greet the bishop and to hear Black Harry preach. Dr. Benjamin Rush, the famous Philadelphia Quaker and humanitarian, called Harry, "the greatest orator in America." Bishop Coke, with whom he traveled in 1784, regarded him as "one of the best preachers in the world . . . even though he cannot read." His lack of education and literacy was made up in his uncanny ability to sense and to speak to the peculiar needs of his audiences, whatever their color and to dramatize the gospel response to those needs.[87]

Hoosier, virtually like many slave preachers, was gifted with a most musical voice, the miraculous ability to retain emotional sermons delivered by white ministers, reproduce them and memorize large segments of the Bible. When he was questioned as to his preaching abilities, complete command of voice, aptness in language, and free delivery as to Scripture and doctrinal truth, Harry replied, "a description of the Elocution of Faith: I sing by faith, pray by faith, preach by faith, and do everything by faith: without faith in the Lord Jesus I can do nothing."[88] Believing in God to be the conviction of their initial credibility, Harry Hoosier and other slave preachers were divinely authenticated.

Jupiter Hammon

The first African American to publish a poem, essay, and sermon, according to Sondra O'Neale, was Jupiter Hammon. He was born October 17, 1711, as a servant of the royal British aristocrat, Henry Lloyd. Hammon received enough rudimentary literate and vocational education to become a productive writer beginning with his first published poem "An Evening Thought, Salvation by Christ with Penitential Cries," December 25, 1760. Later, a printed sermon entitled, "An Address to the Negroes of the New York State" was reissued by the Pennsylvania Quaker Association in the early nineteenth century. O'Neale asserts:

Thus very early in his ministry, Hammon learned to wield that two-edged sword: offering the worth of rightful, guiltless equality to the Black slave while at the same time delivering gloved but scathing condemnation to his white readers. Of course, the gospel itself afforded him that tool and no other method would have worked as well in the more Biblically aware eighteenth century. He was indeed the unsung Black Poet Laureate of America.[89]

Most of Hammon's poetic works reflected a distinct hypnotic four-three beat such as was chanted in an antiphonal chorus of the early African American slave church. Phyllis Wheatley, a protege of Hammon, continued to carry the mantel striving for peace where Christ, the citadel of truth and justice, would be King.

Other Pioneer Preachers

Another celebrated preacher during this era was George Liele of Virginia, who received his freedom from George Sharpe, because of his gifts and effect on fellow bondsmen. He received much attention in South Carolina and in 1784 organized the First Baptist Church in Kingston, Jamaica. Also, John Chavis, a mulatto who preached frequently to whites in North Carolina, became a Princeton graduate and a recognized Presbyterian pastor in Virginia and North Carolina. His final sermon preached around 1837 when he formally retired from the pulpit ministry was published in pamphlet form and had a wide sale around the country.

Brutality Towards the Slave Preacher

The majority of slave preachers were often brutalized, flogged and imprisoned for preaching the gospel. Whether authorized or unauthorized by their masters, slave preachers were exempted from preferential privileges. Lincoln states:

Pioneer black preachers like Andrew Bryan of Georgia who preached to whites as well as blacks were whipped repeatedly in a determined effort to discourage their zeal. Joseph H. Evans, a free black, risked his freedom and his life when he began preaching in Fayetteville, North Carolina, around 1780, because he found the blacks there "suffering greatly for want of moral and spiritual uplift." Whipped for preaching in Fayetteville, he held clandestine meetings in the outlying sandhills and other remote places. Because of his persistence and their faithfulness, the slavemasters permitted him to build a small church in 1790. This was the first Methodist Church in that part of North Carolina, and so many whites eventually came to hear him that the black congregants were crowded out of the sanctuary and separate sheds had to be built for them.[90]

Throughout the North and South, independent churches were organized by African American clergy, in spite of the opposition. In the 1780s, Moses, a black man, was taken up and whipped for preaching to a group of colored Williamsburg Baptists. His successor Gowan Pamphlet, and the congregation became members of the Dover Association in 1791. By the final decade of the eighteenth century, the presence of black preachers no longer surprised white congregations. William Lemon, a black preacher, who pastored the largely white Petsworth Church in Gloucester County, Virginia was received as a delegate to the local Baptist Association in 1797, 1798, and 1801.

African American Preachers and the
Abolitionist Movement from 1800 to 1863

The early African American preachers were definitely natural leaders, men and women of substantial ability, forceful personalities and possessors of what today one might consider as stage presence. They were indeed figures of importance for their slave communities and churches as those slaves revered them because of their guidance and leadership.

Two prominent ideas of God surfaced in the preaching, songs and prayers of these early independent churches: first, the compensatory, with a focus upon "the after-life" and secondly, ideas promoting, social reconstruction and rehabilitation.[91] It was the consuming passion of "immediate" liberation that finally found expression and attraction through the voice of the early African American preacher. Joseph Washington believes that the root of the Black Church Tradition is racial unity for freedom and equality, hence every ecclesiastical expression of Negro congregations and institutions is but a variation of this theme.[92]

The main purpose of slaveowners and their white missionaries was to extol the virtues of this world, while the African preacher and his followers were much more interested in the freedom of this world than with the religion of the next. Harry V. Richardson, former President of the Interdenominational Theological Center, writes:

> Yet from the beginning the church served as the main outlet through which the slaves could express their sufferings and dissatisfaction. Although it was done covertly, the church rendered two great needed services to slaves. First, it kept alive the consciousness that the slave system was wicked; and second, it kept alive the hope that in the plan of a good, just God, the wicked, brutal system under which they lived would have to pass away.[93]

Slave preachers were resourceful enough to perceive that the best way to freedom in this world was through the religion of whites, sanctioned by their masters and overseers as a means of harnessing one's energy from labor productivity.

The Nineteenth Century African American Church

The first African American church to emerge in the North during the new century was the First African Presbyterian Church of Philadelphia, organized by the Reverend John Gloucester, Sr. in 1804. Under the leadership of Gloucester, a tradition for education and community involvement was established at the church and a Sunday School which flourished throughout the nineteenth century.[94]

A Virginia born slave named Lott Carey, moved to Richmond in 1804 and from several accounts was both a prodigal and wicked. After his conversion in 1807, he learned to read and made tremendous strides towards being a scholar. Carey received his license to preach from the First Baptist Church and purchased the freedom of his family in 1813. John W. Cromwell gives the following view of this celebrated missionary:

> He was a man of superior intellect and force of character with a wide range of reading. He organized in 1815 the African Missionary Society, the very first missionary society in the country, and within five years raised seven hundred dollars for African missions. When he decided to go to Africa his employers offered to raise his salary from eight hundred to one thousand dollars a year.[95]

Determined to discover the freedom of his ancestors, he declined the offer and organized the Providence Baptist Church in what is known today as Liberia. One eyewitness compared his last sermon at the First Baptist Church in Richmond, to the burning, eloquent appeals of George Whitefield.[96]

The Reverend Thomas Paul, founder of the First African Baptist Church of Boston in 1805, organized the legendary Abyssinian Baptist Church of New York City in 1807 which had been a part of the First Baptist Church. Joseph Willis, a free slave from South Carolina, founded the first Baptist church west of the Mississippi in Louisiana in 1805 and four other Baptist churches by 1818. Willis, highly honored by the whites among whom he preached, was honored as the "Father of Louisiana Baptists."[97]

The growth of the African Methodist Episcopal Church, prior to the late 1820s, Boston became a major center for antislavery activities, and the doors of the First African Baptist Church were available to abolitionist organizers and orators.[98] The growth of the African Methodist Episcopal Church, prior to the

Civil War, was decisively determined by the missionary efforts of its preachers. They reincorporated the First Great Awakening camp meeting tradition that reached its zenith in the 1830s.

For fifty three years, Lemuel Haynes, the Revolutionary War veteran, served as a Congregational minister in New England until his death in 1833. Even in the South, African American preachers routinely preached to any white who would hear them, and some whites joined their churches despite the inconvenience of slavery. The Alabama Baptist Association purchased the freedom of the slave preacher, Caesar, in 1825 as a token of appreciation for his service to both black and white congregations. Lincoln records this era as a major factor in the personal development of black ministers. He writes:

> The rank and file of black preachers was of course limited to less exotic but no less demanding ministries in the black churches. Their organizational and political skills were in that context second only to their spiritual gifts in importance. The fledgling black churches they led had no secure financial base and no managerial talent except that developed under the leadership of the black preachers, whose life experience was most often limited to the plantation routine. But they did have spirit and they did have staying power. They were the true culture builders who in their singular pilgrimage to religious autonomy and spiritual and cultural respectability survived the wastage of slavery, and gave America a distinctive alternative religious heritage of which she may be proud.[99]

The African American Preacher and Slave Rebellion

Many slave preachers enjoyed this open, independent society where they could manage their own affairs. Richard Wade describes the situation of this new found freedom:

> Negroes did in fact get some experiences in managing their own affairs. Black religious leadership carried a broad status that was not confined to spiritual matters. Though not ministers in the conventional sense, the preachers and class leaders were something more than mere slaves. In the life of these churches the first signs of traditional Negro leadership were visible in the cities even before the abolition of slavery. Already the church had become the cardinal point of colored affairs.[100]

Opposition to the ordination of African Americans as ministers was, of course, due to the slaveowner's fear that to elevate individual slaves would be to promote the entire race as a whole, and thus make it more difficult to keep in subjection. A concomitant, and perhaps stronger fear was that the slave preacher might use their pulpits for insurrection.

As this reaction against Christianized blacks developed, a campaign by southern churchmen began as a reaction to the growing abolitionist movement in the North, which denounced slaveowners as anti-Christian. Some churchmen hoped to prove that when placed solely under white control, religious instruction could be used to make slaves more obedient, docile, and well behaved.[101] The literate slave preachers eventually discarded their submissive, humble and obedient posture and embraced a radical position toward freedom. Stennis writes:

> The fundamental rules of their religious creed was that heaven would provide an opportunity to get even with their enemies. The cornerstone of black religion was the idea of a revolution in the conditions of the whites and blacks, even if this was not in strict accordance with the precepts of the Bible.[102]

In 1802, Gabriel, the Black Samson, became informed of the successful revolution of Toussaint L'Ouverture in Haiti. This information inspired him to adapt the position of the Israelites in rising up against the Philistines—the slaveholders. Although his plan failed, Gayraud Wilmore provides commentary of this revolutionary attitude:

> Despite his failure General Gabriel had reminded the people of Virginia and the nation as a whole of the fact that the temper of the times—the spirit of Jeffersonian democracy, the spirit of the Haitian revolution, and the egalitarianism issuing from the French Revolution of 1789—made it impossible not to expect blacks to demand the application to themselves of the human rights and the principles of democracy to which others had appealed.[103]

While whites viewed themselves as the New Israel in possession of the Promised Land, blacks viewed themselves as Old Israel still enslaved in Egyptian bondage. Because of the inordinate amount of influence the slave preachers were able to exhort over their communities, their congregations were viewed as hotbeds of sedition.[104] Throughout the South, there were several retaliations during this period. Two important slave conspiracies, the Denmark Vesey rebellion of 1822 and the Nat Turner slave revolt of 1831, both emerged from religious activities and inaugurated the abolitionist movement.

The Abolitionist Movement from 1830 to 1863

From the viewpoint of Northern social reform, the most notable characteristic of the African American Church was its independence from white control. Money came from the predominantly black membership, hence it could speak out on such an issue as slavery without fear of losing members and offending someone in the South. Benjamin Quarles, in *Black Abolitionists*, writes:

Negro criticism of the churches for their lack of reformist zeal and Christian example left no denomination untouched, Quakers included. After 1830, the Quakers' protest against slavery had weakened, in part because they disliked the harsh language of the new abolitionists. The doctrine of immediate emancipation troubled many Quakers, who felt that a practice so deeply rooted as slavery called for time and patience.[105]

Most Northern congregations and their pastors made no effort to conceal their anti-slavery position and began preaching a social gospel that articulated the church militant in a fellowship of concern for moral improvement, justice and equality.

Negro leadership in antebellum America was predominantly ministerial and this accounted for the key role of the Negro church. The time had come for the church to demand the promotion of education for its people and the abolition of slavery. Many Northern blacks frequently maintained that slavery was demoralizing and destroyed the opportunity and incentives of slaves to develop morally, socially, economically, and intellectually. Monroe Fordham suggests:

> The newly formed and emerging black ministers, black churches and reform leaders were all active in the extensive effort to spread the gospel of moral improvement among the northern black community. The proposition of a gospel that emphasized the necessity for moral improvement and strict adherence to Christian virtue, not only offered salvation, but would also enable blacks to overcome the negative effects which were the legacy of slavery and caste.[106]

The African Methodist Episcopal Church general conference held in 1833 at Philadelphia publicly announced education as the most important item of business. Moreover, ministers were charged to preach occasional sermons on the subject of the importance of education and ministers who neglected the charge would be subject to the censure of the conference.[107]

In May 1840, eight Negro clergymen from various denominations, including Christopher Rush, Stephen H. Gloucester, and Henry Highland Garnet, founded the American and Foreign Anti-Slavery Society. Garnet, an honors graduate of Oneida Institute in 1840, became one of the most prolific orators of his era. At the seventh annual meeting of the American Anti-Slavery Society in 1840, the speaking ability of Rev. Garnet electrified the audience and captured the significance of the African American preacher. Martin Pasternak writes:

> He began his speech by asking Americans to examine the foundation of their republic. It was conceived, he said in "covenants of blood, seized by the oppressors hands and torn to pieces by his scourge." Garnet found "no fault with the principles of the Declaration of Independence, only with the basest hypocrisy and degeneration" that debased those principles. If the American Revolution was fought with the blood of his ancestors, "did they bleed as wise men or as fools?" Garnet asked. "The apologists of oppression ignore

the black man's tears and blood. The church and state, pillars of Christianity, are immersed in blood," Garnet continued. "Let America blush with eternal shame." In a manner characteristic of his style, Garnet concluded his speech by trying to make his audience feel bound with the slave. "Give *us* our freedom," he exclaimed, "remunerate us for our labors and protect our families," he said, for I can not be free while "three million of my countrymen are wailing in the dark prison house of oppression."[108]

The speech gained enormous applause and drew tears while the rhetorical reputation of this gifted orator remained within the hearts of Americans, both black and white, until his death in 1882. In 1865, Garnet became the first African American to deliver a sermon before the United States House of Representatives and in 1882 shortly before his death was appointed United States Minister to Liberia.[109] As pastor of the Liberty Street Presbyterian Church in Troy, New York, his sermons and speeches championed the Negro cause for liberation against the oppressors of slavery.

In preaching a gospel of moral improvement, African American Christians generally emphasized that such was only possible through the benevolence and redeeming power of God. They believed that the ultimate aim of God was to produce the greatest amount of happiness in the universe.

For churches in the North, racial improvement could be obtained through religious and moral education. The Reverend Daniel A. Payne, a leader of the African Methodist Episcopal Church and founder of Payne Theological Seminary, spent most of his active life crusading for the cause of education. In one of a series of essays published in the *A. M. E. Church Magazine* in the early 1840s, Payne explained "the calamitous fact that our people are entombed in ignorance and oppression forever stares us in the face."[110] All black ministers were challenged by the article to place themselves on the side of moral uplift through education.

Another outstanding scholar and theologian for this cause was the popular Reverend Alexander Crummell, a black presbyter in the Protestant Episcopal Church and boyhood friend of Garnet. In 1844, he delivered an address stressing the advantages of an educated black society:

God created all things to subserve some purpose. Consequently the mere existence of the mind is declaratory of some divine intent and he who possesses intellectual endowment may know thereby, that God instructs him to put it to its proper use, that it may bring forth its proper fruits.[111]

Crummell, who later became the first president of the American Negro Academy and a major influence at Howard University believed that a cultured Negro intellect would achieve three components: "prosperity and success, become ennobled and dignified, and would prepare people to move from servitude to the realities of full freedom and citizenship responsibilities."[112]

The Reverend James W. C. Pennington, pastor of the Fifth Congregational Church of Hartford, Connecticut, who in 1843 preached at the General Anti-Slavery Convention in London, urged his congregation in 1845 with the following exhortation:

> Place your trust in God in the struggle to overcome worldly obstacles. God will enable us to overcome the world, the flesh, and the devil. God is able to aid the sinner and the Christian alike in attaining in every respect a more finished state of Christian morals. The state of moral perfection would represent the liberation of free blacks not only from sin, but from all the negative effects and consequences of slavery and racial caste. He reasoned that a virtuous life would please God.[113]

Frederick Douglass

The leading black abolitionist between 1847 and his death in 1895 was Frederick Douglass, who served his people as a lay preacher in the African Methodist Episcopal Zion Church. As an orator, editor, lecturer, author, writer, U.S. Marshal, Recorder of Deeds, Consul General to Haiti, and advisor to President Abraham Lincoln, Douglass distinguished himself as a bona fide leader during the second half of the nineteenth century. Desiring not to identify with the violent tactics of Garnet, Douglass became a comrade of William Lloyd Garrison and articulated a nonviolent moral suasion rather than insurrection.

Douglass' career was formulated as a slave when his mistress taught him the alphabet and several short words, unaware that slaves were not to be educated. Immediately, Douglass profited from this unexpected blessing. In his autobiography, *Life and Times of Frederick Douglass,* he reflects:

> Filled with the determination to learn to read at any cost, I hit upon many expedients to accomplish that much desired end. The ploy which I mainly adopted, and the one which was the most successful, was that of using as teachers my young white playmates, with whom I met on the streets. I used almost constantly to carry a copy of *Webster's Spelling-Book* in my pocket, and when sent on errands, or when playtimes were allowed me, I would step aside with my young friends and take a lesson in spelling. I am greatly indebted to these boys—Gustavus Dorgan, Joseph Bailey, Charles Farity, and William Cosdry.[114]

At the age of thirteen, Douglass earned enough money blackening boots to buy himself *The Columbian Orator*, a very popular book written by Caleb Bingham to improve youth and others in the ornamental and useful art of eloquence. "I was led to buy these books by hearing some little boys say that they were going to learn some pieces out of it for the exhibition."[115]

It was the argument written by Aiken on page two hundred and forty entitled "Dialogue Between a Master and Slave" which affected the liberation aptitude of Douglass and taught him the value of speech power. He further states:

> . . . this, however, was not all the fanaticism which I found in *The Columbian Orator*. I met there one of Sheridan's mighty speeches on the subject of Catholic Emancipation, Lord Chatham's speech on the American War, and speeches by the great William Pitt, and by Fox. These were all choice documents to me, and I read them over and over again, with an interest ever increasing, because it was ever gaining in intelligence, for the more I read them the better I understood them. The reading of these speeches added much to my limited stock of language, and enabled me to give tongue to many interesting thoughts which had often flashed through my mind and died away for want of words in which to give them utterance.[116]

Originally published in 1821, the book provided Douglass with general rules for speaking through the likes of Quintillion, Cicero and others on the art of pronunciation, gestures, method, style, cadence, accent, emphasis and voice.[117] This book became the foundation for Douglass' gift in rhetorical discourse.

In an 1847 speech to Philadelphia Negroes, Douglass listed "the churches of the land as the chief oppressor of the colored man."[118] This position against slavery and oppression launched the continuing rhetorical ritual initiated in the seventeenth century which offered a special lament on behalf of African Americans. Wilson Jeremiah Moses, in the book, *Black Messiahs and Uncle Toms: Social and Literary Manipulations of a Religious Myth*, notes:

> I use the term "jeremiad" to describe the constant warnings issued by blacks to whites, concerning the judgment that was to come for the sins of slavery. Blacks ingeniously adapted their rhetoric to the jeremiadic tradition, which was one of the dominant forms of cultural expression in revivalistic ante-bellum America. Their use of the jeremiad revealed a conception of themselves as a chosen people, but it also showed a clever ability to play on the belief that America as a whole was a chosen nation with a covenantal duty to deal justly with the blacks. The black jeremiad was not characteristically concerned with explaining the dismal status of the African people during the slavery period. It was mainly a pre-Civil War phenomenon and showed the traditional preoccupation with impending doom. Black jeremiads were warnings of evils to be avoided, not prescriptions for revolution.[119]

The black jeremiad has full range of being an important rhetorical method for protesting against all forms of American racial injustice.

The African American Jeremiad

Sacvan Bercovitch, in his seminal study *The American Jeremiad*, believes that "although the jeremiad strenuously denounces social misdeeds, the essence of the rhetoric is its unshakable optimism by predicting society's imminent perfection and fulfillment."[120] The complete rhetorical ritual has a threefold focus. He observes:

> The sacred promise is that within the New World history will lead inevitably toward perfection. The jeremiad's second component, however, is its claim of contemporary declension from the promise. According to preachers of the jeremiad, God's people were not progressing but showed alarming signs of retrogression. God therefore sent punishment to chastise them. The jeremiad kept faith in the promise, however, by inverting "the doctrine of vengeance into a promise of ultimate success." The jeremiad concluded, therefore, with the prophecy that God would mysteriously use the unhappy present to bring the people to repentance and thus, move again towards fulfillments of their mission.[121]

With this conceptualization in view, the jeremiad has the core ingredients for the purposes of an African American protest. Consequently, this abolitionist jeremiad materialized in the free North and confronted a nation saturated in racial indignations.

Frederick Douglass was a pioneer illustration of those blacks who had voiced powerful jeremiads against slavery before the war. David Howard-Pitney offers the technique of Douglass' jeremiad in the following presentation:

> He tireless proclaimed slavery as an abomination to God and a curse to the nation. Slavery, he contended, was a dire threat to America's present and future health. If Americans continued on their present course, "we shall not go unpunished," he promised, but "a terrible retribution awaits us." It was the patriotic duty of blacks "to warn our fellow countrymen" of the impending doom they courted and to dissuade America from "rushing on in her wicked career" along a path "ditched with human blood, and paved with human skulls," so that "our country may yet be saved."[122]

Douglass remained confident that the eventual liberation of African Americans was proximate and continued defining the prewar decades as a time of severe declension.

The most thorough collection of Douglass writings conveys his 1857 jeremiad combating the infamous Dred Scott decision. Howard-Pitney interprets this proslavery legal victory in the following lament of Douglass:

> The omens seemed unfavorable to freedom. But this view was short-sighted and misleading, he argued. From a higher perspective, he discerned "that the finger of the

Almighty may be . . . bringing good out of evil . . . hastening the triumph of righteous-ness," despite contrary appearances. "Come what will," he still believed that "slavery is doomed to cease out of this otherwise goodly land, and liberty destined to become the settle law of this Republic." The American people, above all others, he claimed, "Have been called" to end slavery and institute a reign of universal freedom. In view of this truth, the Dred Scott decision and the public furor it aroused was "another proof that God does not mean we shall all go to sleep" but would shortly awaken Americans to save the nation and its mission.[123]

In this and other antebellum speeches and sermons one can readily identify the jeremiad components of promise, declension, and prophecy as being central tenants to the relevant rhetoric of the abolitionists.

Reconstruction Era and The Social Gospel Movement
1864 to 1915

The Civil War, the disagreement over slavery, appeared to be the hand of God moving in the liberation and legacy of African Americans. They took full advantage of this catastrophe by gaining greater control of their spiritual and communal lives, especially through the social and economic systems of the racist South. Inspired by the hope which accompanied the termination of slavery, African American preachers established a relief system anchored within both congregation and society.

Admittedly, after emancipation, division ensued among former slaves and their leaders, since many tasted freedom for the very first time. The advancement of the black race rested upon their religion and ministers serving them in their fight for equality. According to historian Floyd T. Cunningham, "preachers believed they knew exactly the kind of people God required them to be and the kind he would ultimately bless."[124] Cunningham further states:

> Black Baptist preachers admonished their people to live righteously, to pray that their situations might be different, and to wait patiently upon God. Violence was not an option for them theologically. As best they could, within the limits of their social structure and their theological world view, preachers made life tolerable for their people. Too many parishioners, they thought, failed to live by biblical standards and thereby jeopardized the social advancement of the entire people.[125]

Although former slaves continued their cunning methods of survival even in the newly formed churches, the preacher's chore was mainly to expand their knowledge and appreciation of equality and freedom. Lawrence W. Levine expresses the situation in the following comment:

> The old black preacher discovered that some members of his congregation were claiming to have donated more to the church than they actually had. "De trouble wid you," he admonished them, "is dat de white man done been dealin wid you for so long, some uv you gittin real tricky."[126]

The impetus of this Black folk religion was given leadership by free ministers from the North who aided the establishment of congregations independent of their white sponsors. These new movements maintained similar doctrines and polity, however, prefacing the new denominations with "African."

John Jasper

The most renown preacher of African decent during and following Reconstruction was the Richmond, Virginia native, John Jasper. He was born July 4, 1812, the last of twenty-four children, to a devout Christian mother and a scorned slave preacher father, who died two months before his birth. Jasper began preaching in 1839 and established his ministry by delivering vivid funeral sermons. William E. Hatcher, a long-time friend, in his classic work *John Jasper: The Unmatched Negro Philosopher and Preacher*, indicates:

> There was one thing which the Negro greatly insisted upon, and which not even the most hard-hearted masters were ever quite willing to deny them. They could never bear that their dead should be put away without a funeral. A funeral to them was a pageant. It was to be marked by the gathering of the kindred and friends from far and wide. It was not satisfactory unless there was a vast and excitable crowd. The slaves knew how to demand that a Negro preacher "should preach the funeral" as they called it. The funeral had about it hints of an elaborate social function with festive accompaniments. There was much staked on the fame of the officiating brother. He must be one of their own colour, and a man of reputation. They must have a man to plough up their emotional depths, and they must have freedom to indulge in the extravagancies of their sorrow. It was in this way that Jasper's fame began. He was preeminently a funeral preacher.[127]

Standing over six feet three inches tall, and always handsomely dressed, Jasper attracted a wide spread reputation across Fluvanna County and abroad. He was given special permission by his owners to pastor in the city of Petersburg, even before the Civil War.

The creativity of Jasper developed around the preeminence of his imagination. He had the exceptional gift of painting pictures, defining every detail and unveiling even the most minute incident. Hatcher adds that "his vocabulary was poverty itself, his grammar a riot of errors, his pronunciation a dialectic wreck, his gestures wild and unmeaning, his grunts and heaving terrible to hear."[128] Rarely did even his dullest sermons end, however, without a burst of eloquence or a stimulating, attractive picture, which was always in alignment with his theme. The principle factor in Jasper's growth as a preacher rested upon his constant reading and studying of the Bible. According to Richard Ellsworth Day, in the book *Rhapsody in Black*, he replies:

> He became increasingly familiar with the Word from cover to cover! Its magnificent phraseology and narratives were absorbed into his mind and heart, and thrillingly reappeared in the way a man of his experience would utter them. This, after all, is the secret of pulpit power. Newspaper writers noted that the Word of God was his sole authority, and that he was so deft in using this authority "that it seemed like unbelief to argue against his conclusions."[129]

Jasper, a funmaker by nature, knew the mastery of wit and employed it openly gaining delightful laughter from audiences. His ability to speak effectively depended upon the devices of tensions and releases, which permitted him to captivate the minds and hearts of congregations. Jasper never prepared a manuscript for any of his messages, yet he could remarkably recall his narratives repeatedly, with exquisite exactness. Day explains his unusual method of sermon preparation:

> He never wrote out his discourses. He once described his sermon-making as follows: "First I read my Bible until a text gets hold of me. Then I go down to the James River and walk it in. Then I get into my pulpit and preach it out." These texts, he says, came down on him like a Fluvanna thunderstorm. When no longer able to read, he shut his Bible and walked the James. As he walked, illustrations from his own experience came trooping into mind and begged to be used, as handmaids for the text. Thirty-three years of thus walking the James would make a flaming prophet out of the dullest of men! The James River constantly flowed through his sermons. It served, muddy though it was to represent the River of Life flowing from the throne of God.[130]

Jasper's most celebrated sermon "De Sun Do Move," was delivered in 1878 and served to settle a dispute between two members that the sun revolves around the earth and that the earth was flat. Vigorously denounced by other black clergymen, Jasper delivered the sermon 253 times before packed audiences, including on one occasion to the entire Virginia legislature.[131]

At the ripe age of fifty-five, this honest man of simple tongue organized the Sixth Mount Zion Baptist Church on September 3, 1867 with nine members and nine dollars per week salary. Their initial meetings were held in an old horse stable used during the Civil war. In 1883, the church recorded having over 1,068 members consisting of both Negro and White races. Jasper died on March 28, 1901, following a successful thirty-three year reign as the stalwart preacher of his tribe in the Richmond area called Little Africa. Day contributes a closing epithet, by remarking that "he makes the past, the present; brings the absent to hand, and gives awful vividness to the horror of hell and the glory of heaven."[132]

The Reconstruction Era 1865 to 1877

The most substantial issue affecting this segment of freedom for African Americans was the organizing of southern black colleges. Although financially controlled by major white Protestant denominations, a majority were organized in black churches. During this educational movement, former slaves gained credible knowledge and held numerous positions in both the political and social arena.

Due to the nature of the African American church being a social institution first and a religious body afterwards, the preacher was summoned to continue their fight for equality and justice. However, due to their limited educational and academic training, they were unable to sustain this new found challenge. W. E. B. DuBois offers his insights concerning the new role of the African American preacher:

> Negro preachers are often condemned for poor leadership and empty sermons, and it is said that men with so much power and influence could make striking moral reforms. The preacher is sure to be a man of executive ability, a leader of men, a shrewd and affable president of a large and intricate corporation. In addition to this he may be, and usually is, a striking elocutionist; he may also be a man of integrity, learning and deep spiritual earnestness; but these last three are sometimes all lacking, and the last two in many cases.[133]

The prophetic voice of the African American preacher needed to prick the conscience of those individuals who represented the Declaration of Independence, Constitution and Emancipation Proclamation.

The time had come for preachers to make dreams of freedom a reality in the life and times of their people. Following reconstruction, segregation resumed in the South and discrimination arose in the North. These twin evils restrained the militancy and advancement of free African American people, especially the church. Washington attributes this derailment to the fact that "the Negro minister remained the spokesman for the people with this difference—faced by insurmountable obstacles, he succumbed to the cajolery and bribery of white power structure and became its foil."[134]

Ministers no longer spoke of freedom and equality, but preached on moralities and guarantees of a better after life, much like the white missionaries. During this period, Washington continued his critique by declaring:

The Negro minister increased his control and redirected the enthusiasm of the folk religion for the purpose of gaining personal power. The burning zeal for liberty and justice, the "raison d'être" of the black folk religion was dimmed in the darkness of the whole society's disarrangement. The dominant theme was stymied and could not be articulated in the society at large.[135]

To some, the African American preacher failed to embody what freedom demonstrated for the masses. The nature of their content and delivery incorporated the slave narratives to evoke the past and make it a component of surviving the living present. According to Levine, "they tended to devote the structure and message of their tales to the compulsions and needs of their present situation."[136] Dr. Benjamin E. Mays, a critical scholar of African American religion, supports this view by describing the regression of African American life during this segment:

Following the removal of federal soldiers from the occupied South after Rutherford B. Hayes was declared president in 1877, the destiny of blacks again fell to Southern whites. Between 1877 and 1910, the black man was enslaved again. Segregation, mob rule, and lynching covered "Dixie like the Dew," sanctioned by the United States Supreme Court which overruled what Congress did in 1875 guaranteeing equal protection of the law. Segregation became God in the South. So by 1910 segregation was found in every crack and in every crevice of this nation. The 1896 decision of the United State Supreme Court (Plessy vs. Ferguson) made segregation constitutional provided that the two separates were equal—one for white and one for black, both equal. So it was the black people and the black church to take up the cudgel of leadership to get Congress to restore what the nation had taken away.[137]

The Social Gospel Movement 1878 to 1915

During the Social Gospel Movement, African American preachers such as Martin R. Delany, Daniel A. Payne, Edward W. Blyden, Henry McNeal Turner, Charles C. T. Walker, William J. Simmons, George Washington Woodbey, Matthew Anderson, Alexander Crummell, William Fisher Dickerson, Reverdy C. Ransom, E. C. Morris,[138] founder and first president of the National Baptist Convention, and countless others continued to lead the charge for justice and equality in the wake of Jim Crowism.

With the invention of machinery and the building of factories in America, opportunities for advancement seemed available to every race and immigrant except African Americans. The racial assumptions of the day stigmatized and categorized all African Americans as inferior based in part on interpretations of Charles Darwin's, *The Origin of the Species* (1895). Josiah Strong, the Social Gospel leader during this era, blatantly believed in the superiority of the Anglo-Saxon race.

His racist rhetoric often touched upon the growing evils within urban America caused by the immigration of non-Anglo-Saxon Europeans and the nuisance of former slaves. Most Social Gospel advocates were not as racist as Strong, but few paid attention to the predicament and problems of black people. According to Robert T. Handy:

> These religious reformers ultimately believed in self-help and self-advancement where Blacks were concerned, and therefore urged Blacks to educate themselves and to strive to emulate the standards of white civilization. The problems of Blacks arose basically out of the race's own deficiencies and would be solved by Blacks' own diligence and hard work. It is no wonder that most Social Gospelers were strong supporters of the gradualist self-help program of Booker T. Washington. They considered industrial education to have been the most realistic approach for a backward race.[139]

Refusing to accept this sub-humanizing standard of existence by such overt actions as racial inferiority, again African American preachers sought direction for the betterment and destiny of their church and its people.

By rejecting the notion that they were by nature predestined to exist under the debilitating residue of slavery and discrimination, August Meir states that "Negroes were compelled to rationalize their acceptance of a segregated church life, which embraced a racial philosophy of self-help and solidarity.[140] Black clergy were determined to exemplify their commitment to uplift their race through education and enterprise. In 1887, E. C. Morris validated this concept in a speech published in the *African Methodist Episcopal Review*, stating:

> The solution of the race problem would depend largely upon what Negroes proved able to do for themselves. Prerequisite to this was race pride, and he was persuaded that there was no better way to cultivate this quality than for Negroes to inaugurate enterprises of their own.[141]

Distinguished clerics in the African Methodist Episcopal Church, African Methodist Episcopal Zion Church, and the African Baptist Churches identified the segregated church as a positive motivation for the race as a whole. African Methodist Episcopal Zion Bishop J. W. Hood, writing in 1895, recorded:

> . . . remaining in white churches would have dwarfed the Negro. Excluded from opportunities elsewhere, Negroes received from their churches trained leaders, because to care for the spiritual welfare of the people you must be one of them. A church of their own, for whose support they were completely responsible, provided the freedmen with a lesson in the importance of self-reliance which they could not have obtained so quickly in any other way.[142]

At the Hampton Conference in 1900, Matthew Anderson, a leading Presbyterian clergyman and social reformer in Philadelphia who graduated from both Oberlin College and Princeton Theological Seminary, stressed "the battle against ignorance and improvidence by the Negroes' own efforts, a cooperative racial business, and industrial education as the solution to the race problem."[143] Anderson received adequate support from Black Episcopalians such as Alexander Crummell, John Albert Williams, George Alexander McGuire, and George Freeman Bragg, Jr., who all followed the precedence of their founder Absolom Jones. J. Carleton Hayden describes this remarkable preaching of the nineteenth century black Episcopalians:

> Two general characteristics mark black preaching in this period. First, it was liturgical preaching and Black Episcopalians placed great emphasis on intellect and liturgy. Liturgy was a work to produce a certain quality of person. That quality was called "character." People who had character were cultured and refined persons. Secondly, it was essentially intellectual preaching, persuasive by a process of argumentation and illustrated by literary and historical allusions, especially British, and indicative of higher education. The introduction was aimed at getting the attention of the hearers; the exposition at convincing the hearers of the truth being set forth; and the climax was aimed at moving the will of the hearer to some appropriate action.[144]

After the turn of the century, preachers attempted to deal with the existential situations of their parishioners, searching deeper into their own reservoirs of creativity to fashion a vocational style different from their white counterparts. Cornish R. Rogers details this emphasis:

> Black preaching tends to be more evocative and descriptive than didactic. Its message always stresses the awfulness of the present followed by the glory of the future. The black church operates its interior life as a family. The black preacher became a father figure—invested with power—and not a suffering servant figure, as many white ministers are expected to be. Moreover the black preacher was looked upon as a leader to be followed rather than a model to be emulated. He was for his charges God's holy priest; he was also a power broker between, the black community and the white structures of power.[145]

The provocative thought of another Episcopalian, W. E. B. DuBois, brought a new elitist and contrasting fervor to the forefront of the social developments within the African American community.

DuBois, a most trenchant and sometimes caustic critic, believed that "the black church antedated the black family in America and preserved many functions of African tribal organization as well as many functions of the family."[146] Despite improvements in business enterprise, economic development, and educational advancements, the preacher's influence was on the decline primarily due to two factors. First, the oppressive tactics of President Theodore Roosevelt and the Republican Party, and secondly, the rise of DuBois and Booker T. Washington along with their ideologies of social integration and industrial education. Joseph Washington concludes this period with an epithet:

> The disappointment with the Negro minister and the independent fellowships became apparent early in this century with the loss of widespread support of Negro congregations and the rise of organizations such as the National Association for the Advancement of Colored People and the National Urban League. These racial organizations, led by social workers, took over the leadership of the central concern of the Negro people and channeled their desires more satisfactorily in creative and positive achievements.[147]

Summary

The African American preacher, motivated by the need to survive in a new land and the mandate of God to fulfill their calling as instruments of change, endured the traumatic treatment of the slave masters. Their persistence led to the establishment of the African American church in America for the principles of freedom, equality and justice.

CHAPTER THREE

An Overview of African American
Preaching and Preachers
Part II

The opportunity for African Americans to gain a greater stake in the American dream revolved around leaving the old South for the better conditions of the North. It was during this period of growth in the Black church that the preacher assumed full charge of the lives of those who brought their old-time religion along with their hopes and fears. The quest for citizenship became a continuous struggle involving both human and civil rights. Hence, the Black preacher developed as both a practitioner and peacemaker for the cause of equality, justice, and freedom.

Social Reforms and the Pre-Civil Rights Era
1916 to 1954

The opportunity to leave the old southern plantations became readily available to former slaves for a better quality of life, "up north." Wilmore writes that "the period of the Great Migration which includes the years following the war, had a decisive impact upon the churches."[148] Black churches in northern cities became inundated with a dysfunctional proletariat seeking freedom in the "promised land." The influx started in 1915 and remained constant through World War II. Wilmore clarifies this issue further in the following statement:

> Estimates are that in the three years between 1915 and 1918, from 500,000 to 700,000 blacks migrated to the North and another 360,000 entered the armed forces. It was undoubtedly the most dramatic population shift in American history. This first group became the mass base of the northern churches. However, the second group, a small minority mainly of lighter color, was joining the black congregations of the white denominations. A third flowed into the marginal holiness and Pentecostal churches and the various cults that were spawned during the war years and continued to multiply through the Depression of the 1930s. Still a fourth group remained outside the churches altogether.[149]

Even though the migrants had finally reached what some thought to be "heaven," many still felt like the Israelites in the wilderness who longed for the spiritual sensations of their rural southern churches. Cornish R. Rogers validates this need for religious leadership:

> Most important, the black preacher served as an indispensable cultural linkage figure. During the relentless wave of black migration from the South, he alone represented the link with "home." He created familiar space for rural blacks who found it difficult to feel at home in an alien urban setting. In short he provided continuity and stability for his people.[150]

Joseph R. Washington, an advocate for the Black Church Tradition, argues a forceful rebuttal against the black preacher in terms of his willingness to compromise and succumb to the bribery of the white power structure. He writes:

> Religion of the Negro lacks a sense of the historic church, authentic roots in the Christian tradition, a meaningful theological frame of reference, a search for renewal, an ecumenical spirit, and a commitment to an inclusive church. Born in slavery, weaned in segregation, and reared in discrimination, the religion of the Negro folk was chosen to bear roles of both protest and relief. Thus the uniqueness of the black religion is the racial bond which seeks to risk its life for the elusive but ultimate goal of freedom and equality by means of protest and action. Instead of freedom he preached moralities and emphasized rewards in the life beyond . . .[151]

In many instances, the black preacher was charged with being isolated from the institutions of mainstream American Christianity and its Protestant heritage. Such action allowed the black church to become involved in ecclesiastical politics and social elitism, thus removing itself from the relevant issues of freedom, equality and justice.

During this historical segment of black preaching, gospel music and its message became an inseparable component within the worship experience and greatly enhanced the effectiveness of the preacher. Marion Franklin, a noted off-Broadway gospel music director-arranger writes:

> A great influx of Blacks to the Northern urban industrial centers brought about problems of congestion. It should be noted that it was the Black church in the North which aided the mass of Blacks in their adjustment from the Southern setting to that of the Northern living setting. The theme of Black preaching during this time was a theme of hope and trust. Black preaching advocated that "God has heard our pleas and has pitied our every groan . . ." It was this period that gave birth to the Black gospel song. This song expressed succinctly the problems that were unique to Blacks in the urban environment. These songs

became conduits of expression which languaged the pain and the issue of disruption that Black people had to deal with in the ghetto.[152]

With this view in mind, the ensuing section endeavors to study the greatest preacher-composer of the African American tradition. In order to comprehend how the black church and their preachers handled earthly oppression, suffering, and injustice, it is necessary to connect the relationship of gospel music to black preaching.

Charles Albert Tindley

During this growth segment of the black church, one of the most renowned and esteemed urban ministers to lead the clarion charge towards independence and progress was a slave by birth who pastored one of the leading congregation in America. A concise description of Tindley's ministry is given in the book, *Charles Albert Tindley: Prince of Preachers*, by Ralph H. Jones. He expresses the following:

> When World War I came and the manpower shortage hit industry, blacks, already signed up for jobs, were brought to Philadelphia from the deep south. They became part of a black ghetto in south Philadelphia. Tindley, the foremost black clergyman, urged his ten thousand members to take these blacks into their homes as roomers. Tindley also called up fellow clergy to open the homes of their members. There were no hotels or other housing available for this influx.[153]

Tindley learned to read at night by the light of fire as a hired-out worker in the Quaker community of Berlin, Maryland. He became the leading pastor in the Delaware Valley from 1885 to 1933 and created a new thrust of enthusiasm within the Black church. Gifted with a personal magnetism and astute administrative skills, he quickly advanced within the African Methodist Episcopal ranks, having been appointed a Presiding Elder in 1900.

From one hundred and thirty members at the Bainbridge Street Methodist Episcopal Church in 1902, to the East Calvary Methodist Episcopal Church (formerly a white Presbyterian church on Broad Street), to the building of Tindley Temple in 1924, this tall massive preacher, with the asset of a powerful voice, became the leading pastor in Philadelphia. Not only noted for his preaching, which contained literary gems of description and spiritual insight, Tindley was a gospel singer and composer of hymns. Often Tindley would punctuate a point in his sermon with a familiar hymn from camp meetings, gospel song fests, or prayer sessions or sing an unfamiliar tune he had written.[154] John Summers, an admirer of Tindley, provides an accurate assessment:

> Reverend Tindley was the outstanding Negro in the city. Reverend Tindley was called by
> the mayor in everything. He was the spokesman for the blacks at that time. He played a
> leading role throughout the city, no question about that. Not only [in] the city, but
> Reverend Tindley was known nationwide because of his ability to speak. He was an
> outstanding orator.[155]

The ministry and messages of Rev. Tindley focused upon helping the social
outcast, through a vigorous street ministry, who needed financial, physical and
spiritual support. This belief became a standard battle cry in his sermons, especially
the highly praised and often preached sermon "Heaven's Christmas Tree" taken
from Revelation 22:2.

The powerful preaching of Tindley centered upon the fact that God had
endowed him with Spirit-anointed eloquence and a fervent love for the Word,
united with compassion for those to whom he preached. Lee Heinze writes:

> A humble proclaimer of the simple gospel of Jesus Christ, he preached the glory of an
> eternal heaven, the terror of an endless hell, and the reality of a personal devil named
> Satan. He believed the Bible to be God's holy Word. He did not shun to declare the
> sinfulness, hopelessness, and ruin of all men apart for the mighty redemption made by
> Christ on Calvary, but he did shun modernism, atheistic doctrines, and evolutionary
> philosophies. Through his years of preaching, Tindley stood boldly and firmly, like the
> prophets and apostles of old, courageously proclaiming his belief in the fundamental
> doctrines embodied in the bible. Although men all around him catered, cringed,
> compromised, and cowered before world-loving congregations, Tindley never bowed his
> knee to anyone but the Saviour. Once he said that his goal was to live "so that I will be a
> better Christian than people think me to be."[156]

Tindley represented a new style of preacher in the black tradition who brought a
musical element to the art of proclamation. He concentrated on texts that gave
attention to such important concerns of black Christians as worldly sorrows,
blessings and woes, as well as the joys of the after-life.[157]

The unique gift of composing sermons through song became the trademark
of Charles A. Tindley. As he wrote his songs with a particular audience in mind, he
reflected upon black Christians freed from slavery, just arriving in the North, who
were destitute and illiterate, but valued the highly emotional spiritual life which
Tindley shared. Horace Boyer states the commonness of this approach:

> Tindley was a master in calling forth through imagery and symbolism the biblical and folk
> heroes that were so dear to the hearts of his people and, as well, to his own. Even today,
> ministers quote his texts in the midst of their sermons as if the texts were poems, as indeed
> they are. He made a special effort to use the meters so beloved in the black church of
> yesteryear; short meter, common meter, and long meter. Tindley's lyrics most often

recount a story or propose a situation. A story line is established in the first part of the song and continues throughout, but is punctuated with the major theme or a moral of the situation as the story progresses. He would interject the moral or the ideal conclusion.[158]

This masterful storyteller knew his Bible and had the innate ability to translate its archaic language into the soft, picturesque and sonorous language of not just black people, but every person dependent upon God. Tindley was musically illiterate, but it did not hinder him from writing and publishing forty-six gospel songs, representative of which can be found within the hymnal of every major denomination. Note the following tribute by Boyer:

> Tindley was the first black composer to recognize the validity and potential of sacred songs characterized by simple—almost predictable—melodies, harmonies, and rhythms, and messages which dealt forthrightly with such subjects as the joys, trials, and tribulations of living a Christian life in the twentieth century as well as the rewards of heaven. Most concerts of traditional gospel music are still programming his songs, particularly such direct and ear-catching ones as "When the Storms of Life are Raging, Stand By Me" and "We'll Understand It Better By and By."[159]

A pulpit legend, who stood for his people and with them as an urban pastor for over thirty-one years, he also had a profound influence upon the "Father of Gospel Music," Thomas Andrew Dorsey. The latter declared that "Tindley originated this style of music [i.e., gospel songs], and what I wanted to do was to further what Tindley started."[160]

The Musicality of African American Preaching

Admirers of the African American preaching tradition are well aware that the old time delivery styles were far from removed during this segment of history. As a matter of fact, with an increasing appreciation of musical rhythms and intonations, most preachers of this era continued in the same vein as their slave forerunners. In James Weldon Johnson's 1927 classic, *God's Trombone*, he graphically explains this phenomenon:

> The old-time Negro preacher of parts was above all an orator and in good measure an actor. He knew the secret of oratory, that at bottom it is a progression of rhythmic words more than it is anything else. Indeed, I have witnessed congregations moved to ecstasy by the rhythmic intoning of sheer incoherences. He was a master of all the modes of eloquence. He often possessed a voice that was a marvelous instrument, a voice he could modulate from a sepulchral whisper to a crashing thunder clap. His discourse was generally kept at a high pitch of fervency, but occasionally he dropped into colloquialisms and, less often, into humor. He brought into play the full gamut of his wonderful voice, a

voice—what shall I say?—not of an organ or a trumpet, but rather of a trombone, the instrument possessing above all others the power to express the wide and varied range of emotions encompassed by the human voice—and with greater amplitude.[161]

These preachers had a highly imaginative approach to the gospel story and its heroes. As interpreters of the Bible, their sermons were designed to meet the current needs of people in a cold and hostile world. Through the eyes of songstress Geneva Southall, who shares the connection of religious music to African American preaching, she states:

The effectiveness of the Black sermon lay in the preacher's tone of voice, dynamic and rhythmic nuances, and emotionally-charged oratory rather than in his vocabulary and intellectual message. Because this style has been passed down from generation to generation, the Black sermons belong to the oral tradition in the same manner as folk music and is to be distinguished from sermons belonging to the historical tradition in which ideas are circumscribed and closed in by the written word.[162]

It was necessary for the preacher to move beyond the instrument of Negro dialect because it limited the scope of possibilities to only two complete stops, pathos and humor. Johnson believed that the preacher needed a broader range of methods. He notes:

He needs a form that is freer and larger than dialect but which will still hold the racial flavor; a form expressing the imagery, the idioms, the peculiar turns of thought and the distinctive humor and pathos, too, of the Negro, but which will also be capable of voicing the deepest and highest emotions and aspirations and allow of the widest range of subjects and the widest scope of treatment. The old-time Negro, though they actually used dialect in their ordinary intercourse, stepped out from its narrow confines when they preached. They spoke another language, a language far removed from traditional Negro dialect.[163]

Moving beyond these idioms towards a larger vastness of speech, the toning of voice, and spiritual fervor enabled the African American preacher and the congregation to rise up and take flight in the sermonic exchange. Gardner Taylor comments:

Music is the language of the soul when it is too filled with ordinary speech. The music of the ghetto comes out with a kind of staccato, a sharpness and anguish cry, a stream that is sometimes a dissonance in rhythm. This music grows out of struggle. The greatest music is not a music of contrived rhythms but one forced up out of enormous contest and difficulty.[164]

A direct correlation of the numinous African-music retentions in African-American preaching consisted to a large degree of melody, harmony, rhythm, the responsorial principle, aesthetics, form, instrumentation, counterpoint, also referred to as chanting, and improvisation. Hence, William C. Turner writes:

> . . . there is no chance of coming to terms with the musical aspect of black preaching without a backward and sideward glance to Africa, for in African culture we can clearly observe the structures of meaning embedded within the religious consciousness of its people which has allowed for the sustentation of music as a means of communicating the "surplus."[165]

Music, with all of its rhythmic qualities, is undoubtedly a crucial element of the African American oral culture, especially within its preaching event. This moaning, groaning, whooping, and shouting stimulated congregations into emotional frenzy. The affective domain penetrating the African American oral preaching tradition depends largely on many shadings and nuances which are communicated vis-a-vis intonation. African American preachers have come to know that it is not "what" you say but "how" you say it that matters. Johnson elaborated upon this etiology even further when he said:

> . . . the inner secret of sheer oratory is not so much in what is said as in the combination of the how, when, and where, the how is the most important of these factors and its chief virtues lie in the timing; that is, in the ability of the speaker to set up a series of vibrations between himself and his hearers.[166]

The African American preacher through spiritualized language developed the art of communicating to a people who continually struggled to gain respect and personhood. This method of preaching came to be known as kratophany, or a manifestation of power which is spoken word and rendered gesture.[167] Drawing upon the wisdom of repetition, reinforcing the old, the imaginative-filled preacher charismatically utilized improvisation in order to create a temporary release from "the troubles of this world." This insight led Cornel West, the militant African American scholar, to describe this oppugnancy as:

> The same atavistic influence operated upon the adherents of Afro-Christian faith: rhythm and music in preaching, operating beneath the structures of rational and discursive communication, moved the hearers away from the history that unleashed terror upon them. Only through perpetuating their quarrel with history while simultaneously sidestepping its terror could they forge a positive identity for themselves.[168]

The other worldly traits of this "singing in the spirit" have provided the homiletical musicality of the African American tradition credibility to live on, as a wholistic remedy.

Lacey Kirk Williams

One of the most prominent, celebrated pastor-preachers ever to ascend a pulpit was Reverend Lacey Kirk Williams, former president of the National Baptist Convention, USA, Inc. and pastor of the Olivet Baptist Church, Chicago, Illinois. Williams, a Texan by birth, forged toward his historic place in Afro-Baptist life through a persisting desire to gain the necessary education to lead God's people. After years of teaching in rural schools and pastoring sometimes four churches simultaneously, he graduated from Bishop College, Marshall, Texas in 1912.

Rapidly advancing as a gifted preacher from Marshall, to Dallas, then to the famed Mount Gilead Baptist Church of Fort Worth, he was a long time president of the Baptist Missionary and Educational Convention of Texas and vice-president of the National Baptist Convention, USA, Inc., destined to become president. Upon receiving the call to Olivet in 1917, he faced the great migration of the Negro northward. Within five years, the church had taken in over four thousand new members who filled up the recently purchased First Baptist Church at Thirty-first and South Park Avenue.

Upon the death of Dr. E. C. Morris in 1922, Williams led the charge to build what has become the National Baptist Publishing House in Nashville, Tennessee. During the campaign to raise a needed sum of money, a reporter named J. D. Crum recounts in the book, *Crowned with Glory and Honor*, a discourse by Williams:

> President Williams began his address in a homelike conversational manner; it was interspersed with wit . . . when he became animated by the brilliant truth of the Negro in America, the strength of the Baptists, the publishing house being built by Negro skill, Negro brain and Negro muscles, he burst into a blaze of oratory that stirred the hearts of those who heard him. Afterwards, he appealed for pledges to be paid by the time of the dedication in May or the Nashville session of the convention in September.[169]

A man of faith, Dr. Williams loved preachers, both old and young and of all classes. His home was always open as well as his pulpit to any gospel preacher. Even during the time when Olivet was the most outstanding church in the denomination, any preacher received the opportunity to stand before the awesome crowds that Williams' eloquence had drawn to the site.

As only the second African American at that time ever to address the students and faculty of the Divinity School of the University of Chicago, he spoke to a

standing-room audience on the subject "Making the Church a Community Asset."
An observer reports the event:

> The audience followed the speaker almost breathlessly, not due to the novelty of seeing
> a Negro speak in the chapel, but because of the strength of the message. It presented
> Olivet as a church with the task of saving the souls of men from fear, oppression, mental,
> economic, or political, by taking hold of the problems that have to do with their everyday
> lives. When he came to the conclusion, the hearers, men and women, students and
> teachers, bent forward to catch the significance of his words. He said that a church must
> do something more than administer to the physical needs of men, that a church must have
> a message. In its message, the church must excel other organizations; a church must
> believe in itself and in God. He said that Olivet believed in both, that Olivet has a morale.
> Then he closed with a prayer that God might give us a thirst for Him, and power to find
> Him that He might unite our hearts and hands in the service of God and man.[170]

In appearance, he was well structured, above medium height, and poised with
neatness and good carriage. The depth of his spirit became contagious through eyes
that had a strange shining, glow when his soul encountered something of supreme
interest. Seemingly unaware of his turf, his vision captivated even the slightest
movement like a cobra, head erect and ready to strike. Whenever the threat
subsided, he recoiled into his relaxed, nonchalant position as to appear numb, but
ever ready quickly to spring at will. After Williams delivered a message in Louisville,
Kentucky at the Lyric Theater, an eyewitness stated:

> Dr. Williams is a calm, cool, deliberate speaker with an analytical mind, marvelous gift of
> exposition, and a keen sense of humor. He talks in an easy natural conversation tone rising
> now and then to flights of impassioned eloquence that swept its audience off its feet. He
> is an entertaining, inspiring, and instructive, speaker.[171]

Dr. Lacey Kirk Williams became vice-president of the Baptist World Alliance at the
1928 meeting in Toronto. He held the position until his fatal plane crash on
November 17, 1943. Williams was known as the leading Colored leader of the
Christian world. Ms. Horace offers a fitting tribute to this denominational leader:

> There was little of the hullabaloo of voice or contortion of the body. When he talked he
> conversed informally; his tones rose or fell naturally and with ease according to the
> emphasis he placed upon his words. The listeners thought of him as challenging the whole
> world for a great cause representing a Great Force, and they swung into it from the great
> outside. He rose to heights of intellect and emotion, took his hearers with him, and when
> he burst into an exclamation of adoration or cried from the hearts as of all the Christians
> of all the world. He was never alone in his ecstasy. Ministers have said that they would
> sermon we quote, must to some extent fall flat without the man's bristling personality
> beside it—his body, his tones, his eyes, his fervency, his interpretations, his voice, his

interpolations, his quixotic deductions, his simple, clear, delivery. His words we may save, but the things that go with them God must prepare for us in another.[172]

For seventy-two years the world came to love, honor, and admire a worldwide leader of humanity, uplifting the cause of Christ and His church.

Several preachers deserve recognition for their contribution to the homiletical renaissance of the African American tradition during this period of church growth and community development. They include Adam Clayton Powell, Sr., J. Pius Barbour, Father Divine, Mordecai Johnson, Vernon Johns, Washington Taylor, Elder Lightfoot Solomon Michaux, Martin Luther King, Sr., Miles Fisher, Benjamin E. Mays, Roscoe Conklin Simmons, Lorenzo King, William Holmes Boarders, Edler Hawkins, Bishop Charles Manuel "Daddy" Grace, T. M. "Lawd, Bless My Bones" Chambers and L. Venchael Booth. Moreover, a stellar preacher who gained nationwide attention for his ministerial efforts, was the poet, mystic, philosopher and theologian, Howard Thurman.

Howard Thurman

The valedictorian of the 1923 class of Morehouse College, Howard Thurman would become a premier example of both spirit and intellect, majestic and mystic. He became to the African American church and academic society what Albert Einstein earned through nuclear physics, the consensus of a pure mastermind. Upon receiving his Bachelor of Divinity degree from Colgate Rochester Theological Seminary in Rochester, New York, Thurman served as the pastor of the famed Mt. Zion Baptist Church in Oberlin, Ohio for two years. Luther E. Smith, Jr. writes:

> Thurman gives two primary reasons for taking this position: 1) the location of the church in a college town offered significant advantages for his personal development; with Oberlin College and its theological program he had the opportunity for graduate study and other educational resources (i.e., lectures, library, special work with Bible professors) which would continue to challenge and feed his mind; and 2) his temperament fitted the expectations for ministry of this college town church; he would not have to whoop, holler, or resort to any other such preaching styles in order to reach his congregation.[173]

In 1928, he joined the faculty of Morehouse College and Spelman College in Atlanta, Georgia as Director of Religious Life and Professor of Religion, and the rest is history.

A distinguished career as lecturer, preacher, and theologian took Thurman to Howard University in 1932 as Dean of Rankin Chapel and Professor of Theology. There, he teamed with Mordecai Johnson, its President, and other noted scholars to formulate the premier institution for African Americans. His appointment made him the third person in America to have such a privileged audience; the others being Chicago and Princeton.[174] Thurman remained until 1944 after which he moved to San Francisco and became Co-Founder of The Church for the Fellowship of All Peoples. An inclusive ministry was developed at the church with a membership representing a vast cross-section of ethnic and cultural backgrounds.[175]

Thurman, who independently studied with the Quaker scholar Rufus M. Jones at Haverford College in the late twenties, reaffirmed his ability as a critical thinker. This laid the foundation for him to become dean of Marsh Chapel, at the all white Boston University. The Boston Globe sent a reporter to report the first Sunday service in the chapel who remarked, " . . . I wouldn't miss staying in Boston to see what is going to happen to you and to this chapel."[176] For twelve years, the intellectual prowess of Thurman electrified the capacity filled chapel services. He received special recognition from *Life Magazine* in 1953 as one of twelve "great preachers" of this century and honored by *Ebony* in 1954 "as one of the ten greatest Negroes in America."[177]

The author of twenty-two books, as well as being a contributor to countless articles and journals, Thurman's quest to find meaning and assurance through identification with God and creation became the mainstay of his travels, lectures, and relationships. Thurman dialogued with men such as Ghandi and Nehru which broadened his perspective of God. After his retirement in 1965, he founded The Howard Thurman Educational Trust, a service for assisting worldwide religious and college communities. As its Chairman, the organization remained the focus of his life until his death in 1981.

Thurman was also viewed as a pastoral theologian whose caring personality very naturally attracted persons to him. Paul Chaffee analyzes this perspective in his essay entitled, "The Spiritual Ground of Pastoral Theology:"

> For Thurman it means first and foremost an extraordinary care for his audience, the auditor or reader. The care can be seen in how he uses word and thoughts. In both writing and speaking, he has taken generalization, with all its attendant dangers, and made it a fine art. It succeeds because it strives to plow the common ground of every individual's experience at such a deep level that to participate in the dialogue, even as listeners, creates a distinct impression of intimacy.[178]

The "caring motif" became a communicated trademark upon the preaching style of Thurman. It enabled him to share his perspectives on truth and religion so that those who heard him might readily opt for the transformed life.[179] Doctrines, creeds, and biblical dogmas did not appeal to his method of preaching the gospel.

His basic concern for community centered upon the essence of Christianity. Marcus Boulware adds:

> If one were to examine his written sermons, he would discover that the minister commands a language of power. When preaching, he makes his case and gives the audience intellectual meat for our times. The sermons are food, not froth. Where numerous ministers are emotional and pedantic, Dr. Thurman possesses a profound learning supported by a genuine mystical experience and persuasive logic. A dramatic preacher known for his undertones, pointing finger, and mystifying presence, his oral composition embodies a style similar to prose set to music. He has no axe to grind and preaches to soothe the spirits of the dispossessed of humanity.[180]

The tranquil preaching style of this brilliant orator permitted his listeners the unique opportunity for a realistic experience of God. Smith describes the nature of the preaching event:

> The audience is not witnessing a performance, a rehearsed act; the audience is there with Thurman as he, completely absorbed in a thought that permeates his being and affects his appearance, explores the meaning of life.[181]

James Earl Massey analyzed Thurman's preaching with regard to substance and style. He notes:

> Very early in his ministry Howard Thurman decided that he would present himself and deliver his message in a way that would match subject matter and personality. The typical sermon pattern in Thurman's preaching revolved around a single idea or insight, one point to which every aspect of the sermon directly and logically related. Thurman's deliberate style demanded close attention and a patient hearing because he did not deal in "asides," nor did he rush through his message. Thurman did no shouting, and he used no rhythmic rhetoric to arouse the emotions. Thurman's style worked always to help the hearers experience a climax of impression. Thurman's rhetoric, imagery, illustrations, deliberate timing, spirit of worship, sincerity and voice all worked effectively when he preached, and the usually produced a climax of impression for those who listened with openness to "what" he said. Thurman did not let sermonic forms bind him. The shaping element for his sermons was not some predetermined arrangement or design but the meaning and mood of the truth or insight he sought to share.[182]

For Thurman the most important aspect of preaching he conveyed to his students was the communication of meaning and the sharing of a mood. "This is what I wanted them to learn."[183]

The Struggle for Human Dignity and Civil Rights

The African American preacher, often uneducated and burdened by a desire to serve respectfully the people within the community, was repeatedly the focus of attack by those who sought opposition. Due to the rise of the second generation educated Negro, a new intelligentsia emerged influenced by the NAACP, Urban League, Universal Negro Improvement Association, social clubs, fraternal lodges, black trade unions, and college Greek-letter sororities and fraternities. This group undertook many of the privileges sanctioned in the black church by its leadership. Gunnar Myrdal, a Swedish economist, conducted an important study of race relations in the South during in 1930s and 1940s. He recorded a paradox within the black church both stimulating and inhibiting black activism. In his book, *An American Dilemma: The Negro Problem and Modern Democracy*, Myrdal reports his observations:

> The church on the one hand is depicted as a place where over the years blacks have gathered together to pursue common causes—it was frequently the only community center blacks had. It was a place where black leaders, many of whom were black ministers could reach large numbers of blacks and, in the long run, build up a spirit of protest among blacks. On the other hand, the black church in general has been conservative and accommodating and that poverty prevented black churches from paying salaries that could attract ambitious young black men. The other worldly outlook preached in many black churches was itself an expression of political fatalism.[184]

In order to overcome this negative, stigmatized image, the Black preacher again, moved to the forefront of the African American's struggle for human rights, justice and respect. Utilizing their experiences within national and international ecumenical bodies like the Baptist World Alliance and the YMCA, according to Raboteau, "northern and southern black ministers played active roles in several movements for interracial cooperation antedating the civil rights movement."[185]

George Edmund Haynes, a founder of the Urban League and its first executive director, was also a Congregationalist churchman. He used his influence as the executive secretary of the Federal Council of Churches' Commission on Race Relations from 1922–1947 to bring whites and blacks together to discuss, study, and act upon racial issues. A Black Baptist minister and college professor from Richmond, Virginia, named Gordon Blaine Hancock, organized the Southern Racial Council in 1943 at Atlanta University as one of the few interracial organizations in the pre-civil rights South. Raboteau adds the following commentary highlighting the leadership of one family of black ministers:

In 1935, Martin Luther King, Sr., led several thousand black demonstrators on a march from Ebenezer Baptist Church to the Atlanta City Hall to protest the denial of voting rights to blacks. A decade earlier, Adam Daniel Williams, Martin Luther King, Jr.'s maternal grandfather, organized rallies at Ebenezer to protest a municipal bond issue that contained no plans for high-school education for black youth.[186]

In the midst of racial bigotry and human injustice, what the African American church needed was someone who could articulate their demands at the highest level of the American social justice system. From a blood line of prophetic witness and protest, God raised up a fourth generation preacher named Martin Luther King, Jr. to lead the Negro charge for civil rights, justice and equality and tell ole Pharaoh "to let my people go."

The Black Preacher and The Civil Rights Movement
1955 to 1970

In May of 1954, two major events happened that changed the course of history. First, the United States Supreme Court in its historic decision, Brown vs. Board of Education, overruled the racist segregation ruling of Plessy vs. Ferguson which for fifty-eight years relegated black people to second class citizenship. Secondly, Martin Luther King, Jr. preached his first sermon as pastor of the Dexter Avenue Baptist Church in Montgomery, Alabama. Since the populace believed that all one needed was a building, a few chairs, and a "call" to become a preacher, the majority of black clergy were men and women of little or no educational training. In a 1955 study of the need for trained clergy in the black church, Ralph A. Felton observed the following crisis:

There are 17 Negro schools in the United States that are offering B.D. training. The total enrollment in these 17 schools is: 90 juniors, 68 middlers, 66 seniors—224 in all. This means an average of 5 juniors, 4 middlers, 4 seniors, or an average total enrollment of 13 ministerial students per school. In one year, including those Negro ministers trained in white seminaries, 96 new trained ministers graduated. According to the above table, 862 new Negro ministers are needed annually by Negro churches to serve the 14,894,000 Negroes in the U.S. This is a disgraceful situation.[187]

The black church desperately needed trained men and women to fill the void of progressive leadership. Because black people needed strategies, solutions, and support for their current problems, the "pie in the sky" concepts began to lose their spiritual attractiveness. Johnston wrote:

Audiences today are not especially interested in an other-worldly sermon; they prefer a sermon in which religious teachings are directly related to life. Churchmen increasingly desire a sermon which offers information on current local, national, and international topics, which offers instruction on methods of improving conditions under which they live, and which relates specifically to the application of religious principles to life. Audiences prefer a sermon in which the speaker combines the intellectual and the emotional appeals. Increasingly a need is being felt and a desire is being expressed to hear practical sermons which instruct members regarding voting, farming conditions, education and so on. The practical sermon bears direct application to life as religious teachings are related to current social problems.[188]

The most eloquent expression depicting the immorality within the American justice system was formulated in the cadences of the black church and its prophet Martin Luther King, Jr.:

Studded with frequent references to biblical images like Exodus and Promised Land, King's speeches marshaled the evocative power of the black sermon to convince Americans of both races that desegregation was a religious, not a political cause.[189]

Martin Luther King, Jr.

Nurtured in the home of religious grandparents and parents, it was of little doubt that the spiritual inclinations and dreams of young Martin would grow into giant like accomplishments. Most of King's adult faith had greatly been impacted by his childhood experiences and spiritual roots. Martin Luther King, Jr. was born on a cold, gray, overcast Saturday, on January 15, 1929. As the first son born to M. L. and Alberta King, and the first grandson of A. D. and Jennie Williams, Frederick L. Downing writes that "young Martin grew up with a sense of favor and entitlement that came from the warmth and affection that was bestowed upon him at home and at church.[190] Martin recorded his first encounter with segregation at the age of six. After being denied service at a downtown shoe store because Martin and his father refused to sit in the rear, the elder King explained to his son:

I'd never accept the stupidity and cruelty of segregation, not as long as I lived. I was going to be fighting against it in some way or other as long as there was breath in me. I wanted him to understand "that." He still looked puzzled, but he nodded his head and told me that if I was against it, he would help me all he could.[191]

Determined to fulfill this "destiny compulsion," the young Martin consciously vowed to help his father overcome the evils of racism and the dehumanization of the Negro.

Martin became a fierce competitor in all aspects of life. Full of anger, aggression and astucity, he could handle himself both in dealing with the boys in the neighborhood and the books in the classroom. A B+ student, he entered high school at thirteen because he skipped over grades in both elementary and junior high school. Stephen B. Oates noted the following about the young King:

> At fourteen, M. L. was a sensuous youth who played a violin, liked opera, and relished soul food. Physically, he was small and plump-faced, with almond-shaped eyes, a mahogany complexion, and expressive hands. But the most memorable thing about him was his voice. It had changed into a rich and resonant baritone that commanded attention when he spoke in class or held forth in a nearby drugstore.[192]

In the fall of 1944, King entered Morehouse College at the age of fifteen. Soon, he met Gladstone Lewis Chandler, a professor of English, who taught him the art of lucid and precise exposition and also polished King's forensic style which enabled him to place second in the Webb Oratorical Contest. Guided by the likes of George D. Kelsey, Walter Chivers, and Benjamin E. Mays, the college president, young Martin came to grips with what it meant to become a "Morehouse Man." Inspired by the sermons of Mays in chapel, King finally accepted the will of God to become a minister at the age of seventeen. In 1947 the elder King ordained Martin into the gospel ministry and made him assistant pastor at Ebenezer.

In 1948, King graduated from Morehouse College at nineteen, with a degree in sociology and a minor in English and decided to study at the Crozer Seminary, in Chester, Pennsylvania for his Bachelor of Divinity. King was quite impressive on the campus and in the classroom as one of six black students attending the nondenominational seminary. The quest to engage a philosophical method to eliminate the evils of social injustice eventually consumed the young scholar. In his readings of Walter Rauschenbusch, the leading exponent of the Social Gospel Movement of the early twentieth century, King found his theory for Christian activism. But he also needed an example to demonstrate this power of love and nonviolence. A lecture by Dr. Mordecai W. Johnson, president of Howard University, who returned from a recent visit to India, explicated the life and teachings of Gandhi. King read everything he could about Gandhi, his celibate life, method of temper-control, and concept of agape, a love for all humanity. Lerone Bennett believes that this initiated the conversion point in Martin's concept of the civil rights movement. He states:

> The opening to Gandhi was facilitated by two factors: King's propensity for large ideas and concepts; and the further fact that the movement was already based on the solid rock of the Negro religious tradition. What King did now was to turn the Negro's rooted faith in the church to social and political account by melding the image of Gandhi and the

image of the Negro preacher and by overlaying all with Negro songs and symbols that bypassed cerebral centers and exploded in the well of the Negro psyche.[193]

The meeting King and Gandhi eventually shared in India became a treasured reality for the one who would lead the greatest non-violent movement in America.

Upon graduation in June of 1951, King, the valedictorian of his class, won a $1,300 scholarship to the graduate school of his choice. With his father's approval, he decided to attend Boston University School of Theology for Ph.D. studies. Having been greatly influenced by the scholar, Edgar Sheffield Brightman, since his days at Morehouse, King desired a greater appreciation in the philosophy of personalism and systematic theology. While studying in Boston, Martin met the attractive and intelligent Coretta Scott, a voice student from Marion, Alabama who eventually married the eligible bachelor becoming his faithful and devoted wife on June 18, 1953. Boston University awarded King the Doctor of Philosophy degree in 1954, four months after he had accepted the pastorate of the Dexter Avenue Baptist Church.

Although King had preached in major pulpits up and down the east coast, he now founded himself back in the segregated South, a place of nightmares and distorted dreams. He remembered a statement that he had written in a preaching class at Boston, "keep Martin Luther King in the background and God in the foreground and everything will be all right. Remember you are a channel for the gospel and not the source."[194] The preaching of King became a symbol of redemptive scholarship and spiritual vitality. Washington describes the preaching style of King:

> King is an outstanding example of the Baptist preacher. He has that Baptist hum which makes what is said only as important as how it is said. The key to being a successful Baptist preacher is being able to speak at once as a philosopher and as a man of religion, without distinguishing between the two. This is accomplished by using a tone of voice which so absorbs one's audience in the emotion that anything which is said is cushioned. The usual approach is to begin a sermon with a philosophical statement such as, "One of the great glories of democracy is the right to protest for right." This is followed by numerous examples of the present situation: "We have no alternative but to protest. For many years we have shown amazing patience. We have sometimes given our white brothers the feeling that we liked the way we were being treated." Then comes the Biblical injunction "to turn the other cheek." Other scriptural passages are added to suggest the way in which one would thereupon enter jail "as a bridegroom enters the bride's chamber." As the climax nears there is an admonition to love drawn not only from the Bible but perhaps from some past tower of strength such a Booker T. Washington, who said, "Let no man pull you so low as to make you hate him." As the sermon or lecture is concluded, such words as these may be heard: If you will protest courageously, and yet with dignity and Christian love, when the history books are written in future generations, the historians will have to

pause and say, There lived a great people—a black people—who injected new meaning and dignity into the veins of civilization." There is our challenge and our overwhelming responsibility. Then comes the climax: "In this spirit the victory is assured. Glory hallelujah! Glory hallelujah!" Anyone who has heard the ringing "Amens" which always follow such an oration knows that therein is spirit and motivation enough.[195]

Naturally gifted within the oral traditions of black preaching over the course of years, King, in his sermons and especially his titles, augmented his pivotal role as a social activist. The general homiletical theme of this inspiring pastor, according to Lewis Baldwin, Professor of Religious Studies at Vanderbilt University was "the brotherhood and sisterhood of persons as a necessary precondition for a proper relationship with God."[196] One of the overarching attributes of King's preaching lies in his ability to preach effectively to any audience, rich or poor, black or white. Baldwin describes King's style:

> Significantly, King planned and structured his sermons with particular audiences in mind, knowing, for instance, that a sermon that strongly appealed to whites was not likely to evoke enthusiastic responses from blacks. When preaching to whites, he employed reasoned argument with little emotion, and usually drew on Euro-American intellectual sources that were regarded as persuasive authorities in the white community. King's sermons before black audiences freely employed folk idioms and were expressed with high emotions and eloquence in order to reach the people to move them, to uplift them, and to inspire them to act.[197]

King often utilized the gift of humor to introduce his sermons and establish a folksy rapport with a black church congregation, which never failed to respond and appreciate his comments. "King's skillful use of humor as a way of connecting with his audience," according to Baldwin, "was one indication of the high level of creativity he brought to the preaching art."[198]

Mervyn A. Warren, in a doctrinal thesis entitled "A Rhetorical Study of the Preaching of Doctor Martin Luther King, Jr., Pastor and Pulpit Orator," offers a vivid explanation on the responses to King's sermons:

> There are responses to his preaching—or for what purpose does a speaker speak? Principal responses to the pulpit address of Dr. King as interpreted by the researcher are termed (1) Local, spontaneous responses, (2) Local, delayed responses, and (3) General, implied responses. Local, spontaneous responses are those which auditors make during and immediately following the sermon. Especially when his listeners include what are generally thought to be typical Southern Negroes. Local delayed responses are principally those which have been observed particularly in letters written to Dr. King from academic institutions and therefore, do not typify responses made by the ordinary audience. General implied responses to Dr. King's oral communication refer to those observed in

organizations and various echelons of the government in terms of revised policies in favor
of racial integration and in terms of legislative measures, judicial decrees, and executive
orders. In a very real sense, then, his sermons are eventually delivered to the entire nation
and the world, even if only quoted in parts.[199]

Hortense J. Spillers' analysis of King's sermons has stood long within the credibility
of black preaching. For him, the human ear was the most effective witness of
King's style. Since the popular speaker always preached a sermon, whether in
church, at a political assembly, or a civil rights rally, the focus always appealed to
the conscience of the audience to share in the common goal of full integration for
African American people. Spillers writes:

> In King, the rhetorical style as he learned it in the Academy met the poetic style of his
> Fathers as he experienced it in the South. His oratory carried the emotional stuff, while his
> analysis carried the moral message. In King, the two were compliments. The prominent
> linguistic feature of the [King's] sermon is their nominality where a greater number of
> nouns, adjectives, and adjectival clauses abound than verbs and verb forms. Modification
> (adjectiveness) and nominality in King combine to create a picturesqueness and grandness
> of speech that were his hallmark. This particular feature (adjectives and nouns) in all its
> variations is at the heart of King's metaphors—the dominant poetic quality of his message.
> The argument, then, proceeded by way of the figure which always gave rise to a mental
> picture or image. King, while working in the conceptual and ideological, knew that the
> Word came alive in a figure, and he was a man of the living Word with his sights fixed
> clearly on this earth.[200]

King could see the dream because he articulated its message via cadence, repetition,
rhythm, humor, passion, words, phrases, a sense of euphony and resonance. This
preacher vocalized the reality of freedom and justice for all.

The Need for Liberation

The Civil Rights Movement facilitated enormous changes in America and every
aspect of the African American lifestyle—socially, politically, and economically.
The results of protest speeches, marches, and rallies produced three types of black
clergy, according to Ronald L. Johnstone, who were not all in agreement nor
supportive of the mission to overcome racism. He elaborates on the three
stereotypes:

> The militant is a preacher who identifies himself as a member of inner-core planning and
> executing civil rights action groups. He is an aggressive, take-charge activist who not only
> speaks out on civil rights issues but also acts on the basis of his beliefs. The moderate is
> inclined to be a peacemaker, the gradualist, the treader-down-the-middle-of-the-roader.

> While opposed to racial oppression, his form of protest is more subtle and accommodating. The traditionalist is a minister who believes his role should be confined to meeting the spiritual needs of his congregation, and not political things. He is passive with regard to challenges to the prevailing social order, preferring never to enter the battle arena in any case, they are acquiescent.[201]

Even though dissension existed within the ranks of leadership, there was one who continued to strive for a cooperative effort both at the local and national levels for jobs and integration. He is the Rev. Leon Sullivan, former pastor of the Zion Baptist Church of Philadelphia, author of the "Sullivan Principles" (methods to eliminate Apartheid in South Africa) and founder of the Opportunities Industrialization Centers (OIC), which initiated better jobs training methods for inner city people, both black and white.

Sullivan, along with four hundred other African American Philadelphian preachers, organized what came to be known as the Selective Patronage Program from 1959 through 1963. Initially, these leaders boycotted the products or services of twenty-nine corporate businesses which discriminated against blacks in employment. This strategy created many job opportunities formerly closed to minorities. Sullivan explains:

> The crucial key to the success of our Selective Patronage Program was the colored preacher. Although he had been criticized by nonchurchgoers through the years for what has been called lack of leadership in the colored community, the fact is that without the influence he has exerted through his church, black people would never have come as far as we have. The contributions of the black preacher and the black church to the black advancement are incalculable.[202]

It was Rev. Sullivan, a graduate of Columbia University with a Master's degree in education, who desired to provide a theological basis for motivating black clergy towards developing the social and economic development of the church as it related to business matters. In his book, *Alternatives to Despair*, Sullivan, a former board member of General Motors, responded to the challenge of preaching self-reliance and stability. His sermons and addresses focused upon the need to become more involved in Black economic development.

These tactics became so successful that the Southern Christian Leadership Conference, under the leadership of its founder Rev. Martin Luther King, Jr., organized a similar program called Operation Breadbasket, in 1962. Over a period of twenty years, OIC offices were organized in every major urban city in America and helped in recruiting, training, and employing many of the corporate leaders of today. Sullivan proclaims that "to be truly emancipated, a man must be emancipated economically as well as psychologically and physically. He must be emancipated in his pocketbook, otherwise he fools himself."[203]

Due to the slow development of the Civil Rights Movement, aggressive leaders like Adam Clayton Powell, Jr. began to attack the NAACP, SCLC and even King himself because of their "coaptation" by the liberal white politicians during the Kennedy administration. Eventually, the cry of the neglected urban dweller became "Black Power." At a baccalaureate address at Howard University in 1966, Powell spoke these words:

> Human rights are God-given. Civil rights are manmade . . . Our life must be purposed to implement human rights . . . To demand these God-given rights is to seek black power—power to build black institutions of splendid achievement.[204]

After the assassination of Dr. King, on April 4, 1968, massive killings and riots erupted across America, especially in the black communities where businesses were looted and burned. The call for "Black Power" by Adam Clayton Powell, Jr., and later by Stokley Carmichael, a leading member of SNCC, the Student Non-violent Coordinating Committee which supported King and the movement, divided the masses pitting the young radicals against the patient conservatives. The militant concepts of the new hour changed from desegregation to liberation, from integration to self-determination. Thus, a new theology was created, a Black Theology to substantiate and perpetuate this magnetic force, Black Power. A young theologian named James H. Cone combined the two phrases in creating viable alternatives for the Black Church.

A Theology for Black Preaching and Womanist Perspectives on Preaching 1971 to the Present

The modern concepts of Black preaching derived from the need for a theology expressive of a new Black religion and a challenge for the church to intensify procedures in eliminating the racist system of the American political, social, and economic system. With an increasing awareness of the high percentage of women in the African American Church, Black women accepted the challenge, along with other daring Black men to pursue a quasi-revolutionary course towards freedom and equality.

Black Power and Black Theology

The quest for a relevant interpretation of the term "Black Power" became a major factor for black theologians as James H. Cone, Gayraud S. Wilmore, J.

DeOtis Roberts, and especially the black preachers who may have reluctantly subscribed to it. Cone, in his pivotal work *Black Theology and Black Power*, assesses this concept:

> To what object does it [Black Power] point? What does it mean when used by its advocates? It means complete emancipation of black people from white oppression by whatever means black people deem necessary. The methods may include selective buying, boycotting, marching, or even rebellion. Black Power means black freedom, black self-determination, wherein black people no longer view themselves as without human dignity but as men, human beings, with the ability to carve out their own destiny. Black Power means T.C.B., Take Care of Business—"black folk taking care of black folk's business" not on the terms of the oppressor, but on those of the oppressed.[205]

The concept brought immediate fear and tension within the ranks of both the white establishment and black leaders who did not want to conform to a new way of believing. The reality of a power based urban community for self-help, also became a concern of how this new found community would respond to God. This necessitated Cone to provide a functional concept of Black Theology. He further states:

> Black Theology must take seriously the reality of black people—their life of suffering and humiliation. Though the Christian doctrine of God must logically precede the doctrine of man, Black Theology knows that black people can view God only through black eyes that behold the brutalities of white racism. The task of Black Theology, then, is to analyze the black man's condition in the light of God's revelation in Jesus Christ with the purpose of creating a new understanding of black dignity among black people, and providing the necessary soul in that people, to destroy white racism. The purpose of Black Theology is to analyze the nature of the Christian faith in such a way that black people can say Yes to blackness and No to whiteness and mean it.[206]

The sources of this theological construct developed through the black experience, black history, black culture, revelation, scripture, and tradition. The scriptural reference for Black Theology focused on Luke 4:18–19, as Jesus Christ being the foundation for human liberation:

> The Spirit of the Lord is upon me, because he has anointed me to preach the good news to the poor. He has sent me to proclaim release to the captives and recovering of sight to the blind, To set at liberty those who are oppressed, To proclaim the acceptable year of the Lord. RSV

The context of black preaching for these times is centered upon the theme of liberation, redemption, and reconciliation. Cone offers a thorough conceptualization of the meaning of liberation in his book, *God of the Oppressed*. He writes:

> Jesus Christ, therefore, in his humanity and divinity, is the point of departure for a black theologian's analysis of the meaning of liberation. In this sense, liberation is not a human possession but a divine gift of freedom to those who struggle in faith against violence and oppression. Liberation is not an object but the "project" of freedom wherein the oppressed realize that their fight for freedom is a divine right of creation.[207]

Olin P. Moyd, a Maryland pastor and protege of J. Deotis Roberts, wrote a dissertation on the subject, "Redemption in Black Theology." His book provides biblical and theological dimensions of liberation for a better appreciation of the black theology movement:

> Black theology seeks to explicate the Black community's understanding of God's promise and the goal toward which He is directing the world while Black people in America are and were going through dehumanizing experiences. Redemption in the Black tradition is seen as a voluntary act on the part of the Redeemer on behalf of human kind in need of redemption.[208]

While the discontented majority joined the ranks of the new age Afro-Americans in response to over three hundred years of racism and dehumanization by whites, a black theologian named J. DeOtis Roberts sought to gain the necessary blend of both White Theology and Black Theology. His acclaimed work, *Black Theology: Liberation and Reconciliation*, tended to maintain the pacifist actions of Jesus instead of the need to rob, kill, and destroy. He explains that "reconciliation is a two-way street; it depends as much upon what whites will do to make conditions in race relations better as it does upon what blacks will not do."[209] Roberts, who primarily maintained this version of Black Theology in contrast to Cone and his group, adds a refined perspective after some years of reflection:

> Black theology addresses itself to a liberating understanding of reconciliation. Jesus becomes a radical and he is understood as the oppressed one or as a suffering slave because of his involvement in the liberation of the oppressed. Reconciliation is not merely vertical, it is horizontal as well. It involves understanding what God is doing in the world to set humans free and join him in the liberation push. Reconciliation does not exist from sharing power. It means whites giving up self-glory, the worship of white skin, and participating in a new humanity in which there are no slaves or masters but human beings.[210]

Thus, this new era of Black Theology conveyed a message which desperately needed to be shared in the context of faith, worship and the black church. To validate its urgency, at the annual convocation in 1969 of the National Committee of Black Churchmen, a prospectus defining Black Theology was adopted. The following statements are excerpts from the document:

> Black Theology is not a gift of the Christian gospel dispensed to slaves; rather it is an "appropriation" which black slaves made of the gospel given by their white oppressors. Black Theology is the product of black Christian experience and reflection. It comes out of the past. It is strong in the present. And we believe it is redemptive for the future. White Theology sustained the American slave system and negated the humanity of blacks. This indigenous Black Theology, based on the imaginative black experience, was the best hope for the survival of black people. Black Theology is a theology of black liberation. It is the affirmation of black humanity that emancipates black people from white racism, thus providing authentic freedom for both white and black people. It affirms the humanity of white people in that it says No to the encroachment of white oppression.[211]

This profound development of a new theology did not become the mouthpiece of every Black preacher; however, for the most part, their rhetoric did take on a more meaningful expression of pride, self-determination, and the call for reparations. The image of Black preaching stood between the crossroads of respect and responsibility and its effectiveness became a major concern.

Black Preaching

Although the term "black" has been articulated repeatedly in this section, its effect upon preaching during this historical period of realization took on a more aggressive posture towards liberation. The second book written in the C. Eric Lincoln Series in Black Religion was *Black Preaching* by Henry H. Mitchell. He presents a theological basis for the new voice:

> Black preaching is conditioned by the sociology, economics, government, culture—the total ethos of the Black ghetto. It is also affected by (and producing and changing) both a Black "summa theologica" and, in particular, a theology about itself. Much of this body of thought is unconscious and unformulated. However, the process of analysis and writing has begun. Professor James H. Cone's writings are especially good cases in point. Giving the primary emphasis to the immediate needs of men and putting the intellectual questions in their secondary place, the message for "now" has been proclaimed. The Black pulpit must give Blacks insights and inspiration to survive today's social jungle, while at the same time, arming them with the insights and inspirations to liberate themselves and eliminate oppression.[212]

Since the basis of Black preaching resolves more around experience than explication, it centers upon a kinship to ancient Israel and the prophetic traditions in the Old Testament. Mervyn Warrens believes that "if Black preachers are saying anything to the church today, it is a loud and clear message that religion must first meet a person where he is and whatever he is."[213]

The primary dilemma during this period of transition in the African American pulpit presented itself as a need for a corrective language of freedom. Hycel B. Taylor, a former professor of homiletics at Garret-Evangelical Theological Seminary in Chicago, states:

> The critical difficulty for black preaching for the present period of history when black redemption must be seen in terms of total liberation of the black man from the snares of racism, is that it has yet to translate its mythological language, both in word and deed, into eventful language that can deal with the possibility and actuality of black freedom. Black freedom is no longer a future possibility in the subconsciousness and consciousness of black men; it is a thoroughly conscious present reality that seeks the fullest expression by any means necessary.[214]

One of the key features for communicating the message of liberation and redemption in black preaching is style. Warren appraises this rhetorical element in quadripartite categories: effects, truth, ethics and methods (or artistics). Lawrence Carter, dean of the Morehouse College Chapel, goes further to describe the language mannerisms of black preaching as being that of poetry and not prose. He notes this distinctive element for several reasons:

> This language is not an ethnic dialect limited to pathos and humor; nor is it a regression to ghettoese which is merely a mutilation of English pronunciation. At its best black preaching expresses the racial spirit of Afro-American originality; it expresses the imagery, idiom, the peculiar turns of thought, and the distinctive humor and pathos punctuated by intense crescendo and diminuendo. It also expresses universal ideals, provincialistic facts, and profound feelings covering the widest range of subjects and variety of treatment.[215]

William A. Jones, renown pastor, preacher, and author, in an unpublished paper, states that there are five salient characteristics that accompany the posture of black preaching: the art of dialogue, the use of parallelism, cryptic language, the union of body and soul in delivery, and an uninhibited voice towards freedom and fearlessness. These factors might also be coupled with the five factors that John A. Blackwell, in his concept of the nature of black preaching, observes as "double memorization, double dialogue and identification, double vision, double freedom, and double consciousness."[216] These descriptions are more than significant to authenticate and appreciate the thrust of Black preaching and the memorable effects upon its hearers.

Due to the increased educational opportunities afforded most church attendants in the 1990s, the values of Afrocentricity[217] have frequently recreated economic coop-activism, as with Jesse Jackson—both on national and international levels. Most black clergy, as well as their ancestors, are involved in the rights of their people because politics and religion are inseparable in the African American community.[218]

Recently, C. Eric Lincoln and Lawrence H. Mamiya conducted an in depth empirical analysis on the conscious movement of the black church. They report:

> Our study is one of the first systematic, empirical attempts to begin charting the influence of the black consciousness movement upon the black clergy since the civil rights period. Given their strong leadership role in African American congregations, we assumed that this clerical elite will have an influence upon lay members through their sermons, personal theology, and educational methods. Our study was limited to the views of the clergy, and a further examination of the views of congregational members needs to be done in the future.[219]

Question six of that study asked the impact of sermons upon the changes in black consciousness since the civil rights movement. Clergy under forty and with more education tended to have attitudes toward explicitly emphasizing black pride, black power, etc., by responding with a 79.4% positive average. Older ministers over sixty and less educated did not feel the same high intensity for a black social consciousness and responded more negatively with a 53% average. In the same study, 65% of the clergy acknowledged that they had not been influenced by black theology or its theologians. At the 1983 annual meeting of Society for the Scientific Study of Religion, Lincoln and Mamiya presented a paper which reported that 92% of the churches surveyed expected their minister to be involved in social and political issues and another 91% felt him or her to be involved in protest marches on civil rights issues.[220]

The role of black preaching has basically remained unchanged since its inception on the slave plantations of the South and the abolitionist pulpits of the North. For these times, however, James Henry Harris, in a prophetic voice offers a convicting challenge for the African American preacher. He states:

> Preaching is an awesome responsibility, and our modern society harbors some equally awesome realities. Consequently, effective preaching cannot be limited to style and form or the substance of traditional Eurocentric theology and hermeneutics. Today, in addition to theological training, the black preacher needs to understand economics, history, and political theory in order to address the many needs of the Black Church. The context of

black preaching is one of urban and rural poverty, joblessness, homelessness, discrimination, and to lesser degree, black individual success, educational achievement, and economic independence. The context of the Black Church is a geographically urban and politically indifferent infrastructure, where despair and hopelessness are bred and nurtured. The preacher, both black and white, is compelled to prick the conscience of the oppressed and the oppressor in order that the cataclysmic message of Jesus might be heard in the ghettos, gentrified neighborhoods, suburbia, and rural hamlets throughout the nation and the world.[221]

Those who dare to accept the calling and challenge to proclaim that there is a Balm in Gilead to make the wounded and sin sick whole, will identify with liberating the oppressed.

Womanist Perspectives on Preaching

Although black women have acknowledged their personal rights to "the call" as God's chosen instruments long before the turn of the eighteenth century, their biblical and theological framework has recently come full circle. When Sojourner Truth stood to her full height of six feet and with a voice one observer likened to the apocalyptic thunders, she told an 1851 convention during her famous speech "Ain't I A Woman?" that

> . . . if the first woman God ever made was strong enough to turn the world upside down all alone, these women together ought to be able to turn it back, and get it right side up again. And now they are asking to do it, and the men better let them.[222]

The persistent struggle of black women to claim their rightful place in American society has been an ongoing religious, political, and social battle. Through the trials and tribulations of slavery the black woman believed in herself and in a God who allowed faith to prevail in the midst of racism, classism, and sexism. Dr. Thomas Kilgore, a supporter of women clergy, believes "the raising up of women to preach is God's way of saying that blacks must come of age and let the church be the church. Its ultimate purpose is to glorify God."[223]

The womanist perspectives on preaching, however, no longer rest upon the views, actions, and acceptance of a dominant, patriarchal board of ecclesiastical overseers. Black womanist theologians[224] have ably provided the theological arguments for their inclusion in the Black Theology movement which did not directly, nor ultimately address the human suffrage of black women. Jacquelyn Grant, Professor of Systematic Theology at the Interdenominational Theological Center, and an ordained A.M.E. clergy, writes:

> Just as White women formerly had no place in White Theology—except as the receptors of White men's theological interpretations—Black women have had no place in the development of Black Theology. By self-appointment, or by the sinecure of a male-dominated society, Black men have deemed it proper to speak for the entire Black community, male and female. Many Black women are enraged as they listen to "liberated" Black men speak about the "place of women" in words and phrases similar to those of the very White oppressors they condemn. If the liberation of women is not proclaimed, the church's proclamation cannot be about divine liberation. If the church does not share in the liberation struggle of Black women, its liberation struggle is not authentic.[225]

In order to overcome the oppression of a male, white, feminist oriented church atmosphere, a Womanist Theology emerged as the definitive voice for black woman clergy. Because of the black women's experience, they have identified oppression coming from both genders of the white world. Delores Williams argues that "since white women join white men in oppressing black women (and in maintaining white supremacy), black women need nomenclature and language which reflect this reality."[226]

In Pulitzer Prize-winning novelist Alice Walker's book, *In Search of Our Mother's Garden*, the language describing the black folk expression, "You acting womanish" originated, as she fully explicates the concept:

> The term means wanting to know more and in greater depth than is good for one . . . outrageous, audacious, courageous and willful behavior. A womanist is responsible, in charge, serious. She can walk to Canada and take others with her. She loves, she is committed, she is a universalist by temperament. Her universality includes loving men and women, sexually or nonsexually. She is not a separatist. She loves music, dance, the moon, the spirit, food and roundness, struggle, the folk, and she loves herself. "Regardless." A womanist is a Black feminist or feminist of color. Womanist is to feminist as purple is to lavender.[227]

The theological relevance of this language has become the symbol of the black woman's experience in America. It resonates in what some womanist theologians term "holy boldness." Ethicist Katie G. Canon offers a concluding commentary on the beginnings of this black feminist consciousness by stating that:

> this tradition identifies those biblical texts (Gen. 1:26–28, Mark 7:26–30, Luke 4:18, Acts 2:17 & 9:36, and Gal. 3:28) which help black womanists to celebrate and rename . . . innumerable incidents of unpredictability in empowering ways.[228]

The responsibility of doing theology from a tri-dimensional experience of racism/sexism/classism support these and other interpretations for the role of women preachers.

The Methodist Church and Women Preachers

The earliest documented recollections of a black woman preacher were in the writings of Jarena Lee, the first woman evangelist identified with the African Methodist Episcopal Church. She acknowledged her call at the age of twenty-four and requested a license to preach from Rev. Richard Allen, organizer and pastor of the Bethel A.M.E. Church of Philadelphia. In her autobiography, *The Life and Religious Experience of Jarena Lee*, she recalled her conversion experience to proclaim the gospel:

> Between four and five years after my sanctification, on a certain time, an impressive silence fell upon me, and I stood as if some one was about to speak to me, yet I had no such thought in my heart. But to my utter surprise there seemed to sound a voice which I thought I distinctly heard, and most certainly understood, which said to me, "Go preach the Gospel!" I immediately replied aloud, "No one will believe me." Again I listened, and again the same voice seemed to say, "Preach the Gospel; I will put words in your mouth, and will turn your enemies to become your friends."[229]

Although she never received an official license to preach, she organized several prayer meetings, preached throughout the new America, and became the pioneer preacher for all aspiring black women. Other women, such as Sophie Murray, Elizabeth Cole, Rachael Evans (Bishop Handy noted congregations considered her a better preacher than her husband), Harriet Taylor, Zilpha Elaw, the internationally known evangelist, singer, Amanda Smith, and the Zionists preachers Harriet Tubman and Julia A. J. Foote, the first woman to be officially ordained in 1891, all became the avant garde for A.M.E. and A.M.E. Zion preaching women. Theirs was a personal divine call to preach the gospel and evangelize the community, "not to look after the females . . . [and] assist the stewards, class leaders, and pastor of a single congregation."[230]

In 1884, Bishop Henry McNeal Turner led a movement for the licensing and ordination of women as deacons in the denomination. The ordination of women preachers eventually became a reality in 1948. Today, there are over 700 women pastors in the denomination. One of the most stellar leaders in an old-line A.M.E. Church was the Rev. Dr. Vashti McKenzie. She ministered in her hometown of Baltimore, Maryland at the Payne Memorial A.M.E. Church and became the first woman bishop of the denomination in 2000.[231] Hopefully, she and others will follow the first African American woman bishop of the Episcopalian Church, Rev. Barbara Harris and the Rev. Leontine Kelly, the first African American woman Bishop of the United Methodist Church.

The Baptist Church and Women Preachers

Opportunities for women entering the preaching ministry of black Baptist denominations have been limited, stifling, and even nonexistent in some places. The Progressive Baptist Convention has initiated a proactive stance in accepting black women as clergy, even in the pastorate. This has been the result of timely perseverance, continuous training and theological preparation, and God's fervent anointing upon "all flesh."

The growth of the black Baptist church from 1780 to 1880 was primarily due to the fact that white plantation owners allowed slaves an opportunity to hear the gospel, the role of the slave preacher, and the development of schools and colleges for former slaves. During Reconstruction, the American National Baptist Convention was organized which "provided a much needed intellectual outlet for many of the younger and more progressive brothers and sisters graduating from Northern-sponsored Southern black schools."[232]

Virtually every black Baptist state convention organized a women's missionary unit for the sole purpose of raising money and doing missionary duties. Some men believed such a division would provide the women a feeling of superiority over them. Virginia Broughton, a staunch supporter of the women's convention in Tennessee, traveled extensively up the Mississippi River as a missionary. She recalls going to Cooter, Missouri "a place where few Negro men dared to go to preach, and a woman missionary of no race had ever gone."[233] Evelyn Brooks offers a constructive insight on the issue of the women's growth and the minister's hostility:

> The black women's movement in Tennessee met with strong opposition from black ministers. Ministers carefully studied the Bible, Broughton observed, to learn if aggressive missionary roles for women were sanctioned. Several ministers became jealous of the growing popularity of women leaders among their black Baptist sisters. Male hostility became especially intense after the ninth annual meeting in Durhamville. Broughton attributed the cause for the hostility to the powerful spiritual manifestations that some of the women revealed to the crowd: "Several sisters came with revelations, visions, and prophecies that made indelible impressions." The pressure of the male opposition grew so strong during the following year that women's bible bands were forced to discontinue in many churches.[234]

Eventually, women began advocating more positions reflecting female authority, including that of deaconness and speaker at the largest yearly fundraiser, the church's annual Sister's Day or commonly known today as Women's Day. These actions prompted men in Alabama to complain that "the women do not allow them to talk enough in their meetings."[235] Leontine T. C. Kelly clarifies this expression by acknowledging a woman's right to speak on this day:

The institution of Women's Day in the black church of practically all denominations gave opportunity for the development of "women speakers," who always began with the demure excuse, "Now, I'm really no preacher, but . . ." Then they would proceed to preach the Word, really preach the Word in the completely identifiable black style, receiving the same response—even from the men. As long as it was a Women's Day celebration, this expression was acceptable.[236]

The womanist theology of the black Baptist Church during the closing two decades of the nineteenth century centered upon racial equality and salvation for the world. According to Brooks, who writes:

Despite the broad number of roles that Broughton believed the Bible authorized, she explicitly warned women against the danger of aspiring to those that had no female precedents. She denied that women should have access to the clergy or perform the clergy's role of establishing new churches, baptizing converts, and administering the Eucharist. Notwithstanding these proscriptions, Broughton argued for woman's presence on the executive boards of both state and national conventions of the denomination.[237]

It would be only a few "risings and settings" of the sun before spirit-filled women assumed complete authorization to preach in black Baptist churches.

At the 1895 convention of the newly organized National Baptist Convention, U.S.A., it was decided to allow the women to have their own convention and officers; however, "the new convention of black churchmen did not grant women power to make policy or to vote as delegates."[238] In 1900 a talented and eloquent orator named Nannie H. Burroughs of Washington, D. C. became corresponding secretary of the women's convention. She also held a secretarial position at the office of the Foreign Mission Board of the convention in Louisville, Kentucky. The heady Ms. Burroughs represented her convention at the World Baptist Congress held in London during July 11–19, 1905. It was here that Burroughs' oratorical abilities and genius gained her the favor and admiration of the crowds present at Exter Hall and Hyde Park. In the same year, after a four year debate, she finally received permission by president Dr. E. C. Morris "to establish a national woman's training school to prepare black women to work as home and foreign missionaries, to teach Sunday School and to give better domestic service."[239] On October 19, 1909, the National Training School for Women and Girls officially opened in Washington, D. C. with Nannie Burroughs as its founding president. The school soon became the "prize" of all National Baptists. Bishop Kelly in her review of the black preaching tradition adds:

The unordained black woman has long been preacher-spiritual leader. When you read the words of a Sojourner Truth, you sense her style as traditional preaching. Harriet Tubman moved on her faith and "preached" freedom on the journey. Ms. Nannie Burroughs, Baptist woman educator, "preached" women into early morning prayer meetings in Washington, D. C. years ago. I remember hearing the feet of many women who responded to her powerful messages by walking to the early morning prayer meetings in protest of the treatment of blacks and women in the capital of our country. We were told to stay in bed until our own mother returned from the meetings.[240]

It was from such beginnings of a standard prayer service that Baptist women formulated their talents and developed skills of communication. These women were not always literate, but they stood firm on the Word of God and used their wisdom and pride to advance the culture of their mothers, by leading a race of people to "de Lawd."

In many instances, such traditional prayer services became the setting for female "preaching." Harold Carter, a leading African American pastor, lecturer, and revivalist from Baltimore, Maryland takes this issue of prayer bands into account:

> Black women who lead in some form of prayer ministry across America seem to owe some of their calling to the inherited role of the African priestess. This is especially true where women, using the title "Mother," minister to persons in the general areas of healing, family advice, and the normal problems of life. Examples of women founding churches from prayer bands and carrying on community ministries are indeed numerous. Every major city in America would seem to have some Black woman with a prayer ministry of some sort, calling herself under the general heading "Mother." These women cannot be ignored. They continue to have a following among the poor, the socially dispossessed, and among those who feel that more established doors to solutions are closed.[241]

Drs. Ella and Henry Mitchell, both Baptist theologians and preachers, provide a critical overview of the historical role of women preachers in the book, *Women: To Preach or Not To Preach*.[242] Of the twenty-one sermons supporting women preachers, notable, prominent Baptist pastors and scholars namely Charles G. Adams, John W. Kinney, W. Franklyn Richardson, Anthony C. Campbell, J. Alfred Smith, Gardner Taylor, Samuel D. Proctor, and G. Daniel Jones favor women preachers in the Baptist Church.

Lincoln and Mamiya, who have further explored the historical accounts of the development of black women preachers in their epic work, *The Black Church in the African American Experience*, note that all three major black Methodist denominations have ordained women clergy. The Colored Methodist Episcopal Church granted full rights to women in 1954. The authors give the following indictment on black Baptists:

> For women in the three black Baptist denominations (National Baptist Convention, U.S.A., Inc., National Baptist Convention of America, Uninc., and Progressive National

Baptist Convention), the struggle and quest for full ordination into the ministry has been even more difficult. The complete history of black preaching women among the Baptists is undocumented and difficult to trace because the independent church polity of the Baptists ensures the autonomy of each congregation in matters of faith and practice. While there is no specific policy against the ordination of women in any of the black Baptist denominations, the general climate has not been supportive of women preaching and pastoring churches. However, in recent years there has been a small minority of black clergymen who have sponsored women candidates for ordination in their associations. The Baptist principle of congregational autonomy has been helpful in these cases since the independence of each church and pastor cannot be challenged by any denominational authority.[243]

When the Reverend Suzan Johnson Cook became pastor of Mariners' Temple Baptist Church of Manhattan, New York, it marked an historic "first" for African American women within the American Baptist denomination. She currently serves as president of the Hampton Ministers Conference, the largest African American ecumenical body in America. Other women pastors, who also have gained solid reputations as leaders of black congregations include Rev. Millicent Thompson, Ed.D. co-pastor of Baptist Worship Center Church of Philadelphia, Rev. Ernestine Cleveland Reems, pastor of the Center of Hope Community Church, Oakland and daughter of the late Bishop E. E. Cleveland who was a maverick preacher from northern California, the legendary Johnnie Colemon of Christ Universal Temple in Chicago, Dr. Barbara King of the Hillside International Truth Center, Atlanta, Dr. Cynthia James, Landmark Ministries, Inc. in Oakland, Evangelist Iona Locke, of Perfecting Church, Detroit, and Dr. Audrey Bronson, Sanctuary Church of the Open Door, Philadelphia. Wherever Baptist doors have been shut, other nondenominational opportunities have always been readily available to black women.

The Sanctified Church and Women Preachers

The salvation of African American woman preachers realized itself when they were literally forced to go outside traditional religious bodies for their vocational interest. While the Church of God in Christ (COGIC) strictly forbids ordaining women as elders, bishops, or pastors, the Holiness and Pentecostal movements have traditionally welcomed women in whatever capacity they needed to be. The Sanctified Church, a symbolic phrase by Zora Neale Hurston, represents these black sects and cults which needed their own expressions of faith. Cheryl Townsend Gilkes cogently remarks:

The Sanctified Church encompasses those independent denominations and congregations formed by black people in the post-Reconstruction South and their direct organizational descendants. These churches arose largely in conflict with the older denominations (Baptist and Methodists). The Sanctified Church is important because its small size carried with it a large cultural impact. The Sanctified Church had a respect for and positive redefinition of black women's special historical background. It came to prominence at a time when the role of black women in their community and the larger society was under tremendous negative pressure. In light of the repression of the nineteenth century, the Sanctified Church affirmed "the freedom of womanhood" in a number of ways.[244]

Here, the black community in general and black women in particular found positive support, especially all those who suffered the worst injustices in the slave system. Women were taught the finer mannerisms of being "ladified" along with a deeper appreciation of religious morals and values. With possibly over ninety percent of the members being female, the church appeared to be a woman's movement. Moreover, Gilkes further states that "the success of Sanctified Church evangelists was often due in large part to the response of other women to their preaching."[245] The strategy behind organizing a church of this caliber rested upon the women evangelist preaching revivals to gain members, then finding a building, and requesting a pastor from headquarters, usually in the South. In these storefront ministries, women adopted the role of pastor-teacher throughout the process of urban ethnogenesis. This process enabled black people who had made cultural choices in favor of tradition to maintain their choice within the context of a like-minded constituency.[246]

Elder Lucy Smith, a former member of two distinguished Chicago Baptist churches, Olivet and Ebenezer, ultimately found spiritual freedom among white Pentecostals and received a calling of divine healing. Joseph R. Washington writes:

> This calling was responded to by scores of migrants, who aided her move from the single-prayer meeting sessions that began in her home in 1916 to the establishment in the 1930s of the all Nations Pentecostal Church on a fashionable street. Elder Lucy Smith was a "black puritan preaching holiness," variously described as elderly, corpulent, maternal, dark-skinned, a simple, ignorant, untrained woman with deep human sympathies, who believed absolutely in her own power to help and heal other people. "My church is for all nations and my preachin' for all Christians."[247]

Another Pentecostal personality who capitalized on this movement during the early twenties was Bishop Ida Robinson, founder and organizer of the Mt. Sinai Holy Church of Philadelphia in 1924. In *Black Gods of the Metropolis*, Arthur Fauset describes her pastoral authority:

Bishop Robinson is tall, sharp of feature and eye, medium brown in color, probably of mixed Indian-Negro blood. Her education has been limited, but she is extremely intelligent, and a competent leader. She is, of course, a keen student of the Bible. Her authority is said to come directly from God. All during the sermon there is much shouting, "Amen! Praise the Lord!," etc., and from time to time the preacher interrupts her discourse with a song which is taken up by the congregation. If the preacher senses that her words are not getting over, or that there is a lassitude creeping over the congregation, she will cry out "Help me!" or she will plead, "Holy Ghost speak through me!" The sermon varies in length, sometimes being relatively brief, twenty minutes to a half hour, at other times an hour or more. When the sermon ends usually with a song rather than a spoken prayer, the preacher may sit down and relax after the strenuous performance or she may start at once to take up the collection.[248]

Though the Sanctified Church seemed meaningless to the black establishment, it afforded those African American women, who knew that God had called and sanctioned them for the purpose of preaching, a legitimate locale to exercise their gifts, skills, and talents.

Woman as Preacher

The argument against black women in pulpits has become at best an odious, remote discussion among the trained and educated womanist theologians and clergy. In the book, *African American Religious Studies*, Dr. Cheryl Sanders, Professor of Ethics at Howard University School of Divinity, offers a comparative analysis using thirty-six sermons, eighteen by men and eighteen by women, of the differences and similarities of black women and men preachers in relation to "the use of inclusive language, central themes, biblical texts, sermon form, and homiletical task such as exhorting, testifying, and teaching."[249] The focus of study centered around whether the distinctiveness of women's preaching enabled God to speak with a womanist voice. A summation of her analysis resolved the following:

There appears not to be much difference between women and men in the selection of sermon form. The women and men in the sample appeared to be more alike than different in the selection of biblical texts for their sermons. Three themes were common to the preaching of both women and men: the church and its mission, Christian virtues, and racial identity. I have identified seventeen homiletical tasks that the preachers in the sample have undertaken in their sermons. There seems to have been a consensus among both women and men preachers not to lend great importance either to celebration or to liturgical concerns. We can say that women and men preach the same Word but with distinctive "accents"—women tend to emphasize the personal and men the prophetic.[250]

It is through academic scholarship such as that provided above which validates a woman's human rights to proclaim her love for God, experiences with Christ, and full endowment of the Holy Ghost.

Catherine Louise Peck, in her Master's thesis, raised other key concerns towards the oratorical abilities of women as preachers and pastors in the African Methodist Episcopal Zion denomination. She interviewed four leading pastors, an ordained minister, and Evangelist Shirley Caesar who all minister in North Carolina. Each woman affirmed their overall style and development not to male preachers, but to the traditions of African American folklore. She explains this phenomenon:

> All of the women in this study—from Reverend Council who claims she is inexperienced to Reverend Brown who has been preaching for thirty years—witness to the fact that they have absorbed and preserved the traditional hortatory techniques as faithfully and precisely as men have. One may discern many traditional elements in their sermons: direct references to people in the congregation, stock phrases such as "I heard somebody say," or, "They tell me that . . ." preceding a Biblical passage. That these sermons, like those Rosenberg recorded are "composed largely by using language that is formulaic" seems clear. In form and style of delivery, their sermons follow the formulas that any student of folk sermon will recognize. In the content of their sermons, too, these women follow tradition. They exemplify those traditional artists whose material arises organically from his or her personality and experience in that their sermons are often blatantly feminine in subject and imagery.[251]

African American women preachers have made themselves available and accessible to the hereditary genius of their ancestors, the oral traditions, and narratives in sharing the gospel witness. In the spirit of compliment, the distinguished Pastor Emeritus of the Concord Baptist Church of Christ, the Reverend Dr. Gardner C. Taylor sanctioned women preachers when he declared:

> I came to appreciate women as I taught women in school. I began to see an inkling of spiritual and religious leadership in them. I am open to this if a woman has been properly trained in the ministry.[252]

African American women are being trained at the best theological schools worldwide and their acceptance into the gospel ministry which has been long overdue is now evident in our midst.

Summary

This study of African American preaching has produced an opportunity for the reader to gain a better perspective of the historical approach to the discipline. The intention is to lay sufficient groundwork for evaluating Taylor's sermons in their proper capacity.

Since a comprehensive overview of African American preaching as a rhetorical study has yet to be done, this effort has attempted to present the methodologies and backgrounds of historically celebrated preachers during the ongoing development of African American people in America. Slaves were captured and forcibly brought to this land with nothing more than their cultural heritage of God which fortified their existence and survival as a people.

It was necessary to discover that the early slave preachers established a precedent for preaching against the evils of society. This voice of prophetic protest remains a vital part of the contemporary African American preaching tradition. One must also conclude that women preachers are not some new prodigy within the Black church. Their place in the pulpit has been solidified by a resilience to overcome rejection and become an integral part of the African American preaching tradition.

There are significant challenges for the Black church to determine its course of action in the coming days. Black Theology of the sixties and seventies will find a wider audience through seminary trained men and women. The future of African American preaching, however, must continue to climb upon the backs of those gallant heralds who would not take "no" for an answer. They knew that "God would make a way somehow."

In the context of an historical overview of African American preaching, these chapters offer a greater opportunity to study and analyze the ministerial life, preaching methodology, and rhetorical talents of Dr. Gardner C. Taylor.

CHAPTER FOUR

The Life and Ministry of
Gardner Calvin Taylor

To appreciate, analyze, and reflect upon the preaching ministry of Taylor, one needs some understanding of the major influences on his life and the development of his professional identity as a person, preacher of the gospel, pastor, and pedagogue. The purpose of this chapter is to provide a concise history of Taylor's life, calling attention to the important events and relationships as they help to fashion the man and his ministry. What is set forth here is by no means an attempt at a complete biography; rather, the historical information is given as a descriptive background for a more thorough study of his preaching. This is necessary because an analysis of his preaching ministry through the artistic canon cannot be complete without some understanding of his background.[253]

Taylor is the primary informant about his background, and the materials collected during personal and telephone interviews were recorded and preserved on microcassette tapes.[254] Additional information was obtained from Taylor's wives, family members, previous church members, former students, and colleagues. A more comprehensive history would demand that more personal references be secured as well as "cross-checking" dates, events, which are beyond the scope of this research. The goal pursued here toward understanding Taylor is to trace his identity and to translate important factors discerned in the process.

Interpretations of the data stated in this chapter are given by Taylor, this writer, and additional informants. Unless otherwise cited, all of the material comes directly from the interviews with the phrases in quotation marks as direct quotes from Taylor. To facilitate reading and writing style, footnotes are used only to cite informants other than Taylor.

His Early Influences

On June 18, 1918, Gardner Calvin Taylor was born to a Baptist preacher-father and an educated mother. He was the only child of this union and was considered special early on because he came thirteen years after his parents were married. (There was also an eighteen year difference in their ages.) The young Gardner was reared on South Boulevard in Baton Rouge, Louisiana. After the death of his father, a great aunt, Miss Gerty, moved in to assist with the raising of the precocious lad. Taylor described her as a rough-speaking little woman who virtually "ruled" their neighborhood, which was white and black. Outside of his father, she was the only one who could kept young Gardner straight. "She saw a little meanness in me, and did not mind or excuse laying her hands on me." Later, a foster sister, Theresa, came to live with them and helped his aunt and mother care for Gardner and persons who roomed at their home.

His Father

The Reverend Washington Monroe Taylor, born five years after the end of slavery in 1865, often told his son that "you could almost still hear the echo of hounds baying on the trail of runaway slaves." Gardner remembered his father as one who did not finish high school, but was always reading constructive literature. Gardner's father was impressed by some insights from Charles Darwin's *Origin of the Species*,[255] often talking about the "battle of the fittest." As they would be driving past the Louisiana State University Agricultural Facilities in the middle 1920s, the senior Taylor lamented out loud "that their livestock had better housing in the fields than many Negroes living in Louisiana."

At Gardner's birth, his father preached regularly to the largest crowd in Baton Rouge, many of whom had been in slavery. Washington Monroe Taylor addressed the issues of his day and continually kept a ray of hope before the congregation that a better day was on the horizon. The Mt. Zion Baptist Church ministry attracted several local educators, prominent community leaders, and the common laborers. It was because of his aggressive ministry that Wash Taylor, as he was commonly known, eventually became president of the Louisiana State Baptist Convention and a Vice President in the National Baptist Convention, U.S.A., Inc. He was known everywhere, and with his large heavy-set build and dark complexion, he carried weight in more ways than one. Mr. Herman Stewart, a boyhood friend of Gardner Taylor stated:

> He was the man at that time, Wash Taylor was. When he said something, "That was it!" He would even give the governor's inauguration prayer in Louisiana. When he married you, he didn't have no book. When he would bury you, he didn't have no book, he did not read nothing.[256]

Wash Taylor's popularity increased through his gifted use of language, a style of preaching uncommon at that time. Gardner Taylor characterized his father as "having a natural gift for the language, a graphic language formation that came natural to him."

Although the respected pastor only had some high school education, he was well read and possessed an above average library for a Negro preacher, at that time. Dr. C. D. Simmons, a former Louisville, Kentucky pastor who, at fifteen years of age, heard Wash Taylor preach a baccalaureate sermon around 1924 at Foster's High School in Washatau Parish, Louisiana, recalled that "he preached like the old style, much emotion and power, but with eloquent language. His method was different."[257] Having heard his father's sermons as a child, Gardner remembered the terms, expressions, and wording which later came natural for him to follow in that line of preaching. Using various notebooks that Gardner's mother kept of his father's sermons in long hand, "one could easily detect a similarity in the phraseology and diction between he and his father."[258]

In 1931, Washington Monroe Taylor, passed from this life leaving a preaching legacy that his son would forever cherish.

His Mother

Selina Gesell Taylor was a small, gentle, light-skinned woman with gorgeous black hair who genuinely loved her only son. An extremely intelligent woman, she attended college but never finished. She did, however, complete what was known as the "normal course" which black people and white people taught in Louisiana. Selina Taylor did not work outside of the home until the death of her husband. She then became a school teacher at Perkins Road School, attended by the Negro children. Gardner Taylor remembered that "after my father's death, we were land poor; we had some land but no money and the land was not worth anything back then. She had to go to work and she did, supporting the two of us."

Remaining a few steps ahead of poverty was difficult, but Selina Taylor was industrious and steady. Wash Taylor's death left his wife and son in major debt to several people, but she was faithful in arranging payment for their bills and paid every one of them off from her fifty-two dollars a month salary, while white teachers were getting a hundred and four doing the same job. Despite conditions, the Taylor family survived the times.

Gardner's mother was a staunch educator and it reflected in the way her son learned, read, and recited quite early as a child. During the annual Youth Days at Mt. Zion when children assumed the roles of church leaders, her son always gave the sermon speech. Ruby Taylor Harris, a first cousin, explained "she drilled him over and over again, until he had that sermon speech memorized word for word, flawless."[259] The primary interest her son later showed toward biblical narratives was initiated through his mother's reading them to him. Gardner vividly recalled:

> Yes, she used to read me stories from *Great Stories of the Bible Illustrated for Children* which early enhanced my imagination. I could actually see those people and I would go to bed with those figures, and what they were doing and why they were doing it. It was a wonderful experience.[260]

In a sermon based on Genesis 6:3–6 which he delivered at the McCreary Center for African American Religious Studies in Cleveland, Ohio, Taylor stated that "as a boy my mother would read that story of Noah to me and I could almost hear the taunts of his neighbors, interspersed with the echo of the ringing of Noah's hammer." The imaginativeness of the preacher-to-be was nurtured and encouraged by his intelligent and godly mother.

When his Aunt Gerty died in Baton Rouge in 1955, Gardner Taylor brought his mother to Brooklyn, New York to live. Selina Gesell Taylor thus spent the last fourteen years of her life listening to her son preach before one of the largest Black Baptist congregations in America. She departed this life in 1969 at the age of 81.

His Formative Years

Those who observed and knew the only child of Pastor Wash and Selina Taylor, perceived that he had what some people called "old folk's sense" due to his late birth. Gardner was quite active and playful as a child, and being the son of a prominent minister, everybody made much over him. Though he was not a spoiled child, he was boisterous and sometimes noisy. Theresa, who came to live with the Taylor family when he was four years old, recalled a few of the young Gardner's traits:

> He was always the leader of the group among the children in the neighborhood. And whenever they had anything to say or do in the church with speaking lines, his friends at an early age started calling him "Rev." and it just seemed to follow him.[261]

Gardner was the pride and joy of his father who called him "Marster," which meant "Master" in their Louisiana bayou idiom. Mrs. Foster notes that "his father's eyes were not large enough to see him; and when his father said, "Marster," he said it all."[262] This father-son relationship became a cornerstone in the personal development and faith of Gardner Taylor.

To aid their son's eagerness to learn, every evening Rev. Taylor would have the nine-year-old read him the daily newspaper as one of his chores. Indeed, this helped Gardner gain an appreciation for a wider vocabulary and detailed expressions. Since Gardner was an only child, his parents constantly kept other young people in his company so that he would develop naturally and build personal and lasting relationships. Taylor has stated, "I have been blessed to have had people around me all the days of my life."

The young Gardner was fascinated with books, and loved to read which became a key asset in his rhetorical training. Because Negroes were not permitted to attend public libraries during that era in Baton Rouge, Theresa, a student at Southern University, would supply him with books from the college library. She recounted:

> He would stay up all night to read a book if he had to give it back the next day. The furnished libraries were for White people, and even though ours was not the best equipped, it was the best that we had. He would tell me to bring him a book home because there were not any he could get from the library here. And when I would bring them home, he would read them so fast, that the librarian asked me, "Are you reading all of those books?" I told her no, "I'm taking them to Gardner so he could read them." She said, "Ask him what kind he likes." And so I did, and he replied, "Mysteries, mystery books." She sent those and others that he needed to read as well. All while I was in college, I had to keep him supplied with books to read, 'cause that is one thing he would do; he would read.[263]

Blessed with intelligent parents, a healthy family environment, and a community of caring friends and fellow church members, the young Gardner C. Taylor received steady encouragement to excel in life spiritually, socially, and scholastically.

Public Elementary and High School Education

During his early elementary schooling, Gardner showed exceptional promise as a student. While in Mrs. Tody Thomas' fourth grade class, a psychologist came from Louisiana State University to give him and a few others an IQ test. Gardner's test scores were the highest ever recorded in the state.[264] Because the majority of white educators believed white children were superior to black children in learning aptness, the scores seemed unrealistic. However, when the department determined that the highest score was achieved by a black child, they returned to the school and gave Gardner a similar test. He again scored the top IQ rating of any elementary child, black or white, in Louisiana during the mid-1920s. Taylor has reported:

> When I came home from school that day, my people had all of this candy for me and I could not understand it. I really did it. And then the man came back and I took another test, and he said that I had a certain IQ. He was a white university professor. They said, "I had the best mind in the schools, but I told them that did not say much, because in Louisiana schools, there were not many minds there no way."[265]

Later, however, Taylor did not always show such genius when he barely got by in high school with grades of 75, 78, and 80. Having lost interest in the school's curriculum, along with a deep dislike for mathematics, geometry, and algebra, he discovered a deepening appreciation for history, literature, and civics. "Things I was interested in I did well. I read widely in history and that was interesting." During the public assembly when grade averages were announced monthly, Professor Paige would call out Gardner's average and remark, "Uh, uh, uh, a good mind going to waste with a grade of 76."

Dr. Milton Froyd, an executive with the American Baptist Convention and a professor at Colgate Rochester now deceased, pursued the initial case study and tracked Gardner Taylor's academic accomplishments from that time and beyond seminary, substantiating his rare aptitude.[266] The teenage Taylor overcame his early lack-luster performances, and became valedictorian of his class and captain of the McKinley High School varsity football team.

College

After high school, Gardner Taylor received a football scholarship to attend Leland College, a Negro Baptist school in Baker, Louisiana, twelve miles north of Baton Rouge. The president of the college, Dr. J. A. Bacoats, used to ride down and preach for Wash Taylor after Taylor's health declined. Bacoats eventually succeeded him as pastor of Mt. Zion. This allowed a closer relationship with Bacoats, and Gardner continued to develop academically, showing excellence in his studies.

It was during this increasingly fruitful time in Taylor's life that his dream of becoming a lawyer gained momentum, since it had long been his ambition. His college friends never considered him becoming a minister, even though his father had been a prominent one. Instead, he spent considerable time studying public speaking and rhetorical discourse while anchoring the debate team. Daniel Haley, a college roommate commented:

> In the dormitory, the only thing that separated us for three years was a wall. My room was right next to his room. And often times I would walk out of my room and Gardner Taylor would be in his room a lot of times alone and you could hear him speaking and going through lectures. At that time it did not seem as if he was inclined to become a minister. When he debated, you already knew which side was going to win. He had a well trained mind and was very skillful, but even with all of that he was modest and well-liked. He was kind of like a Churchill. He carried himself portly.[267]

Taylor enjoyed his friends and college life. Honoring his jovial bent on several occasions to tell jokes about himself, he had a special way of putting those around him in a relaxed atmosphere. Several years later, a friend, Dave Means, on their fishing trip, told him that "when you went into the ministry, the stage lost a comedian." Being a well-liked person and "one of the fellows," he possessed a great sense of humor along with his academic capabilities.

During his college days, Taylor used his rhetorical aptness to attack and dismay the young preachers in his dormitory. On several occasions, he made many of them look ridiculous during their debates over biblical issues. Having his father's library at his disposal, Gardner read many theological books. One of them, Robert Green Ingersoll's *Some Mistakes of Moses*,[268] lodged questionable notions in Taylor's mind. Having read the book out of curiosity prior to entering college, he was aware of that agnostic writer's views about Moses and myths in the Bible. He put embarrassing questions to fellow students and others who were preachers, giving occasion for the other students to laugh at them and scorn their inability to respond effectively. Years later, Taylor ashamedly commented:

> When I think about it now, tears almost come to my eyes, because it was unworthy. They were young men who were sincere and had declared themselves and I guess through all of that I was struggling against my call into the gospel ministry.[269]

It was a time in his life when he thought there was something absurd about religious faith.

Struggling against the call into the gospel ministry during this time in his life, Taylor experienced a momentary sigh of relief in his senior year, when he was accepted into the University of Michigan Law School. His acceptance was conditional because Leland was not an accredited institution, but Taylor unwaveringly believed that he could become the best politician and criminal lawyer in the country. He confessed feeling strange about it, "not knowing how in the name of God they accepted me, at a time when no black person ever had been admitted to the Louisiana State Bar."

While attending Leland College, Taylor served as a chauffeur for Dr. Bacoats who was now pastoring the Mt. Zion Baptist Church. In a Johnson Publication book, *Why I Believe There Is A God*, Taylor described his conversion experience:

> Late on a spring afternoon of my senior year at Leland, I was rushing back to the campus along Highway 61 in Dr. Bacoats' car when Death brushed ever so close. Two white men in an old Ford suddenly veered across the highway. I slammed the brakes and steered the car toward the ditch. Too late! One man was dead or dying, blood gushed out of his nostrils and mouth and ears. The other was lying groaning on the side of the road. The

only witnesses were a poor farmer ploughing in his field by the road and a local Baptist preacher named Jesse Sharkey who was on his way from work at the Standard Oil Company. Remember, this was rural Louisiana and the year was 1937. Lynching was then more than a dark memory in the national reflection. However, a strange calm came over me that April afternoon and a Strong Figure whom my father and mother had first mentioned to me came back to stand at my side. God was real again, very real. The next morning at the inquest, both of these poor white men testified that I was in no way responsible for the fatal accident. My quick brush with death that afternoon, either from the accident or at the hands of a mob, turned me imperiously toward consideration of the meaning of my life and the ultimate purpose of human existence. Consequently, upon the recommendation of Dr. Bacoats, I went to the Oberlin Graduate School of Theology, sure that the "Old Blessed Figure," God, about whom I had first heard from my parents, willed it so.[270]

Later in the summer of 1937, Gardner Calvin Taylor acknowledged his call to become a minister of the gospel. He preached a trial sermon at the Mt. Zion Baptist Church before a standing room only congregation. He titled his sermon "Come and Follow Me and I Will Make You Fishers of Men." Taylor said, "I got the outline from Spurgeon, but I put the flesh on it."

Seminary

In the fall of 1937, Taylor began studies at Oberlin Graduate School of Theology, following the recommendation of his mentor. His goal was a Bachelor of Divinity degree. Dr. Bacoats had received his Master's degree from Oberlin College. Gardner chose the seminary at Oberlin over Colgate Rochester Divinity School even though Professor Hudson, an instructor at Leland College had given him a recommendation for the New York school. Taylor was so eager to be preaching that he became impatient after he got to Oberlin; he was ready to quit school and go save the world. But one day he came to himself and said, "I am about the biggest fool you could think of; what good will that do me. I have not anywhere to pastor, in school or out of school. I had not thought of that . . . ." Fortunately, his mother remembered some of his father's friends and sought their help. They were A. L. Boone, a pastor in Cleveland, Ohio, and Dr. W. H. Jernigan, a leader in the Baptist World Congress who was pastor of the Mt. Carmel Baptist Church in Washington, D.C. Both men wrote to the energetic and impatient seminarian and encouraged him to remain at Oberlin.

While at Oberlin seminary, Taylor used every opportunity to enhance both his preaching skills and his political ambitions. Some weeks after Taylor began at Oberlin, Dr. R. M. Cable, pastor of Bethany Baptist Church in Cleveland, asked for a seminary student to come and preach. "I do not know how it got around to me, but I said, 'Yes.' It was the second time I had preached." Convinced that the more you preach, the better you become, Taylor preached as often as he could. He preached often at the local Church of God in Christ, and in churches located in the nearby towns of Elyria and Lorain. Young, aggressive and politically minded, Taylor held a little forum at the Second Methodist Church in Oberlin every Sunday evening at six o'clock p.m. The community residents from the various churches would come and discuss issues of the day that affected them.

Throughout his theological training, Taylor demonstrated an uncanny ability to "translate" and adapt each professor's lectures into his own context as a black person. Taylor posited, "I do not know how I did it, but I did, and it served me well." Thus, in later years, he was able to take European religious thought and see it in its context almost without thinking about it. On a certain occasion, a friend jokingly raised a question in class about church music and the National Baptist Hymnal, to which the professor made some condescending remark. But the outspoken Taylor arose and said, "Class, this comes out of where [*we*] are; this is [*our*] background, Professor Johnson! The instructor did not say it any more." In May of 1940, Gardner Calvin Taylor became the third person of African American descent to graduate from Oberlin School of Theology.

Courtship

Taylor's occasion of meeting Laura Bell Scott of Oberlin, Ohio was perceived by him as an answer to prayer. With commitments at Leland focused on academic goals of becoming a criminal lawyer and political leader, and football, it left very little time for serious dating. In 1937, one day before leaving for Oberlin, he and a friend, Dan Nash were sitting on his mother's porch. Taylor noticed in the *Pittsburgh Courier* the picture of a young lady who had just graduated Phi Beta Kappa from Oberlin College. He considered this an unusual feat for a black person. He said, "Nash, when I get to Oberlin, I am going to meet this girl."

Not long afterward, the Mt. Zion Baptist Church in Oberlin, the young lady's home church, sponsored a social gathering and extended invitations to all the new students at Oberlin. It was during that social time that Taylor's dream to meet Laura Scott became reality. She recalled:

> I saw him when he first came to Oberlin, but it was at the social when he introduced himself to me and stated that he had seen my picture in the *Pittsburgh Courier*. I must admit that I was interested in the fact he had seen my picture in the newspaper.[271]

It did not take long for the young minister to make his desired impression upon the lovely Laura Scott. Charlie Walker, a ministerial colleague, asked Taylor to speak at the Vashti Club meeting, in which Miss Scott held membership. Taylor asked, "'Are you and Charlie Walker seeing each other?' and she replied, 'No!' and I never said another word about Charlie Walker."

The Rev. Homer J. Tucker, pastor of Mt. Zion, invited Taylor to speak at the Lenten Services the following semester, and he preached from the subject "There is a Balm in Gilead." It was upon hearing him preach that sermon that Miss Scott, an English major, saw that the young preacher had talent:

> I realized after listening to that first sermon that he had a command of the English language and how beautifully phrased it was. And the more he began to preach the more honed those skills became, until people came to hear him because of the way he expressed things. The way he used language and imagery during his sermons, made whatever he was talking about come alive. I had heard many of the student preachers, but none of them impressed me as he did.[272]

Shortly after, Taylor began visiting Miss Scott and they developed a deeper interest in one another. The courtship lasted about three years. A year after graduating from Oberlin, she gained employment as a teacher at the Avery Institute in Charleston, South Carolina, and they were separated except during the summers and special holidays. On August 25, 1941, they were married in a simple ceremony in her mother's living room. After the wedding, Laura returned to Charleston to teach, while Taylor finished his final year of seminary, during which time he also served as pastor of a local Baptist congregation. The marriage of fifty plus years proved to be a primary example of Taylor's ability to cultivate and manage durable relationships. Taylor has written:

> Well, the course of true love never runs smoothly, it has been said, but I met her in church and the years have clearly taught me that God gave her to me and, I hope she feels me to her. She has been a loyal wife, the dearest of friends, the severest of critics, the warmest of supporters, partner in a romance still growing with the years. I believe that God did that.[273]

Marriage

The distance in their marital relationship ended when Taylor was called from his student pastorate in Ohio to a church in New Orleans, Louisiana. There, the Taylors united with a struggling congregation and learned how to make ends meet and look for the best in every situation. Upon moving to Baton Rouge, Taylor pastored while his talented wife contributed to the family income by teaching in the English department at Southern University. On several lecture tapes, Taylor referred to her as his "in-house grammarian" because of her trained ear and technical understanding in the field of language arts and public speaking.

It was Mrs. Taylor who encouraged him to discontinue taking the condensed version of his prepared manuscript into the pulpit because she noticed that he rarely referred to it when preaching. She reported:

> I said to him one day, since you refer to it so little, why take it up there? You seem to know everything you have down there, so why not try without it. Because having been in several public speaking classes myself, learning that eye contact and all that sort of thing is very important, I said to him "that would give you better rapport with your congregation. Then you could look at them and talk directly to them." So he took my suggestion, and he tried it the next Sunday and was surprised at how well he did, and from then on he did not use it anymore.[274]

Laura and Gardner Taylor were a compatible team for Christian ministry. She remained as the same delightful, intelligent and attractive woman who supported her husband faithfully in his ministerial assignments as a devout Christian wife until her untimely and most unfortunate passing on February 5, 1995. He, the tall, handsome, strong, concerned mate, was precisely what she came to appreciate and respect in a husband. They have one daughter, Martha, an accomplished vocalist, who lives in Los Angeles, California.

The Taylors traveled extensively throughout the world. They both enjoyed the theatrical and musical performances on Broadway. Mrs. Taylor admitted that their traveling had enriched her husband tremendously as a preacher, because "it gave him entree into other facets of life which in turn were used as illustrations in his sermons, education, political views, and other facets of a cosmopolitan life."[275] Everything made an impression upon him and has been used in some way to develop or bring light to his preaching.

Mrs. Laura Taylor's skills and gentleness provided the perfect balance to blend within the temperament of Taylor and his desire to become an effective preacher. She would not let him talk to her about sermons or even preach them to her, because she wanted to hear them fresh on Sunday morning like everyone else. Detecting early on his relentless pursuit of artistic excellence, she would make their home available to him on Saturday to get his sermons together for Sunday. She further added:

> Because I realized early in our marriage that I was dealing with an artistic temperament, I made accommodations to him. You know that artist are difficult to deal with, and as much an artist in the pulpit as those who sing or act or whatever they do, they are people who are very vulnerable. If there was something that should not have been said or could have been improved, whatever comment I had to make was not said until Tuesday or

Wednesday. They do not need anybody standing around making unkind or unnecessary remarks that would not do good until after the performance is over.[276]

The considerable talents of the Taylors were combined to establish an elementary school in 1960 at the Concord Baptist Church of Christ in the Bedstie area of Brooklyn. Laura Taylor organized the curriculum and later served for thirty-one years as the school principal (unsalaried). She retired from her position when Gardner Taylor became senior pastor emeritus, but she continued tutoring children three days a week.

Their lives together served as a living testimony to the goodness of God and their special ability to touch people's lives through their congeniality and commonness. Members of the Concord Church stated "you will never find another couple anywhere like the Taylors."[277]

The sudden death of Mrs. Laura Taylor created an immediate void and loneliness in the life and ministry of Gardner. After much prayer and a brief courtship, he married the former Ms. Phyllis Strong, a member of Concord, at the church on July 30, 1996. A Brooklyn native, she too was an educator, having taught history for over thirty-two years in the New York City school system. She received her undergraduate degree from Bennett College in Greensboro, North Carolina and a graduate degree from Teacher's College at Columbia University in New York City.

Upon becoming a member of Concord at the age of twelve, she states, "my aunt Eunice Jackson, a graduate of Union Theological Seminary in the '40's, was the director of Religious Education at Concord during this time."[278] She recalls joining the church on Palm Sunday in 1956, after the church relocated to Adelphi Street due to the fire. She was baptized by Dr. Taylor. When asked about the preaching style of her acclaimed husband, she recounts:

> I remember his sermons being so descriptive. He went to Radio City Music Hall on Easter Sunday morning and I recall hearing him preach about the dawn and I could just see the sun rising and Jesus appearing from the grave. He also talked a lot about art and culture and things which he had seen on Broadway.[279]

Mrs. Taylor confirms that Garner Taylor has multiple gifts. The most notable, that I find very credible is "he is able to touch people where they are. If you are a housewife or a preacher, he is able to touch both people at the same time in his sermon. It's personal. People come up to him all the time saying that you were talking to me today and they will repeat whatever stories were used as illustrations."[280] During their recent trip to the General Conference of the A.M.E. Church, where Dr. Taylor preached, she adds:

We were walking down this long hall when a man came up and said, "Dr. Taylor, Dr. Taylor, you know my thirteen year old son committee suicide last year. Your sermon today helped me understand his death." We hear that frequently. The most important factor in his preaching is his love for people and his love of the Lord. His father instilled in him early on an appreciation of the Lord, current events, a world view, and people. These traits along with his God given gifts are what made him the preacher that he is today.[281]

Bethany Baptist Church, 1938–1941

At one particular Sunday evening forum, Deacons Jim Crown and Ben Barrett from the local Bethany Baptist Church in Oberlin, told the young minister, "We would like for you to come and preach at our church next Sunday morning," to which the anxious Taylor, with delight replied, "Alright." He preached from the subject "Gathering Around the Table." They were so impressed with his preaching ability and pulpit style that they requested him to supply their pulpit until they called a pastor. "Sounded like Beethoven to me until they asked an awful question, "Reverend, what would you charge us?" Nobody had ever asked Taylor anything like that before, and he was scared that he might price himself out of an opportunity; he responded, "Would three dollars a week be too much?" For the next eight months he supplied the Bethany pulpit and was eventually called to become pastor of the church. Taylor accepted.

Understanding the needs of the membership was not difficult for the new pastor. With many of the members being from states like Alabama, Mississippi, and Kentucky, Taylor's southern roots proved beneficial. He always found himself preaching to a situation, to a point, sometimes sharp and other times not so well defined. Hence, from the beginning, "most of my preaching had to do with fitting, or arming, or equipping black people in terms of the Christian faith for their journey and for their situation." The congregation consisted of hard people and the church was in a mean part of town. The people more or less accepted that kind of arrangement and "my job was to tell them about their responsibility to themselves and to their future." Negro people, having moved North in the 1930s and just out of the depression, were struggling to hold on to some semblance of hope and a sense of being.

Each Sunday, Taylor traveled by bus, thirty cents each way, to preach to the congregation. He generally missed dinner at the seminary and stood around waiting for someone to invite him to dinner because there were no public restaurants where he could eat. Many dinners were eaten at the tables of Bill and Essie Triplett, Deacon Ben Heady and his wife who lived in a coal yard and at the home of Mrs. Mary Kendal. She recalled:

I was a member of the church when they called him. He had a good reputation at Oberlin, a nice gentleman, very down to earth with a good appetite. He loved macaroni and cheese. He was from my home state, Louisiana where I had heard of his father, Wash Taylor, but I did not know him. He was just starting out and everybody liked him, so that kind of made it easy for him. We loved him. My daughter's wedding was the first one he had ever performed, and he was more nervous than they were. He was the kind of person you could have a lot of fun off of. He did not put on any airs, just accepted that we were poor people from the south.[282]

It was a great experience for the young minister, who built the church up from twenty-five members to a congregation of respectable size. On Sunday mornings the church was filled to capacity and Taylor's reputation had begun to spread to all the nearby towns where he was invited to preach. "I learned some things about preaching and thank God it was a good ministry. From the first day, I never had any problems with those people." Both Oberlin and Bethany were preparing him and his preaching for greater challenges.

Beulah Baptist Church, 1941–1943

After graduating from Oberlin, Taylor received a call from the Beulah Baptist Church of New Orleans, Louisiana. Gardner had a friend pastoring there who recommended his name to the church which was vacant at the time. The pulpit committee extended an invitation for Taylor to preach and shortly the church members elected him as pastor. He was not known for his preaching at the time. The native was known only through the family connection of his father. However, Gardner C. Taylor immediately began establishing his own unique style as a preacher of the gospel. He conveyed:

The transition from Ohio to New Orleans was really not that great, but in the delta, the preachers tunes are much more emphasized, like the old Creole preacher, Cashmere Esdalon, a.k.a., "Sunshine money." Their kind of music was not my style. I nor my father ever had what was called a "whoop," but I never had a problem with it, because I preached among whoopers and was warmly received.[283]

With Laura having completed teaching the school year at Avery Institute, she met him in New Orleans, ninety miles from Baton Rouge. Taylor continued to establish himself as a bona fide pastor and preacher while unknowingly groomed to return home.

When Taylor arrived at Beulah, the congregation had a mortgage of several thousand dollars. Immediately, the pastor and his members began working on the debt. The church had no parsonage and were unable to offer a decent salary, but it became an opportunity for him to become engaged in what he liked to do best, preach the gospel. Beginning with a membership roll of about ninety, the church increased extensively and within three months the morning and communion services were filled. Members as well as those around the community experienced an attraction towards his preaching. "People in that congregation were a warmer people."

The Beulah congregation differed significantly from the seminary church. During those times, black people were beginning to stir in New Orleans. Mass rallies were held after morning services in nearby Shakespeare Park with the likes of A. L. "Jack" Davis and Ernest Wright. Davis, a local pastor and first black elected councilman in New Orleans, interceded for Taylor at Beulah. Wright, a local labor leader and civil rights activist, assisted Davis in leading voter registration drives in the city. Taylor assisted both men in public affairs for black people. The political uneasiness of the times suited Taylor's preaching to a tee. "Everything in society sought consciously and unconsciously, deliberately and coincidentally to wring out of them and beat out of them and signal out of them their insignificance." Being faced with the inhumane treatment of his people, according to Taylor, "my beginning years in Louisiana, I preached to salvage their innate dignity in a society which totally sought to crush them."

He accepted minimum pay and the Taylors sacrificed and struggled in the midst of people who heard freedom bells ringing every Sunday morning and evening from the Beulah pulpit.

Mt. Zion Baptist Church, 1943–1947

Gardner Taylor returned to Baton Rouge on several occasions and preached before his family and friends with whom he had been raised at the church, and members who knew him as a child. Many members did not know his father, Wash Taylor, but readily accepted the masterful gifts of the former pastor and church's son in the ministry. When Dr. Bacoats decided to leave Leland College and Mt. Zion for the presidency at Benedict College in Columbia, South Carolina, he staunchly recommended Gardner, the favorite son. Taylor's wife expressed:

> The congregation was accustomed to a trained ministry. They wanted somebody trained. Having roots in Baton Rouge, gone away for a seminary education, and being well trained made them particularly interested in him. Then after they heard him preach and found out that he was a preacher on his own, that is when they decided to extend an invitation to become pastor of the church.[284]

The nostalgia of leading the same church in the exact same location and standing where his father once stood was an overwhelming challenge for the twenty-six year old Taylor. "The pulpit committee literally persuaded him to accept Mt. Zion because he did not want to come and follow in his father's footsteps."[285] This was the same congregation where Wash Taylor in the 1920s set empty barrels next to the offering tables and encouraged members to give money so that their son could receive a quality education.

The preaching success of Taylor along with his instant popularity took the Mt. Zion congregation to higher heights, as the largest church in the city. Able to identify with the social issues and stigmas of their day, Taylor gained an immediate following from the students and professors from Southern University. According to Herman Stewart, a student at the university during that era, "I appreciated his delivery, the way he addressed issues; he never used a script, he just gave you the scripture and went on ahead with it."[286] Even Dr. F. G. Clark, the president of Southern University, whose parents shared membership under the elder Taylor, supported his childhood friend. On the first Sunday, the university would charter buses for students and faculty to attend communion service at the church. His following became evident wherever he preached.

Invitations began coming from various colleges to conduct their Week of Prayer, Easter Services, and Baccalaureates. Laura shared:

> . . . [that] several invitations from universities and churches of which he had no contact, started coming one right after another. So we assumed they came from the university president and faculty members, the National Baptist Convention, and from people who heard him there.[287]

Taylor was contemporary even then with an approach to preaching that went beyond scripture. His unique, creative employment of words brought the scriptures right before the ears and eyes of listeners in such a way that they could understand exactly what he was speaking about. "Although they did not understand all of the words, the way he said them made you visualize the scenario without giving you a definition of what he was saying."[288] Never assuming the people did not comprehend his subject, he phrased the context with such picturesque language that people effortlessly experienced the message.

The blossoming church began a radio ministry for the community and those who were not members listened intently to the young preacher every Sunday night. After the broadcast, the men would meet on the corner at South 13th Street and South Boulevard, two blocks from where Taylor lived, and repreach his sermons from the morning, afternoon, and evening services. "He demonstrated a relationship between whatever was currently happening, whether social, political, or educational, vividly in tune with the scripture."[289]

C. D. Simmons, who formerly pastored in Louisiana, heard Taylor preach his first sermon in the state convention after he went to Mt. Zion. Although his delivery style differed from the atypical Negro southern preacher, he was just as effective:

> Taylor was not a whooper, it was not him. Whatever arousing he did came from what he said and how he said it. He told J. B. Huey, a down home, old fashion preacher, after a convention sermon, "I wish I had what you got." He attempted it a few times, but soon accepted that it was not for him and he had to go his own way. Taylor was on the intellectual type, logical and deep as well. He was a type of orator and there were not many preachers on that order, so it was kind of a new thing that was breeding among people who had not been use to hearing it on that order. He was profound, with a terrific mind. There was a lot of teaching in his preaching, instructive, but also argumentative.[290]

Taylor was a devout National Baptist Convention, U.S.A., Inc. (NBC) supporter. He represented the convention as its delegate to the United Nations meeting in 1945 at San Francisco, California. In 1947, Taylor also addressed the Seventh Baptist World Congress, in Copenhagen, Denmark. Amidst a thriving, state capital congregation in the South, and the notoriety of being a renown preacher, all seemed well in Zion.

During this time, the popular churchman traveled extensively to various parts of the country preaching special church anniversaries, dedications, commencements and the like. In Atlanta, Georgia at the 1946 September NBC, Dr. James B. Adams, esteemed pastor of the Concord Baptist Church of Christ, Brooklyn, New York approached Taylor getting out of a taxi and said, "I want you to preach the centennial celebration of our church." Regrettably, Dr. Adams never heard the sermon, for he died three weeks later with a brain tumor.

The centennial committee of Concord pursued the request of their deceased leader and invited Taylor to preach at their prestigious church. His preaching of the "Prodigal Son" was so ingenious, that the church invited him back on two other occasions. After Taylor preached a Religious Emphasis Week at Shaw Divinity School, President Robert Daniels said to him as he was getting on the train returning home to Baton Rouge, "you ought to be heard at the Concord Church." Orlando Carrington, a prominent African Methodist Episcopal Zion minister from Brooklyn, came to Southern University to preach a baccalaureate. The following Sunday, Dean Harvey, a Zion Methodist, brought him to hear Taylor at Mt. Zion. Upon returning home, he too spoke favorably of him to the members of Concord. Also, Dr. J. H. Jackson, chairman of the Foreign Mission Board of the NBC, wrote a letter informing the Concord congregation of Taylor's leadership and preaching skills. It was soon ordained by God that the Concord Baptist Church of Christ in Brooklyn, New York would call the Rev. Gardner C. Taylor as their next pastor.

When members of Mt. Zion became aware of his resignation, they were devastated. It was beyond everyone's spiritual imagination. Several board members, including his former football coach, K. L. Craft, traveled to Concord with Taylor. They wanted to see what the church had in New York, which could attract him away from his father's church in Louisiana. Even his mother was deeply saddened by the decision, but accepted the fact that God wanted him in Brooklyn. When Craft returned, he reported to Taylor's mother, "Selina, we saw the surroundings up there, and they have everything!"[291] Taylor accepted the opportunity as the will of God, but had no idea of the future challenges awaiting his arrival.

Concord Baptist Church of Christ, 1948–1990

Several members of the Concord Church were from Louisiana cities such as Baton Rouge and New Orleans and they felt honored to have a man from their home state pastor a church as Concord. The church already held an active membership of five thousand in the late forties when Taylor arrived.

Having known from the friendly Adams, the great history of the church, the membership, its organized ministry programs and progressive position against segregation, the challenge to lead a congregation of this magnitude sensitized the young pastor of seven years. However, he did not alter his methods or approaches to the task of preaching that brought him there. Anna Belle explained:

> When he came that first Sunday morning, he electrified the congregation with his mastery of the English language. I had not heard of anyone with the ability to describe any situation or anything the way he does. He had us on our feet. He was on target when he arrived and never strayed. The entire congregation accepted him because he made a big presentation and seemed very humble. You could tell he was a very intelligent young man.[292]

Again, another congregation flourished from his homiletical craft, organizational skills, compassionate personality, and pastoral demeanor. The maturing, extemporaneous preacher won the congregation over with his preaching, and eventually, became the pastor of the people. "The ministry was firmly entrenched when we arrived, but the more I preached the more they began to trust me and realize my talents not only as a preacher but also a pastor."

The pastor elect arrived in New York at a time when the Christian community was reaching out for some black representation. Taylor admitted that "there were some fine preachers before me, but they came too early. I just happened to appear at the right time." There were great disparities among Black people. Many were suffering, but in addition there was a sense of homelessness and being uprooted which caused inhabitants to feel like strangers in a cold, alien land. His earlier sermons confronted this lonely, abandoned sensitivity of misplacement which brought him closer to the hearts of the community.

In 1950, at the interracial Baptist World Congress meeting in Cleveland, Ohio, Taylor represented Concord Church as the guest preacher for the Sunday morning sermon. Dr. Jernigan, a former friend of his father and a member of the governing board, suggested the invitation. This moment for the thirty-two year old minister became a zenith for his preaching career. The sermon entitled "They Shall Ask The Way"[293] received thunderous applause and a standing ovation. All of his rhetorical abilities, language, memory, eloquence, phraseology, delivery and so forth came to the forefront that day.[294]

On a chilly night, October 2, 1952, by some freak accident with an electric cross in the church, the relatively new home of the Concord Church completely burned in a tragic fire. The congregation had moved from their old building on Adelphi Street into the modern facility previously owned by a white congregation during the tenure of Dr. Adams. Taylor, having been the pastor only four years, confronted his biggest ministerial challenge to date.

The well organized leader, set forth a plan of action to rebuild. However, a particular Dime Savings Bank in the city refused to loan the church money because the bank officials did not know how a group of black people would repay it. On the following Sunday, Taylor told his people who were depositors at the bank, to withdraw their funds and the people did. According to a member, after the fire, Taylor held a meeting in his home and announced:

> We are going to go forward because I have a community of baptized believers who believe in me and in what I have said in the four years of my preaching here and with them and their faith in God and my leadership, we cannot fail.[295]

Being without a church facility four long hard years brought Taylor and his people closer in faith and practice. On April 1, 1956, the people of Concord marched into their new edifice at the cost of one million, seven hundred thousand dollars.

The sermons of Gardner Taylor gained an immediate audience in the American Baptist Convention, where he served as a member of the General Council and the NBC. He ripened as a preacher through the Baptist World Alliance, delivering sermons at five consecutive world meetings. His political views of democracy and social justice anchored his stance on equality for black people. He was arrested on several occasions for picketing building trades and protesting against the New York Board of Education, where he eventually became an elected member. As a resolute and principal supporter of the Civil Rights Movement, Taylor preached at the first anniversary of the Montgomery Improvement Association in Birmingham, Alabama.[296]

From 1959 through 1960 he served as the first black minister to preach weekly for the National Pulpit Radio Broadcast. During the summer of 1959, he spent six weeks as the guest preacher for the Baptists of Australia. Taylor also became the first Black Baptist President of the Protestant Council of Churches in New York. He preached either the Easter morning sermon or the Christmas sermon in the pulpits of council members' churches for many years. He added a startling commentary about the transition of his preaching during this era:

> I think my preaching expanded into the realization that there are not only the specifics of a particular circumstance in society, but there are the great universal considerations, our hopes, our fears, the fact that we are born, we love, we hate, we sicken, we die, we laugh, we cry, all the things in among those things. If indeed I was liberated from being a preacher exclusively to black people, it was in the mid 1950s, even when I began to broaden my sense of the needs of people.[297]

Moving into 1962, Taylor continued to identify with the necessities of freedom through nonviolence, but reaffirmed God's call to preach the gospel and not move headstrong into strategic political deployments. It is from such a position that the Brooklyn minister successfully lead his congregation in establishing an elementary school grades 1–6, a nursing home with an annual budget of 4.8 million dollars, a senior citizens residence, a clothing exchange, home care services for the elderly, a federal credit union with assets over 1.8 million dollars, countless ministries and "a million dollar 'Christfund Endowment' for black children and community uplift."[298]

The final command to position himself primarily as a proclaimer of the gospel was realized through Taylor's attempt to become president of the National Baptist Convention, U.S.A., Inc. His popularity had risen to international heights through preaching and leadership. Due to the conservative views and soft position on civil rights of President J. H. Jackson, the timing was indeed right to seek the gavel. Jackson was probably the most powerful Black man in the United States,[299] but it only seemed proper for Taylor to take his rightful place among those gifted generals like E. C. Morris, L. K. Williams, and D. V. Jemison who had ably led the convention.

Offered the Vice Presidency of the convention by Dr. E. D. Billups, President of the Louisiana State Convention who held the position, supporters of Taylor encouraged him to seek the top post. At the 1961 convention in Kansas City, Kansas, Jackson soundly won a monitored election over Taylor amid massive confusion. Bewildered, the disenchanted moderate delegates along with their chosen hero, formed the Progressive National Baptist Convention.[300]

In June of 1990, Dr. Gardner Calvin Taylor laid down his mantle as the industrious, acclaimed leader of the Concord Church. His preaching legacy will long remain within the hearts of those he tenderly touched and inspired to live the faith of Jesus Christ. While still actively preaching, he currently serves as Senior Pastor Emeritus of Concord and Adjunct Professor of Preaching at Yale Divinity School in New Haven, Connecticut.

The Progressive National Baptist Convention

Although it was never the intention of Gardner Taylor, the presidential candidate to lead the "Taylor Team" towards organizing another convention,[301] it seemed to be the only avenue remaining for others who sought a fair and legitimate voice in the convention, especially on the issue of civil rights. Because the household of Black Baptists had no platform to advance its causes for freedom, equality, and justice, the Progressive National Baptist Convention, Inc. (PNBC) received its birthright, November 14, 1961 in Cincinnati, Ohio.

Dr. Taylor became the second president of this newly organized body, serving from 1966 to 1969, and the first president of a National Baptist Convention ever to receive the gavel from his predecessor.[302] It was at Taylor's suggestion that Dr. Martin Luther King, Jr. made his debut appearance in 1966 at the convention in Memphis, Tennessee. In the dramatic annual sermon as president in 1968, during the Seventh Annual Session at the PNBC Washington, D.C., Taylor stated:

> There is the gift and power of black people as members of the "disestablishment" to see the society in its splendor and in its shame. There is the power of a rhythmic beat orchestrated by trouble and mourning and hope and which one hears in the strange sad music of the black preacher when he moves honestly within the cultic setting. There is an apocalypticism, a Christian anticipation in vivid imagery of new structures produced out of cutting moral judgment, a beholding born of stillborn societal aspirations and aided by the better midwifery of rejection and scorn.[303]

In the throes of the black power struggle and racism, the voice of the church continued to be a source of hope and inspiration through the preaching of ministers such as Gardner Taylor.

Known by many today as the "Father of the PNBC," Taylor's voice still persists within the hallmarks of decision-making, as realized in the recent appointment of Judge Clarence Thomas to the Supreme Court. At the 1991 PNBC annual session in Pittsburgh, Pennsylvania, during a heated debate over supporting the jurist, Stan Hastey of the *Christian Century* wrote:

> The 20 minute debate ended on a strong note of opposition. Former PNBC president and founding spirit Gardner C. Taylor, the revered pastor of Concord Baptist Church of Christ in Brooklyn, left the dais where he had been seated with other past presidents to join other delegates at the microphone on the main floor. "We must not stand hand in hand with Jesse Helms or David Duke," he declared. Referring to the argument that Thomas might change his views once on the court, Gardner said he would not have spent 50 years in the ministry had he not believed in the "redeemability" of sinful people. But he clinched the vote when he said, "I do not believe that the person on the mourner's bench ought to be made chairman of the deacon board." Taylor then introduced stronger language to the resolution, suggesting that the PNBC oppose Thomas outright "until or unless in his Senate hearings he expresses support of the constitutional right won in our hard-fought struggles for civil rights." The amended resolution was adopted overwhelmingly on a standing vote, with only a smattering of delegates rising to vote no.[304]

From his precedent position as a denominational champion, Baptists everywhere have benefitted from the gainful expertise of President Taylor as an ally for truth and freedom in our world. In 1969, Taylor was conferred the Knight Commander, Order of African Redemption, by President William V. S. Tubman and in 1973, the Order of Africa, by President William R. Tolbert, Jr., both from the Republic of Liberia.

Theological Educator

Having served as dean of the Union Baptist Seminary in New Orleans during his tenure as pastor of Beulah Baptist Church undoubtedly whet the appetite of the seminary graduate for further involvement. Gardner Taylor's initial opportunity came through one Samuel McKinney, a graduating student at Colgate Rochester Seminary in 1952. Dr. McKinney, now pastor of the Mt. Zion Baptist Church of Seattle, Washington, told the following account of how Taylor preached his class commencement address and was introduced to the seminary:

> I recommended Dr. Taylor; he was a rising star well known to us, but not our white classmates. The thing that helped sell him to the class was the President of the seminary. Dr. Wilbur E. Saunders stated that when he was a student at Union Theological Seminary, he did his field work at the same church where Taylor was pastoring, located on Marcy Avenue. The building, named the Marcy Avenue Baptist Church, had been previously owned by a white congregation before Concord purchased it in the 1940s. So the white fellows assumed he was white because it was the same church building. And when he showed up they said, "You tricked us" and I said, "Keep your mouths shut and you will

learn something." He talked about a "Divine Ultimatum." Taylor went on that night and "toned the bell in Zion." Later, two white guys with tears in their eyes said, "You were right."[305]

From that moment on, Taylor became very popular among American Baptists. He returned to the seminary on several occasions which increased his demand in a lot of places, especially the national convention meetings where in 1955, Taylor initially preached at Denver, Colorado. Shaw Divinity School, Bishop College's L. K. Williams Institute Week, Howard University School of Divinity, the School of Theology at Virginia Union, and Morehouse College kept Taylor among the best and brightest minds in black academia.

However, in 1968, the break came for Gardner Taylor to enter into mainstream American theological education as a forthright professor of the preaching discipline.

Colgate Rochester Divinity School, 1969–1972

Due to the increased numbers of black students attending the seminary, their vocalized concerns to study preaching from an accredited Afro-American minister demanded change. Negotiations were made in the Spring of 1968 to contract Gardner Taylor for the position after a student lock-in. He also became the first black member of the seminary's Board of Trustees.

In his preaching courses, Taylor introduced students to the biographical data of past respected preachers like Martin Luther, Charles Spurgeon, Joseph Parker, Andrew McLaren, Arthur John Gossip, Thomas Chalmers, John Jasper and several others. The resourceful Taylor held a strong belief that students could learn from those who had preached before them and therefore encouraged the class to read volumes of sermons and then analyze and reflect upon them. There was also a fondness in his character for the Scottish and English preachers because of their use of language. Taylor felt that black preaching relied so heavily upon description. Therefore, he admonished students to cultivate a familiarity with the kind of descriptive powers necessary to describe situations, stories, and biblical themes in sermons.

His approach to preaching centered around the responsibility of the preacher to write out complete manuscripts for sermons. Dr. Edward Wheeler, Chapel Minister at Tuskegee University who took the first course offered by Taylor, recalled:

> The class I had with Dr. Taylor was the highlight of my seminary education. For me, it was a glorious experience in academic training. Just having the "master" critique your sermons

made the entire class that much better. He made criticizing sermons a team approach where the entire class would reflect upon a sermon offered by a student. He never made you feel like your sermon was worthless or could not be preached, but he always invited you to look at ways of improving it.[306]

Through his demonstrated humility and pleasant disposition, men and women sought to drink from the same fountain as their "prince among people."

Taylor always articulated to his students the difference between a painter and an artist. Dr. Bobby Joe Saucer, who as a Student Trustee was instrumental in bringing Taylor to Colgate, reflected upon a lecture given in class one day. He said:

Dr. Taylor told us a painter makes broad strokes upon the canvass, but an artist pays careful attention to detail. He told students to find your range, and then mind your gifts within your ability and compassion.[307]

The seasoned veteran assisted students in understanding that there was an art to preaching. "Preaching is a verbal art; the Holy Spirit has to empower all preaching, but it was our responsibility as preachers to treat the sermon carefully, craft it, and follow certain techniques." The Taylor trait of painting pictures and telling stories so the audience could see what the preacher talked about has been a modeled characteristic of his teaching.

Taylor brought the best of both worlds to his students. He shared about the master legends of the past but also integrated the traditions of black preaching of talented preachers such as Sandy Ray, J. Pious Barber, J. C. Austin, and Vernon Johns to name a few, who through natural intuition and instincts could make "roosters crow and mules kick."

Union Theological Seminary, 1973–1974

Teaching in New York City was a welcomed and rewarding challenge for the local pastor. Having been influenced by Paul Scherer, George Buttrick, and Henry Sloane Coffin, his opportunity finally arrived to lecture where the geniuses of his day served. In 1986, Taylor received the coveted "Union Medal of Honor" for his outstanding commitment as a preacher of the gospel to the field of theological education.

While at Union, he had the utmost concern about the demeanor of preachers and how they appeared in the pulpit. He stressed that ministers, (who were primarily men during their era), not wear stripped or colored shirts in the pulpit. A white shirt, for him, always seemed appropriate for the preaching event. Shoes should be clean along with a conservative dark suit. Dr. Calvin Butts, pastor of

Abyssinian Baptist Church in Harlem, stated that "he constantly reminded us that we were ministers and how our decorum should reflect this image."[308]

The class received instructions on how to lift up a subject in the scriptures as if it were a crystal, so that you could see the various prisms and lights within it. He admonished students to lift up a subject from five or six, or however many different perspectives or angles one could accurately determine. So then preachers could develop their thinking around the theme in such a way as to make it more interesting to the congregation.

Rev. Johnnie Skinner, a former student at Union who later became a staff pastor at the Concord Church, shared his experiences in the class:

> His lecture style was not typical. He did not even use a course book, other than some readings he gave us. Basically, we preached and talked about the great themes of the scriptures, salvation, grace, love, etc. He generally taught out of his own experiences, by example. I think he had a few notes, but he never referred to them. He had taught now for a few years and had built up his own method. He told us that we should know the scriptures in terms of the sounds, sights, and smells. We should walk the streets, see the sights and smell the smells. His point was getting us to know the scriptures, and understanding them. I really think that was his major theme. The real benefit that we received was his intense preparation for the upcoming Lyman Beecher Lectures.[309]

Taylor convinced his students to leave their manuscripts in the workshop and bring to the congregation that which was in them. The exercise would be extremely helpful to their preaching. Taylor told his students, "if you do not know what you are going to say, then how do you expect the people to know what you are saying."

Probably, the most recommended task suggested to students focused on reading the critics who review plays, movies, music concerts, albums and books in the New York Times. Because of their colorful use of language, words, expressions and phrases not normally used by people, the familiarity with descriptions would help preachers to dramatically make the word live for the hearer. The task of the preacher was to make the ear into an eye, so people might have an opportunity to experience the gospel.[310]

Harvard Divinity School, 1975–1976

The Boston Theological Consortium consists of seven theological schools in the Boston area. Dr. Daucer, who had studied with Professor Taylor at Colgate Rochester Seminary, served as Director of Black Church Studies for the Consortium. He endorsed the idea to have Taylor teach a course in Preaching at Harvard University Divinity School and the curriculum committee readily extended him the opportunity. In the Spring of 1975, Taylor taught his first course and the class enrollment went beyond the normal limit.

The teaching style of Taylor developed into a spiritual, inspiring, and informative flow of ideas and experiences. The first two or three lectures were on the history of preaching and basically evolved from his knowledge and interest in the field. There was a historical dimension within his lectures. Dr. Frank Reid, pastor of the Bethel African Methodist Episcopal Church in Baltimore, Maryland, who studied under Taylor, commented that "we were always told the importance of understanding the tradition one is standing in and representing at that point of history, for we were a part of an ongoing tradition."[311]

There was much emphasis placed on the craft of preaching which identified the hard work of reading the scriptures, meditating and praying over that scripture, and organizing the sermon. An exertion of preparing both the message and the messenger, Taylor's method assisted students in realizing that preaching a sermon was hard scholarship on the spiritual foundation of the one who preached the sermon.

Following his three of four lectures on history and craft, Taylor led the students into the actual preaching of sermons, and for most that was where the real teaching took place. At the same time, while teaching the class how to prepare a sermon, he also taught them how to listen to sermons. When students preached their sermons, Taylor would close his eyes and listen. Reid anxiously reflected upon the experience:

> Once a student had gone through all the preliminaries and taken their text, he would close his eyes, lift up his head to the heavens and put his right hand on his chin and with the index finger of his right hand, he would either rub his chin or sometimes go to his brow, but invariably his eyes would be closed for the entire message. It was one of the most spiritual experiences I ever had, just watching him listen to a sermon.[312]

The kind and compassionate professor always gave a positive remark about the sermon first, then he very smoothly made the transition into the sermon criticism. Using his great sense of humor and sensitivity, he was that which he taught. Reid believed that "it was an 'incarnational class' because in [Taylor], homiletics became flesh; he taught the class by who he was."[313]

CHAPTER FIVE

Taylor's Sermon Methodology

Gardner Calvin Taylor has taken a prophetic posture in terms of determining the focus of the preaching event. For him, preaching is almost always done in troublesome times, since "man that is born of a woman is of few days, and full of trouble."[314] Taylor considers the "joy-sorrow" quality of black music as the manifestation of the black preacher, "rising up out of heartbreak and hope, apostle at the same time of apocalyptic escape and determined protest."[315]

This chapter initially will be an examination of Taylor's methodology of preaching as it relates to his expressed theory of preaching, his views on the purpose of preaching, and Taylor's preaching preparation method. Since the composition is an attempt to study Taylor's sermons from the artistic rhetorical criteria, a brief examination of the classical rhetorical theories of Aristotle, Cicero, and Quintillion will be presented in the second section to serve as the basis of the critique. The final portion of this chapter will analyze ten of Gardner Taylor's sermons, covering over fifty years of his preaching.

Taylor's Theory of Preaching

The primary consideration for any preacher, according to Taylor is "to become as immersed as one could in the Word of God."[316] This conceptualization has been the fundamental foundation of Taylor's belief since early childhood and the inception of his preaching:

> I am thankful that I was born to parents who, though not highly educated by today's standards, had a natural feel for the essential music of the English language wedded to an intimate and emotional affection for the great transactions of the Scriptures.[317]

For the African American preacher and congregation, knowledge of the Bible and the ability to use Bible verses to apply to any phase of life are the hallmarks of true Christians.[318] The preacher's own conviction about the Scriptures is the initial issue in sermon structure. In *Preaching Biblically*, Taylor offers a practical consensus concerning the Scripture's connection in forming the sermon. The word of God for him has two distinct functions for shaping sermons. He states:

If one sees Scripture as being the precise word of God, then the sermon is likely to take on a quality of 'ex cathedra' pronouncement. This leaves little room for the sermon to muse upon any human traits and insertions that offer an earthy, credible point of association for the lives of those who sit in the pews. On the other hand, if the preacher believes little more about the nature and meaning of the Scriptures than that they are the most elevated human literature, then the sermon is likely to ignore the mysteries of God's self-disclosures and people's uneven responses to those disclosures which are the very kernel of biblical material. A sermon has the greatest chance of accomplishing its proper hoped-for and prayed-for purpose in human life when it arises out of the preacher's own faith that in the words of Scripture a Word arises.[319]

Gardner Taylor does not attempt to prove the authority of the Scriptures, instead he rightfully assumes that authority as being the preacher's point of departure on the sermonic journey. All of the moods, experiences, and thoughts of the human mind are contained in the Scriptures.[320] Taylor's theory of preaching is anchored in God's instructions in the book of Ezekiel, chapter three, verses 1–3:

And he said to me, "Son of man, eat what is offered to you; eat this scroll, and go, speak to the house of Israel." So I opened my mouth and he gave me the scroll to eat. And he said to me, "Son of man, eat this scroll that I give you and fill your stomach with it." Then I ate it; and it was in mouth as sweet as honey. RSV

Taylor takes this passage to mean that "the preacher is to eat as full a grasp, intellectually and emotionally, of the given revelation that we have of God's search for humanity."[321] His theory of preaching is determined by the preacher's calling to visualize the setting, to sense the surroundings, and to speak simultaneously. He comments on this aspect of preaching:

In the sense of what the Word actually says, the disciplines are involved in the exegesis and exposition. I use that in the sense of the intellect. To sense, in terms of the imaginative-ness, one ought to walk up and down a street on which the text lives and see what the neighborhood is like, what the climate feels like. Is there a cloudy atmosphere around it or is it bathed in sunlight? What are its neighbors? When one gets not only the address of the text so to speak, but also the community where it lives. I think that one is able to deal with the Scriptures more effectively. So I use the word 'sense' in terms of the imaginative-ness, which of course must be kept in rein by the seeing. Because there can be a wild, exuberant, and purposely imaginativeness, we sometimes fall. The responsibility of the preacher is to communicate the vision so that what is in him or her becomes alive in those who hear. The gospel is worthy of the noblest language which the human mind and human tongue are capable.[322]

This "burden of the message" placed upon the person who preaches enables one to serve as an intermediary between God and people. The preacher is far more to the human side of the negotiation than to the divine. While the Scriptures have one master theme that runs from one end of the biblical revelation to the other, Taylor argues for a union:

> The Bible has a thread, a theme, running throughout its length. Every preacher, Bible student, and Christian sees that theme—maybe not exactly as I see it, but not completely different either. A preacher's sermons radiate from that central theme like spokes from a wheel. Preachers must have a good grasp of the full sweep of Scripture before they can see it.[323]

For Taylor the Scriptures are of the utmost necessity for the preacher and her or his attitude toward the sermon. He states "that particular theme comes as a "through-line" to each of us in terms of our personalities—not manipulated, not by design, but by nature of the personality."[324]

The Personality of the Preacher

It is the aim of the preacher to discover his or her "through-line" as that distinctive coloration, accent, or thrust of the gospel at this pointed time in history. Taylor states:

> The opportunity and privilege of the preacher is to find his or her dominant response that their personality makes to the gospel. Of course the text will dictate how that through-line is applied, but you will discover it and God deliver you from a deadening, monotony, Johnny-one-note preaching. You will discover it according to your personality that a particular aspect of the gospel will almost invariably come out in anything that you preach. It is authentic, it is your authority, it is the authenticity of your own personality.[325]

The theological connection which Taylor sustains as the necessity of the preacher in understanding one's God-given personality is realized through the incarnation—the Word became flesh. This supreme, ultimate, act of saving humanity which God has taken in terms of redeeming the earth was a step in personality. Taylor offers consolation in the realization that "the Lord who has chosen to put that imperious pressure upon the preacher's personality knows about it also, for it is the only authentic currency which deals with human souls."[326] Entering the contracts of human life, becoming susceptible and eligible for all the experiences which others pass, creates the secrets of whatever internal authority the preacher has in the proclamation of the gospel.

Recognizing and Removing the
Presumptuousness of Preaching

In 1972 Gardner Taylor delivered the Caldwell Lectures at the Louisville Presbyterian Theological Seminary, Louisville, Kentucky. It was in these lectures that he began to dwell significantly upon the "presumptuousness" theme of the preaching craft. He reflects:

> I sometimes feel a revulsion which is almost physical, about trying to confront the deepest concernments of the people to whom I preach with what I see as the will of God for their lives. After twenty four years in the same pulpit, I am conscious of many people in the congregation who have carried far more gallantly very difficult circumstances. And because of that, I feel a certain presumptuousness in trying to address them.[327]

Since the preacher cannot claim any esoteric knowledge of the preaching responsibility nor an eschatological ecstasy in the Christian experience, Taylor drums the question, "How then is the preacher to recognize his or her incapacity, and inadequacy and how is it to be removed?"

Gardner Taylor finds an appropriate answer to eliminate this tempting compulsion of egotistical excellence. He offers a striking commentary on the role of the preacher as both spokesperson for God and sinner among the people. He writes:

> The magnificent anomaly of preaching is to be found in the fact that the person who preaches is in need himself or herself of the message which the preacher believes he or she is ordained to utter. How dare such a person address others, in the name of God, who are no worse off than the spokesperson! The principal presumptuousness is found in the awareness that the person who preaches is part of the guilt and need to which one speaks. The person who preaches is as guilty of the wrongs against God against which he or she inveighs as are those to whom their words address. God help the preacher who is so self-hypnotized that the full brunt of this shame does not fall like an awful weight upon him or her, loading what one says with a becoming humility and hush of the soul that me, of all people, should be sent to say such things about what is wrong with people before God. For what is wrong with the hearers is the same that is wrong with the preacher.[328]

Unless preachers are capable of recognizing their sinfulness and acknowledging their evil, one is likely to address people out of their own hostilities, and deal with them vindictively.

The herald is a component of the human condition and cannot be separated from it. Taylor states "this gives the preacher as his or her presumptuousness is removed by one's guilt, a winsomeness, a pathos, and a power."[329] These attributes accurately substitute for the presumptuousness because the preacher becomes the recipient of a grace which one can never vocalize. The preacher who identifies not only wins the guilt, but also wins the release and deliverance from the guilt, finds preaching power. The preaching of the gospel, according to Taylor, "gets power as we realize to whom it is really aimed and addressed."[330]

While the Word of judgment must be uttered in the proclamation of the gospel, it cannot be pronounced by persons who count themselves different or delinquent from those to whom they are sent. The preacher's words will be given a sense of humility, however sharply and pointedly they must be spoken. There will be a sense of authority, a sense of love, and a winsomeness even in its sharpness.

Once the recognition has been realized and the removal becomes intrinsically evident, the essence of "What does it mean to preach?" is summarized by Taylor:

> It is for a person to sense oneself soiled, stained and scared and to be led in terms of the New Testament to the healing and cleansing fountains. And then to have an eagerness and an enthusiasm within oneself having been led there, to point through all stained and soiled and scared people to the never failing flow.

> It is for a person to have one's own pride and ambition somehow and somewhere broken on the rock of betrayal and disappointment. And then to have them put together in the form and shape of a crucifix.

> It is for a person to despair and to see the willfulness, weakness, and wickedness of humanity in their individual lives and in their great structural installations and to despair that there can ever be a leveling of the way, a lifting of the valleys, a bringing down of the mountains, a straightening of the pathways, and a smoothing of the road. And then find in the New Testament where at the terminus of life, at the place of death, life begins anew and the redeemed in pilgrim humanity come forth out of the womb of that obscure tomb in a cemetery. This is what it is to preach.[331]

Summary

The preachers cannot shun the responsibility of accepting their human conditions as mediators of the Word of God. There is a common preunderstanding of becoming one with the people in order for all to experience the truth and reality of the preaching event. The preacher is the messenger to declare the truth to the people and in no way can he or she feel above those to whom they preach.

The Purpose of Preaching

The sermon contains a wide range of spiritual and emotional components in the context of African American preaching, which also must deal with issues of life and death. The primary responsibility of the African American preacher is to relate and demonstrate the concerns of the everyday life with the redemptive love and power of God. Gerald Davis notes:

> Few scholars who have looked at the African-American sermon have fully appreciated the complexity of the structures of the performed African-American sermon. As a consequence the African-American sermon has been underestimated and underreported more than it has been held in disdain or neglected. The high emotionalism of the African-American church has seemed to be especially problematical for scholars. It is probably one of the major reasons for the underreporting of the African-American sermon.[332]

The conviction of Gardner Taylor to impact the purpose of preaching resonates within the preacher's ability to connect the mundane issues of life with the conditions in the gospel. Davis conveys another salient point related to this affect:

> So careful is the preacher to include specific, contemporary secular elements in one's sermon formulas that the structuring of this element in the preaching seems to claim a greater portion of the preacher's creative energies. In contrast, sacred referencing seems to be casual and is obviously the result of a reasonably stable body of knowledge. The African American preacher may use the perfection of the Christian life as example, as framework, but their focus is riveted on the congregation's need to live a fully experiencing daily, secular existence.[333]

The principal mission of the African American preacher is and always has been to speak to the contemporary needs of the congregation.

Gardner Taylor's idea of the purpose of preaching holds a dualistic view within the theoretical development of African American preaching. In a written interview, Taylor reflected on the question, "How do you determine the purpose of your sermons?" He posits:

> Sermons speak to people's needs. Pastoral experience teaches us many of the needs of people. Also, the preacher's own life, his or her own struggles, teach other needs. Sometimes my sermons consciously meet needs, other times it happens mysteriously. The word of God breaks through the preacher by the power of the Holy Spirit. Other times, in spite of the preacher, the people will be ministered to. Occasionally a parishioner will say at the door of the church, "You spoke to me; this was my problem and you spoke to it." The preacher did not mean to speak to that problem at all.[334]

Incorporating the disciplines of study, observation, and experiences, Taylor addresses the conscious, human need in a term coined by Kyle Haselden, former editor of the *Christian Century*, about the Scriptures being "revealant." "There is no such word in the dictionary, but it's a good word: what is revealed, over against that which is relevant."[335] The preacher's responsibility is becoming fully aware in order to conceptualize, then to visualize, and finally to vocalize how the two terms—revealant and relevant—intersect and connect. Taylor offers a summation of this claim:

> The Bible speaks of a beginning, a quest, a choosing, an emancipation, a journey, a nation, an exile, a restoration, and the appearance of one who incarnates all of that and all that God intends. This is the "revealant," and this record—punctuated by the pronouncements of the prophets—is more than a book of texts. It is the preacher's textbook. Life offers to preachers and hearers the individual concerns all people have and the ageless attempts they have made to establish some form of community. Attempts to contract community repeatedly produce tensions of class, section, race, creed, the threat of war, and now, of annihilation. This is the "relevant." The sermon's task is to swing the light of proclamation, not mechanically, from what is "revealant" to what is "relevant," to show how one touches the others and the demands made in the name of the Sovereign Lord of them both. In structure, design, and delivery, the sermon ought to breathe with the awareness that it is doing business in the supreme matters of human life.[336]

A true care for people and a desire that they be right with God, and restored to themselves requires a looking at them honestly and deeply by the preacher for what they are and are not. Taylor further states:

> My idea of preaching is that it erupts, it happens, it occurs. It is an event which takes place in a field between intentions. Intentions between authority and humility, between thought and feeling, order and ecstasy, as between the humanistic aspect of the gospel and the theistic aspect of it between the Word and the world, between what is relevant and what is revealant. We cannot ever escape that field of tension, as between judgment and mercy, between the contemporary and the apocalyptic, as between matter and manna, the individual and social, as between pleading and commanding, lights and shadows, condemnation and comfort, piousity and cynicism. It is in this field of tension that preaching occurs.[337]

Unless the preacher out of these tensions can become both lover and oppressor, understanding what Taylor terms "the sweet sad music of humanity," the preacher is untrue to his or her calling.

From Where Do Sermons Come?

Taylor believes that the ministry of preaching is ordained by God and is ably set in the task of deriving a power and pathos in passionate avowals of heart, experience, and hearer. In *How Shall They Preach*, Taylor states his sermon building process:

The heart of the preacher's dilemma is how to trust God wholly and at the same time to prepare diligently. Sermons are born of a mysterious romance between preparation and inspiration. The faithful preacher, willing to pay the price in study, prayer and that meditation which is a "sitting silent before God," will find rich reward for his or her pulpit work.[338]

This deep sense of dialogue which carries the weight of divine truth between the one who speaks and those who hear is the result of a prior dialogue. Through the disciplines of study, experience, and observation, Taylor derives seed thoughts from reading books on preaching as well as classic works from notable preachers and scholars, such as W. M. Taylor's work, *The Parables of Our Savior.*[339]

Taylor described his instinctive penchant for human nature and reading as the two primary factors which contribute towards developing his sermon ideas. When asked, "Do most of your sermon ideas come from books or people?", Taylor responded:

My reading, for example, one sentence [idea] will set off a chain of reflection that sparks a sequence of thoughts in my mind. I also get ideas from talking with people.[340]

The preacher must always be ready of mind to grasp the imaginativeness of the biblical record and the current events of the day with a split vision—one eye on the contemporary and the other on God. Hence, preachers have a broad spectrum of life to look everywhere for sermons. "We must be open and ready to hear what humanity have to say about God, consciously or unconsciously, and their need for him."[341] Taylor offers a personal commentary during a lecture on the subject:

My sermons come from this way and that way. I try to save mornings for reading the Scriptures and otherwise. In doing so I find sermons coming along. I find them in pastoral work. I try to view the various plays on Broadway, since many of these writers are speaking very perceptively about life. What they are saying relates to the gospel in many different ways. I try to look into myself and see what are my concerns. There is an inevitable and if your eyes are open, an inescapable relatedness in the Word and world. If he or she is reading his Bible, one has to read it with one eye so to speak there, and with one eye peeled in the other direction, because these things converge, again and again.[342]

There is also a need for every preacher to study the art and craft of the previously recognized masters of the pulpit. Taylor discovered a creative genius anchored by one unique quality that is incorporated within the art of preaching. He writes:

One who preaches must come to know the doubts and hopes, the longings and fears, the strengths and weaknesses of the human heart. He or she arrives at this awareness, first, I think by seeking, not morbidly, to plumb the depths of his or her own being. This has been a part of the genius of all of those who have spoken profoundly and creatively to the human spirit. They were intimately in touch with the deepest sources of themselves, that river of universal being that flows even below the unconscious. So the preacher must be willing to look deeply and honestly into himself, for those depths touched by the light and flame of the Gospel will much of one's preaching find birth and life.[343]

Summary

The preacher must always be alert to the opportunities of discovering sermon materials. One must be consciously equipped to know that God is speaking in a multitude of ways. Also, one must seek to know the craft of preaching from the perspective of those who have mastered the art. Indeed, Gardner Taylor is one who is an example of the preaching tradition.

The Artistic Canon in Classical Rhetoric

The focus of this section will be upon the constructive elements of rhetoric as interpreted by three classical theorists of rhetoric, Aristotle, Cicero, and Quintillion.[344] The common uses of the word *rhetoric* are negative and disparaging. Sonja Foss notes that "*rhetoric* is commonly used to mean empty, bombastic language that has no substance; it means communication as the use of symbols to influence thought and action."[345] The main function in the connotation is oral persuasion as an invitation for hearers to change their lives in some way. Raymond Bailey writes that "rhetoric is best understood in terms of intent. If the speaker or writer intends to move the audience to a new understanding or a new behavior, the work is rhetorical in nature."[346]

Aristotle (ca. 384–322 B.C.)[347]

Rhetoric proper starts with Aristotle; all rhetoric is in some way—more or less—derived from Aristotle.[348] He developed "a theory of rhetoric which outlines the practical details of speech craft and also sets forth a fairly complete rationale for the subject.[349] Aristotle's *Rhetoric*, according to Lane Cooper, is "one of the world's best and wisest books, not meant to be read as a novel; it is a book to be chewed and digested."[350]

The *Rhetoric* is divided into three parts: Book I basically consists of Aristotle's definitions and functions of the art of rhetoric. He defined rhetoric as "the faculty [power] of discovering in the particular case what are the available means of persuasion."[351] Establishing the art of persuasion on the grounds of being either artistic or nonartistic, Aristotle determined that the *entechnoi* or *artistic proofs—ethos*, *pathos*, and *logos* consisted of means of persuasion. He wrote:

> Of the means of persuasion supplied by the speech itself there are three kinds. The first kind reside in the character [*ethos*] of the speaker; the second consists in producing a certain [the right] attitude in the hearer [*pathos*]; the third appertain to the argument proper, in so far as it actually or seemingly demonstrates [*logos*].[352]

For Aristotle, the three-fold dimension of a speech situation consisted of speaker, subject, and audience. This configuration produced three kinds of oratory in rhetoric, the deliberative, forensic, and epideictic. He described them in the following manner:

> The elements of deliberation [counsel] are exhortation and dissuasion. The elements of forensic speaking are accusation and defense. The elements of an epideictic speech are praise and blame. As for the divisions of time which severally belong to these several kinds of speakers, to the deliberative speaker belongs the future, for he gives advice about things to come; to the judicial pleader belongs the past, for it is always with regard to things already done that the one party accuses and the other defends; and to the epideictic speaker, above all, belongs the present, for every one praises or blames with regard to existing conditions.[353]

While chapters 1–3 of Book I focus on general topics, definitions, and the nature of rhetorical arguments as a philosophical rhetoric, chapters 4–14 present detailed descriptions of persuasion through the three kinds of rhetoric. Book II is a continuation of the three characteristics of invention. Aristotle believed *ethos* or character to be the most important means of persuasion. He wrote that "as for the speakers themselves, the sources of our trust in them are three things that gain our belief, namely, character (initial credibility), intelligence (derived credibility) and goodwill (terminal credibility)."[354] A speaker possessing any combination of these qualities will be held in confidence by his or her hearers. In Aristotle's view, *ethos* is to be accomplished through the speech, and not a matter of any previous accolades.

In chapters 2–18, Aristotle dealt with the second mode of proof, *pathos* and how to arouse emotion in an audience through the kinds of character within the speaker. Aristotle observed through extensive writings on emotions that an effective speaker must know the audience and how to create and use emotions in persuasion.[355] Bailey strengthens this argument by stating:

> [*Pathos*] is the power of conviction that exists in the values, beliefs, and feelings already held by the audience. The task of the preacher is to determine how to control and channel the emotions present in every audience.[356]

The final mode of proof in the invention canon is *logos* or subject matter which Aristotle initiated in Book I chapters 3–14 and concludes in Book II chapters 18–26. Although Aristotle's three types of oratory are based on the kinds of audience, George Kennedy asserts that "Aristotle clearly thinks of this part of the work as essentially an exploration of the subject matter of speeches (*logos*).[357]

For Aristotle, the content of the subject matter determines the relationship between the speaker and audience. Arguments can take the form of being either inductive (examples) or deductive (thoughts). Aristotle stated that "whatever the subject on which we have to speak or reason, we must have some knowledge, if not a complete one of the facts."[358] The function of *logos* in the art of rhetoric is determined by the fact that "without it, you would have no materials from which to construct an argument."[359]

In Book III of *Rhetoric*, Aristotle addressed the canons of style, delivery, and arrangement. He defines the term *lexis* to mean "everything that has to do with expression—choice of words, syntax, and delivery."[360] For success, delivery is of the utmost important to the effect of a speech.[361] He further elaborated upon delivery:

> The art of delivery has to do with the voice; with the right management of it to express each several emotion—as when to use a loud voice, when a soft, and when the intermediate; with the mode of using pitch—high, low, and intermediate; and with the rhythms to be used in each particular case. These are, in fact, the three things that receive attention: volume, modulation of pitch, and rhythm.[362]

The essential quality of style is not in diction alone, but syntax, phraseology, and clearness. The style, according to Aristotle, should be neither mean nor above the dignity of the subject, but appropriate.[363] There are four common faults of style: 1) the misuse of compound words, 2) the use of strange words, 3) mistakes in the use of epithets, and 4) bad figures of speech.[364] A speaker needs to be aware of the abuse of and use of metaphors and similes in discourse as relating to good style. Alfred North Whitehead notes that "style, in its finest sense, is the last acquirement of the educated mind; it is also the most useful."[365] Traditionally, the study of style enables the critic to learn about the personality of the speaker and to perceive the spirit and sense of the times.

Arrangement is the final artistic canon described by Aristotle. For him, there are only two essential parts of speech: "Necessarily, you state your case, and you prove it."[366] This process in rhetoric is respectively termed, "Statement and

Argument."[367] The parts of a speech cannot exceed four—Proem, Statement, Argument, and Epilogue.

The Proem or Introduction begins a speech and should "pave the way for what follows."[368] The primary function of the introduction is "to make clear the end and object of your work."[369] The source of an introduction may be conceived in the speaker, the audience, the subject, and the opposition. The basic concept here is removing prejudice from the audience and gaining the attention of the hearer.

The Narration plays a key role in assisting the audience in recalling the events of a past story, which does not exist in deliberative speech. A vivid connection between narration and *ethos* (character) is made through the revelation of moral purpose. Here, the principal of argument is established by Aristotle in order to exhibit character in dialoguing with the current issues being discussed. The speaker's motive is to demonstrate reasons why an audience should prefer one side of an issue over another.

Book III concludes with a chapter on the conclusion or Epilogue. Aristotle believed the final section of a speech consists of four parts. He wrote:

> 1) You must render the audience well-disposed to yourself, and ill-disposed to your opponent; 2) you must magnify and depreciate [make whatever favors your case seem more important and whatever favors his case seem less]; 3) you must put the audience into the right state of emotion; and 4) you must refresh their memories.[370]

Through the four guidelines, one may discern that a generalized description of *ethos*, *pathos*, and *logos* represents the ending of a speech. In the Epilogue you should give a summary review of your proofs.[371]

Cicero (ca. 106–43 B.C.)

Cicero was considered by many to be the greatest Roman orator and the most important Latin writer of all time.[372] In the books, *De Inventione* and *De Oratore*, Cicero defined and explained the basic functions of rhetoric and the concepts involving the five artistic canons. For him, "the function of eloquence seems to be to speak in a manner suited to persuade an audience, the end is to persuade by speech."[373] He further stated and defined the five rhetorical canons:

> Invention is the discovery of valid or seemingly valid arguments to render one's cause plausible. Arrangement is the distribution of arguments thus discovered in the proper language to the invented matter. Memory is the firm mental grasp of matter and words. Delivery is the control of voice and body in a manner suitable to the dignity of the subject matter and the style.[374]

In *De Oratore*, which consists of three books in dialogue form, Cicero expands the scope of rhetoric and develops the basic guidelines and requirements for becoming an effective orator.

The focus of Book I is the qualifications of the ideal orator. Cicero held to the conviction that "eloquence is dependent upon the trained skill of highly educated men."[375] He clearly developed this conviction using the five classical canons of rhetoric:

> And, since all the activity and ability of an orator falls into five divisions, I learned that he must first hit upon what to say; then manage and marshal his discoveries, not merely in orderly fashion, but with a discriminating eye for the exact weight as it were of each argument; next go on to array them in the adornments of style; after that keep them guarded in his memory; and in the end deliver them with effect and charm.[376]

Cicero maintained a firm stand on the necessity of knowledge and natural talent for good speaking, which identify with the canons of invention and delivery. This premise became the personal conviction within Cicero's thesis. Good speakers possess a harmonious, graceful, style that is marked by a combination of polish and artistry. He explained the nature of these attributes:

> There were very many qualifications which an orator must derive from nature. No readiness of tongue is needed, no fluency of language, in short none of those things—natural state of looks, expression, and voice—which we cannot mold for ourselves. But in an orator we must demand the subtlety of the logician, the thoughts of the philosopher, a diction almost poetic, a lawyer's memory, a tragedian's voice, and the bearing almost of the consummate actor.[377]

The best aid for preparing the speaker is to write as frequently as possible. For the pen, according to Cicero, is the best and most eminent author and teacher of eloquence.[378] Both memory and delivery must be consistently trained and practiced, along with the constitution of voice, breathing, and gestures, also known as *chironomia*. Cicero noted that his students become acquainted with history and its poets, but also "study and peruse the masters and authors in every excellent art, and by way of practice praise, expound, emend, criticize and confute them."[379] In Book II, "The Making of an Orator," Cicero saw the need for oratory to be supported with a wide range of learning. He believed that "the art of speaking well, of speaking with knowledge, skill and elegance, has no delimited territory."[380] Rules hinder the exploration and depth of an orator whose ultimate aim is the art of persuasion. This factor, according to Cicero, relied upon three things:

The proof of our allegations, the winning of our hearers' favour, and the rousing of their feelings to whatever impulse our case may require. For purposes of proof, however, the material at the orator's disposal is twofold, one kind made up of the things which are not thought out by himself, but depend upon the circumstances and are dealt with by rules; the other kind is founded entirely on the orator's reasoned argument.[381]

This proof, *logos*, closely connects with the proofs of Aristotle which Cicero uses in winning the favor of audiences through the blending of *ethos* and *pathos* as degrees of appeal to their emotions.

The rhetorical canons, arrangement and memory are given extensive treatment in the latter part of Book II. The decision of how to arrange materials in a sermon for the intention of exposition and explanation is "in the highest degree a task for professional skill."[382] The strongest and most salient points germane to the sermon should be placed at the beginning. Cicero expounded on this issue:

One's opening remarks, though they should always be carefully framed and pointed and epigrammatic and suitably expressed, must at the same time be appropriate to the case in hand; for the opening passage contains the first impression and the introduction of the speech, and this ought to charm and attract the hearer straight away.[383]

A solid introduction should contain either a central proposition on the whole sermon or speech or a strategy to gain some faction of dignity and ornament. Cicero suggested that "the opening passage should be so closely connected with the speech that follows as to appear to be not an appendage, but an integral part of the whole structure."[384]

The memory canon generally is acknowledged as natural, intuitive gifts of an orator. Because memory depends on how a speech is arranged, Cicero made memory a function of order. He wrote that "the discovery of the truth that the best aid to clearness of memory consists in orderly arrangement."[385] The art of performing this canon lies in the formation of mental images that facilitate recall through the ordering of the facts. Hardly anyone exists who has so keen a memory that he can retain the order of all the words or sentences without having arranged and noted his facts.[386] Cicero wrote:

The most complete pictures are formed in our minds of the things that have been conveyed to them and imprinted on them by the senses, but that the keenest of all our senses is the sense of sight, and that consequently perception received by the ears can be most easily retained in the mind if they are also conveyed to our minds by the mediation of the eyes.[387]

The gift of memory in preaching originates within the natural ability of the speaker, but according to Cicero, it also demands the discipline of arrangement. He concluded with the following:

> A memory for things is the special property of the orator—this we can imprint on our minds by a skillful arrangement of the several masks that represent them, so that we may grasp ideas by means of images and their order by means of localities. This practice cannot be used to draw out the memory if no memory has been given to use by nature.[388]

The two canons presented by Cicero in Book III are style and delivery. The former is given extensive treatment due to the nature of public speaking at that time. The latter basically summarizes the operations of the other four canons. Every sermon starts with an idea. Cicero wrote:

> That it is impossible to achieve an ornate style without first procuring ideas and putting them into shape, and at the same time that no idea can possess distinction without lucidity of style.[389]

Cicero's model of style was established upon four requirements of diction, lucidity, ornament, and appropriateness of style. His reflections concerning diction and lucidity are centered upon studying the grand masters of the rhetorical art. He suggested:

> But all correct choice of diction, although it is formed by knowledge of literature, is nevertheless increased by reading the orators and poets; for the old masters, who did not yet possess the ability to embellish their utterances, almost all of them had an eminently clear style, and those who have made themselves familiar with their language, will be unable to speak anything but good Latin, even if they want to.[390]

The final two requisites, ornament and appropriateness, tend to center around how words are clothed in a respectful and relevant language. Every preacher should take this conviction to heart, especially in preaching the Gospel. For Cicero, "the style must be in the highest possible degree pleasing and calculated to find its way to the attention of the audience, and have the fullest supply of facts."[391]

Due to the various degrees of style, the speaker must be cognizant that the delivery fits the occasion. "Delivery," according to Cicero, "is the dominant factor in oratory; without delivery the best speaker cannot be of any account at all."[392] The most pointed characteristic within the delivery canon is the voice. He further affirmed that "for effectiveness and distinction in delivery the greatest share undoubtedly belongs to the voice; the gift of voice is what we should pray for first."[393]

Cicero took the principles of rhetoric established by Aristotle and incorporated them into the standard of Roman oratory as a method of proving, delighting, and stirring. Cicero's rhetoric was "a constant function of oratory, a method of critical analysis, a criterion of judgment, and a test for measuring the effectiveness of speeches."[394]

Rhetorica ad Herennium

The *Rhetorica ad Herennium* is a major work on rhetorical training which consists of four books dealing with the five canons introduced by Aristotle and expanded by Cicero. The *Rhetorica*, written about the same time as the *De Inventione*, contains a briefer, yet no less complete, discussion of 'stasis theory' that is similar to Cicero's.[395]

The unknown author, whom many scholars view as Cicero, builds a solid foundation in Books I & II for rhetorical training by describing the five canons, especially invention. The initial goal of every sermon is to gain the receptive attention of the audience "by promising to discuss important, new, and unusual matters."[396] According to the writer, this aim can be achieved by four methods: by discussing our own persons, the person of our adversaries, that of our hearers, and the facts themselves.[397] These facts should possess curtness, color, and clarity.

The conclusion consists of three forms: summing up, amplification, and appeal to pity.[398] Summing up is basically recalling to memory the facts which have already been mentioned. Amplification utilizes one of ten accepted commonplaces to produce an emotional appeal among the audience. An appeal to pity rests upon changes in wealth, the loss of a verdict, the mercy of others, disgrace of associates, and a committed heart. The appeal to pity must be brief, for nothing dries more quickly than a tear.[399] Since the persuasive functions of a speaker rested upon proof and refutation, the writer stated that "invention is the most important and most difficult of the five tasks of the speaker."[400]

The topic of arrangement brings the writer to declaring that there are six items included in this form of rhetoric. He wrote:

> Our Arrangement will be based on the principles of rhetoric—to use the Introduction, Statement of Facts, Division, Proof, Refutation, and conclusion. This Arrangement, then, is twofold—one for the whole speech, and the other for the individual arguments—and is based upon the principles of rhetoric. But there is also another Arrangement, which, when we must depart from the order imposed by the rules of the art, is accommodated to circumstance in accordance with the speaker's judgment.[401]

The author shares the conviction with Cicero that the most potent arguments should be presented at the beginning and end of a speech, and weaker ones stated during the middle. The writer of the *Rhetorica* conveyed delivery as "the faculty of greatest use to the speaker and the most valuable for persuasion."[402] The detailed description was anchored upon two basic elements: voice quality and physical movement. He wrote:

> Voice quality has a certain character of its own, acquired by method and application. It has three aspects: Volume, Stability, and Flexibility. Physical movement consists in a certain control of gesture and mien which renders what is delivered more plausible. One must remember: good delivery ensures that what the orator is saying seems to come from his heart.[403]

The consensus among the classical rhetoricians was that the key to effective oratory depended upon one's ability to produce a quality delivery.

The memory canon was given considerable attention in the *Rhetorica*. The writer classified memory as "the treasure-house of the ideas supplied by Invention, the guardian of all the parts of rhetoric."[404] There were two types of memory used in oratory: one natural and the other the product of art.[405] He further entailed the origin of each:

> The natural memory is that memory which is embedded in our minds, born simultaneously with thought. The artificial memory is that memory which is strengthened by a kind of training and system of discipline. The natural memory, if a person is endowed with an exceptional one, so often like this artificial memory, and this artificial memory, in its turn, retains and develops the natural advantages by a method of discipline. Thus, the natural memory must be strengthened by discipline so as to become exceptional, and, on the other hand, this memory provided by discipline requires natural ability.[406]

A final instruction was that the best manner of recognizing the gift or "art" of memory may well be through the use of images. Hence, images have a way of being absorbed and maintained in the hearer's memory. The rule here is that the speaker "establish likenesses as striking as possible and set up images that are not many or vague, but doing something."[407]

In Book IV, the entire study is attributed to the canon of style or expression. Two of the key ingredients for a purposeful style, resided in the examples of renowned poets or orators since they "prompted modesty and served the purpose of testimony."[408] A final characteristic was established by the following:

> The highest art resides in this: in your selecting a great diversity of passages widely scattered and interspersed among so many poems and speeches, and doing this with such

painstaking care that you can list examples, each according to its kind, under the respective topics of the art. This, then, is the height of technical skill—in one's own treatise to succeed also in using borrowed examples![409]

The purpose of examples is for a solid, oratorical style and not to provide confirmation, but rather clarification.

Style was characterized as the grand, the middle, and the simple. Each method supported a particular choice of words depending upon the level of speech dictated by the circumstances. The grand style was composed of the most decorative language. The middle style was indicative of a relaxed, warm presentation held by a firm grasp of prose. The simple style offered its hearers a basic common, correct style, for everyday usage. In each style, there was a detriment which made the goal unsuccessful if it was not achieved. These pseudostyles were known as swollen, drifting, and meager.

In order for each style to be of the highest value, three qualities were necessary: taste, artistic composition, and distinction. The writer defined each accordingly:

Taste makes each and every topic seem to be expressed with purity and perspicuity (correctness and clarity). Artistic composition consists in an arrangement of words which gives uniform finish to the discourse in every part. To ensure this virtue we shall avoid the frequent collision of vowels, which makes the style harsh and gaping.

To confer distinction upon style is to render it ornate, embellishing it by variety. The divisions under distinction are figures of diction and the figures of thought. It is a figure of diction if the adornment is comprised in the fine polish of the language itself. A figure of thought derives a certain distinction from the idea, not from the words.[410]

The book concludes with an analysis of thirty-five distinctions, ten figures of diction, and eighteen figures of thought used in the writers three kinds of style.

Quintillion (ca. A.D. 40-95)

Thomas Conley stated that Quintillion's principal work on rhetoric, *De Institutione Oratoria* (On the Education of the Orator) represents "a compendium of theories of rhetoric discussed in the context of the production of the perfect orator" and is "one of the fullest records of rhetorical lore in the Isocratean-Ciceronian tradition ever written."[411] The work, whose lifetime program is the education and training of an orator, consists of twelve books dealing with the five canons of rhetoric.[412]

Book one outlines the principles of pedagogy from preliminary education to retirement age. Books two and three describe the basic functions and scope of the rhetorical art. Books four through six define invention. The focus of Books seven through ten is arrangement, style, and the benefits of imitating master authors. Book eleven contains teachings on the memory and delivery canons. The character of the perfect orator is the topic of the last book.

Drawing upon the foundation of Cicero, Quintillion clearly sets forth his idea of the art of speaking well, especially in practical affairs. He believed that the educated orator would have a broad education, a reputable character, and a willingness to dedicate one-self in arduous study. He wrote that "all language has three kinds of excellence, to be correct, perspicuous, and elegant."[413] Quintillion's primary agenda for *The Institutes* were discussed under the headings: the art, the artist, and the work of art. Quintillion explained:

> The art will be that which ought to be attained by study, and the knowledge of how to speak well. The artist is he who has thoroughly acquired the art, that is, the orator, whose business is to speak well. The work is what is achieved by the artist, that is, good speaking.[414]

Quintillion's objective or rhetorical art not only meant speaking well, but also emphasized the character and integrity of the speaker. He wrote that "my orator and his art, as defined by me, do not depend upon the result; but when he has spoken well, though he may not be victorious, he has attained the full end of his art."[415] The reasoning behind this conviction went beyond the means of persuasion. In reality, only those who achieved honor and respect "as good men," received the appreciation of an audience.

The proof of any argument rested upon a speaker's ability to make correct decisions concerning the gist of the argument. Quintillion further wrote:

> But no less care ought to be taken as to what you advance, than as to the manner in which what you advance is to be proved. Here the power of invention, if not the greatest, is certainly the first requisite; for as arrows are useless to him who knows not at what he should aim, so arguments are useless to him who has not ascertained to what point they are to be applied. This is what cannot be attained by art.[416]

The goal of the orator was not to argue for the sake of decision but to be rich and brilliant. For Quintillion, metaphors, the charms of expression, would bring more light to a subject than an undisguised argument. Once the subject matter was established, the arrangement of the issues gained the attention. Quintillion believed that "art can easily show a way, if there be one; but art has done its duty when it sets the resources of eloquence before us."[417]

In Book VIII, Quintillion placed eloquence as the imperative in all of oratory. The usage of words where necessary, whether singularly or collectively, and should be correct, well arranged, and varied with descriptions. He wrote:

> What is to follow requires more labour and care, since I have now to treat the art of elocution, which is, as all orators are agreed, the most difficult part of my work. For 'eloqui,' "to speak forth," is to express whatever has been conceived in the mind, and to communicate it fully to the hearers. Eloquence, therefore, requires the utmost teaching; no man can attain it without the aid of art; study must be applied to the acquirement of it; exercise and imitation must make it their object; our whole life must be spent in the pursuit of it; it is in this that one orator chiefly excels another; it is from this that some styles of speaking are so much better than others.[418]

The practice of rhetoric depended largely upon the speakers ability to read, listen, and write. Book X deals with the basic components of developing the required background through history, philosophy, and both ancient and modern writers.

Interacting with Cicero's *De Ortore*, Quintillion stressed the importance of memory and delivery as gifts of nature that were nurtured through diligent exercise. He stated that "all knowledge depends on memory; it is the power of memory that brings before us those multitudes of precedents, laws, sayings, judgments, and facts."[419] Memory for Quintillion was the "treasury of eloquence." Good delivery depended upon both voice and gesture, thoughts quite similar to Cicero. The rules for delivery were no different than those for language. Quintillion expressed:

> For as language ought to be correct, clear, elegant, and to the purpose, so delivery will be correct, that is, free from fault, if our pronunciation be easy, clear, agreeable, and polished. If the voice, too, be naturally, so to speak, sound, it will not be dull sounding, gross, bawling, hard, stiff, inefficient, thick, or on the contrary, thin, weak, squeaking, small, soft, effeminate; while the breathing, at the same time, should be neither short, nor unsustained, nor difficult to recover.[420]

The most natural, facial expression affecting a speaker's delivery belonged to the eye which held all the feelings of an orator. Without the use of hands, all delivery would be lacking in "the power of inciting, or restraining, of beseeching, of testifying approbation, admiration, and shame; the language of the hands appears to be a language common to all men."[421]

In the final book of Quintillion's *Institutes*, he characterized the perfect orator as a good man, who was full of wisdom and of high morality. He posited:

> Since an orator, then, is a good man, and a good man cannot be conceived to exist without virtuous inclinations, and virtue, though it received certain impulses from nature, the orator must above all things study morality, and must obtain a thorough knowledge of all

that is just and honourable, without which no one can either be a good man or an able speaker.[422]

The treasure of this classical work on rhetorical training is adequately summarized by Kennedy who writes "what Quintillion stresses is the orator's ability to lead, to influence, to dominate a situation."[423]

Summary

The classical canons of rhetoric, through the initiative of Aristotle, Cicero, the writer of the *Rhetorica ad Herennium,* and Quintillion have become the foundation for both preaching and public discourse. Each canon has its own individual identity, while at the same time serving the whole spectrum of rhetorical criticism. Because of the unique approach of the Black preaching tradition, the opportunity to study the rhetorical techniques of one of its celebrated figures is critical in order to obtain the necessary appreciation of the art. It is to this concern that we will now direct our attention.

An Analysis of Taylor's Theory
and Practice for Preaching

This section of the chapter will seek to analyze and evaluate Taylor's theory and practice for preaching in view of the earlier discussions on classical rhetoric. Each sermon will be analyzed for its use of one canon. These selected messages covering a broad span of Taylor's career are based upon the plight of the Black Church in particular and humanity in general.

"*They Shall Ask The Way.*"[424] This sermon was delivered in Cleveland, Ohio on July 23, 1950 at the Eighth Baptist World Congress, which later became known as the Baptist World Alliance. Gardner Taylor was thirty-two years old and pastor of the five thousand member Concord Baptist Church of Christ in Brooklyn, New York, which was one of the largest congregations in America, black or white. The message will be analyzed from the ethical (*ethos*) proof of invention.

Taylor's initial credibility became evident when Dr. W. H. Jernigan, a member of the board, recommended his young protege as the featured speaker for the Sunday morning worship service. Generally, this hour would have been reserved for a seasoned, renowned Baptist preacher of lengthy tenure with a distinguished reputation. The derived credibility of a speaker, as determined by the audience, comes from the sermon itself through the display of qualities of character, intelligence, good will which are essential to Aristotle's artistic proofs.[425] Taylor's audience consisted of delegates from around the world. The sermon played a major role in opening the eyes of the world to the plight of African American people being persecuted and oppressed. Taylor makes the following comment:

> This was a few years preceding the civil rights explosion. Men had come back from the second war in 1945. There was a new restlessness in Black America. America had taken one of the center places on the world stage, and was pawning itself off, really as a democracy when there were these fearful inconsistencies in our matters of race.[426]

The sermon is epideictic in type and has the immediate and primary concern of the speaker.

Taylor poses several statements relating to the conditions in the world and particularly those in America. His character is grounded in the maxims he uses to anchor several statements relating to the question. The speaker's introduction centers upon "utopia," "new Science," "man's brutality to man," "world of plenty," "backward people" and "poor witness." These fitting examples demonstrate an inductive approach of Aristotle's description of wisdom which allows the audience direct access to the problem and opportunity for giving solutions.

After Taylor offers the text in Jeremiah 50:5, he then moves towards a deductive stance by answering the question in the text from the New Testament text of John 14:6. The intelligence of Taylor[427] that seeks to persuade the audience toward acceptance of this condition becomes the basis of the sermon. The key factor determining his knowledge lies in the contemporary situations of war, peace, unity, and racism which are openly presented to the audience.

The ethical dimensions of the sermon center upon Cicero's view of substantiating the speaker's arguments as valid or seemingly valid.[428] The argument is not one-sided, but two-sided, standing as a benefit to all since "majorities and minorities share the same hatred which is death to both." This is clearly stated by the speaker's ability to mediate the problem which is an attestation of the speaker's perceived credibility as described by Aristotle. The speaker constantly uses the first person pronoun "we" in accepting blame and offering a solution throughout the sermon.

The good will of the speaker might be critiqued as being credible by utilizing the situation to address personally a national problem. After studying the sermon, Taylor uses the historical plight of Israel as the backdrop for developing a social consciousness through historical events of the people of God. "We shall be Christian at the point of race or forced to confess we are not Christian at all." The conclusion is clothed with an opportunity for the audience to answer the question, "Can we be sure?" Terminal credibility becomes assured within the hearts and ears of the audience when the description of Calvary is painted with the flair of a poet as "our way" becomes God's ultimate answer for the redemption of humanity. As mentioned earlier, the sermon received thunderous applause and a standing ovation.

"*The Christian Drama.*"[429] The Bayou-born Gardner Taylor was at the forefront of the Civil Rights movement with the Reverend Martin Luther King, Jr. from its inception, both spiritually and financially. This sermon was preached at Montgomery, Alabama on December 6, 1956, celebrating the November 13, 1956 ruling by the United States Supreme Court that Alabama's state and local laws requiring segregation on buses were unconstitutional. The one year struggle occurred when Rosa Parks refused to relinquish her seat on a bus.

The audience consisted of local, state, and national ministers and officers of the Montgomery Improvement Association, boycott participants, and church folk of all types. Many in the audience knew of Taylor's reputation as a speaker at the National Baptist Convention, USA, Inc. And he likewise knew the audience. Aristotle believed the relationship between a speaker and an audience was essential for creating *pathos* in speaking.[430] The worship atmosphere was filled with high emotions, joyous singing, fervent praying, and spiritual praise. A victorious celebration seemed evident among these people of God who had gained both a moral and spiritual accomplishment in a time of despair.

Gardner Taylor understood the characteristics and needs of his audience as fellow sufferers of injustice and oppression. The discriminating eye of Taylor incorporated Cicero's view of knowing what to say as a means of emotional persuasion.[431] Taylor utilized the attention concept in *Rhetorica* as the means of introducing the audience to the important and crucial issues of the day.[432] In his introduction, the rhetorical questions: "Has the bright dream of human dignity for all men now been dissipated by the rapacity of sinfulness of our society's standards?" sets the tone for controlling the emotions of the audience.

Taylor states the aim of the sermon regarding both his use of intellect and emotion:

> I intended to relate the Montgomery movement to God and to the purposes of God, and to gather the people who were showing such heroism into a confidence relating the sufferings of the people of Montgomery to the sufferings of Christ. And to relate the sufferings of Christ to the sufferings of the people in Montgomery. We have a Christian reflection and reverence in appropriately seeing the great victory in our Lord's death. It looked, I'm sure on the days and weeks of his death, as an abject failure.[433]

The introduction sets the stage to discuss an injustice that has been committed against black people in the south. The speaker instructs the audience by drawing upon historical questions concerning "Western civilization?" and "Has the bright dream of human dignity for all men now been dissipated by the rapacity and sinfulness of our society's standards?" The speaker identifies with the audience by vocalizing "we have separated humanity according to crass human standards, for the satisfaction of our pride and prejudice," "our society—sore, stricken, separated—needs an infusion of a new sense of spirituality."

The sermon text came from Romans 6:5. Taylor set the scene by depicting Rome as the contrast between the "crown and cross," "haughty and humble," "success and service." The theme of the sermon is summarized in the phrase, "a death like his." The death of Jesus, the 'Negro's Lawd' becomes "the guarantee," "the certified" that God honors suffering. Taylor draws upon the emotion of the people by viewing Calvary as the commitment to Montgomery which according to Aristotle produces the proper mindset in the hearers.[434] The quoting of the familiar John 3:16 after a repetition of "He died" and "Jesus died" undoubtedly brought the congregation to arousing shouts and screams of Amen!

The Christian drama, using the image of seed and harvest, is portrayed as one of commitment, patience, and trust in God. Even though the radicals of the Black Power era used this as a means of seizing change and glory, the prophecy of Gardner Taylor did not prove false. He simply states, "planting, seeding, and tilling is human, harvest is not human." Taylor posits upon this redemptive characteristic:

> During the heart of the Civil Rights Movement, the purpose was one of redemption. Dr. King often delineated that America had to be saved and Black people were the redemptive remnant having suffered for so long. We were in a position to save the nation, and this was our idea.[435]

The oratorical powers of Taylor conclude with a vivid description of the Christian drama of Good Friday and Easter Sunday. Taylor tells the story for all to hear truth that "He who began a good work in you will bring it to completion at the day of Jesus Christ." The chorus is repeated once and for all "but if we are united with him in a death like his, we shall certainly be united with him in a resurrection like his." Taylor incorporates the standard close of the Black preaching tradition to arouse the emotions of the audience by quoting the third verse of Charles Albert Tindley's classic hymn "Some Day." This form of preaching resonates with the *Rhetorica* and its proof of *pathos* in the conclusion as appealing to the "committed heart."[436]

"*Hearts Waiting for What?*"[437] Taylor remembers Paul Butler asking him for a sermon to be placed in the *Best Sermons* series. He goes further to state that "he asked me to deal with the society, the gospel as it relates to society, and so this is it."[438] The sermon is listed in the book under the theme "the social gospel." It is to this end that Taylor directs his argument and reasoning. The sermon is deliberative and deals directly with the future expectations of a better day. It will be critiqued from the logical (*logos*) proof of invention.

The sermon was delivered at the Concord Baptist Church of Christ, a congregation with a membership more than ten thousand, in 1958. The audience consisted of people from all walks of life who recently had built a $1,200,000 edifice under Taylor's leadership. In 1958, Taylor became the first African American to be elected president of the Protestant Council of New York City. Later that year, Gardner Taylor became a member of the city's Board of Education. These accomplishments are the high esteem accorded him.

The sermon comes from Isaiah chapter 25, verse 9 and its content centers upon God's presence in the struggle with an oppressed people. Taylor begins by dealing with society's "inward yearning" in a poem by William Wordsworth which offers a picture of Taylor's knowledge and depth of reading. The introduction provides the reader with the idea of expectation, "getting ahead," and "bettering our condition." Taylor's keen observation of society's dilemma probes him to believe that "something big is about to happen." For Aristotle, knowledge of facts was important to the argument[439] and Taylor consciously displays his understanding of the evils assaulting African Americans.

Using the title as a rhetorical tool, Taylor gives the answer to the relenting question with, "we are waiting for God," for the "righting of wrong by the aid of the Divine arm." The plain sense of the *logos* is developed by Taylor's deductive argument of the question, "Hearts waiting—for what?" which resonates with Quintilian's view of making the right decisions concerning what to debate.[440] Using the Aristotilean format of "Statement and Argument,"[441] Taylor moves towards the explication and application of the *logos* by introducing Isaiah who "speaks of the coming of God in power." Our God is One who, "can get in it with us" and whose "power and might are set against evil."

Secondly, the speaker draws the antithesis that the mythical Greek gods "were too far from the needs of men, and so the cause of righteousness never knows a certain and worthy end." For Taylor, justice does not prevail without God. Thirdly, Taylor identifies two persons who "speak with spiritual authority" of God's nearness in "the arena of our troubles," "the theater of our operations." The *logos* of the sermon is the Gospel message: "We have a God Who comes where we are," "We have no less a Gospel than that God is kin to us," and "our hearts wait for a God Who can feel our sorrow and share our hearts' desires." Herein underlies the reasoning behind Taylor's argument.

The legal prowess of Taylor takes the reader through the court system as the NAACP fought against the evils of racism and segregation. He asks, "Is God going with us, even to the Supreme Court?" Another feature of Taylor's logical pursuit is to paint the weak as becoming the strong. His example of the handyman fits this reasoning to the bill. The crux of Taylor's thinking lies in his belief "that God has for [it] some worthier destiny than our bitter divisions of race and region."

There is a "foreseeable future" and a "better day ahead" as the conclusion builds excitement for this inward yearning. Taylor sounds the clarion conviction that hope will never die in the hearts of God-fearing people. The intellect of Taylor passionately moves the audience to a state of silence as he tells the story in James Stewart's memoir of "The Boy" by Coventry Patmore. His classic ending radiates with the staccato of musical rhythms to answer the question, "Hearts waiting for what?" with "And there is the answer of God." Taylor's answer always proves for right in the experience of life.

"*Some Comments on Race Hate.*"[442] The year is 1964 and African American people have gained limited advancements in civil rights, equality, and justice. The initial audience was the Concord Church; however, the sermon now appears in print for the larger distribution to society. In 1963, Taylor was arrested for demonstrating against job discrimination in Brooklyn's building industry. The climate in white America was saturated with racial hatred and prejudice after the signing of the Civil Rights Bill. The sermon definitely deals with the present historical situation. Arrangement canon will be the criteria used in analyzing this sermon and the following Presidential address.

The order of Gardner Taylor's sermons generally conforms to the traditional trichotomic partition of an Aristotolean Introduction, Body (Statement of Facts and Proofs), and Conclusion. The text, John 4:9, deals specifically with the issue of racial prejudice and immediately sets the tone for the speaker. The sermon has the four basic components of a speech which reflect the rhetorical criteria of Aristotle.[443] In this sermon, the introduction is shorter than most, only eleven lines, but it is saturated with a fact, conviction, and warning. The opening sentence, "Race hate is an old and persistent disease in the bloodstream of society," becomes the central idea of the sermon. Taylor takes this sentence, drawing upon Cicero's suggestion for the introduction as the basis of the entire sermonic structure. It's an issue of inherent importance and timelessness from a biblical and societal perspective. The striking facts concerning hatred based upon prejudice and race "offends heaven and shuts so many out from God." Taylor does not exclude "the hater or the hated" from this evil, especially the church. His hearers are a part of the problem, and thereby must become connected to the solution. The introduction is quite appropriate for the theme.

The body in the topical/textual sermon is rather extensive. The text becomes the first division and informs the audience that "prejudice and bigotry blinded the eyes and deafened the ears of the Samaritan woman." The pulpit, according to Taylor, must take the lead in eradicating this evil in our land. He proceeds with a historical overview of how the church instigated segregation in America. Taylor treats each subtheme with a credible belief that "In our life time we shall not know peace between blacks and whites in this country."

The body's third division contains a refutation of separatism and the partial cures which seem only as sedatives and not a realistic solution. This final division is germane to knowing oneself and accepting humanity as the kindred of God. Such a position permits one to become the "authentic nobility" that destroys the issue of race hatred in the soul of America. The main points in the body are arranged in a manner that begins with the text and ends with a Theocentric view towards the solution. All subthemes are examples supporting the main divisions.

The conclusion, by reason of fact and example, offers the audience a solid connection between humanity and God. It brings the Jesus/Samaritan Woman discourse to a fitting end in knowing that the argument is in harmony with the introduction and body. Using Psalm 8 as the proof text, Taylor states that "This is the biography of every human soul." Moreover, the familiar frame of Calvary, the New Testament revelation, reaffirms God's acceptance of our differences. The third description is from a Wordsworth poem which is used as a preamble for the final stoke of expressing the speaker's hope. The historical faith of African American people rings vividly in the Negro spiritual, "Swing Low, Sweet Chariot." This word-picture depicts the imagery of a blessed home in glory validating that the answer is our religion.

"The President's Message to the Progressive National Baptist Convention, Inc. September 1968."[444] Dr. Garner C. Taylor, fourth President of the Progressive National Baptist Convention, Inc., delivered his final presidential address on September 7, 1968, in the nation's capital after two years of service. The American scene lurks with tension, militancy and chaos due to the Viet Nam War and the assassinations of Gardner's dearest friends, Martin King, Jr. and Robert Kennedy. The Convention Hall has overflowed its seating capacity with delegates, still shocked over the death of King, who need to hear a "Word from de Lawd."

Taylor's introduction begins with a historical reflection of Washington, D.C. as the "nerve-center of the political arrangements of the whole earth." The memory of the "March on Washington" in August 1968 opens the door for Taylor and the Convention to pay fitting tribute to "the only authentic spiritual genius America has produced." The introduction is filled with historical references which undoubtedly grips the audience through the oratorical powers of Taylor's expertise.

The assassination of King and Kennedy serves as a staunch reminder of America's neglect of Resurrection City's "cries of hunger and deprivation," and the disregard "to confess and repent of our wrong in Viet Nam." These and other measures of controversy within the republic sets the stage for the body of the message. Taylor's theme centers upon hinting at God's command as to "the direction in which we are to move."[445]

Because of Taylor's involvement with the organizing of the Progressive Convention after it split from the National Baptist Convention, U.S.A., Inc., he reports that "God has called us out for a purpose." The message stresses the remedies which the convention must take, especially at this most critical juncture in Black life. First, the speaker believes that the convention, under God's guidance, is "to initiate the work of reconciliation" to unite Baptist fellowship and bring healing to America.

The grateful President acknowledges the work of his cabinet and officers in the second division. Appreciations and accolades fill the audience with the reassurance that "Progressive Baptists enjoy a very great regard and confidence in our World Baptist family." The third division is fully representative of the primary concern of black people in regard to integration vs. segregation. The integrationist view of Taylor and his allies is being challenged by a younger generation of separatist, Taylor states:

> I had to examine deeply where these young people were coming from. I came to an understanding particularly in New England schools like Mt. Holyoke, Smith, and Wesleyan, especially these women schools where little colonies of black seemed to be engulfed, and they were desperate to find identity. And so I was talking about separatism as a temporary withdrawal to find ourselves in order to return to the society. And there was that alternation in the life of our Lord of retreat and return.[445]

The speaker lists several illustrations of matters evolving around the nation concerning this vital issue. The goal is to position himself upon a solid, biblical text which was Luke chapter nine.

Gardner Taylor placed his listeners within view of how Jesus led his disciples by the statement "that every group must at some time or the other get with itself, find itself." The retreat is beneficial not only for the Church, but black people as well. Using the Scriptures, Taylor suggests that "He called them apart that they might be empowered. He gave them power and authority." Citing biblical examples, the speaker threads the seriousness of the hour with the cruciality of seeing "the society in its splendor and in its shame."

In the conclusion, the "empowerment" motif rests upon Jesus sending black people back into a treacherous world "to lift the hope of life in the colony of death." The dramatization of being sent bears the thought that "as we serve, we must ever tell men who sent us." As representatives of redemption, Taylor says that black people "bare the Crown Seal of Jesus Christ." In conversational fashion, the climatic ending is saturated with poignant descriptions of the One who sends. Taylor's task—to explain, entertain, convince, and persuade—is most effective through the arrangement of his final Presidential address.

"*A Balm in Gilead.*"[446] Style is the focus of the next two sermons. The personality of Taylor the preacher can be vividly detected through his word pictures and expressive ideas. He initially preached this sermon as a first year seminarian at the Lenten service of the Mt. Zion Church, in Oberlin, Ohio on March 29, 1938. It also marked the first time Miss Laura Scott heard him. Taylor remarks, "This sermon got me a wife. Best sermon I ever preached!"[447]

Gardner Taylor proudly admits that the ideas in the sermon, Jeremiah 8:22, belonged to his Father, who first preached the sermon in the 1920s. Through time and testing, however, the amplification and application became the testimony of Gardner Taylor's own spiritual pilgrimage. He states:

> When I first preached this sermon, my thoughts were about my Father and wondering where and how he got those ideas. The idea, it has been one of the strengths of black preaching. I think, at an earlier generation, our preaching at its best has been the "capacitability" to draw parallels.[448]

Words and phrases such as "deep ache," "trapped and suffering," "do you hear the pain?," "deepest mourning and wrung from his heart sorrow and from his eyes copious tears of sympathy," "the thrust and counterthrust of human struggle" provide specific sentiments of the burden upon the protagonist.

Writing in the first person plural pronoun, the speaker analyzes the effects of sin, through terms as "cultural lag," "ignorance," "this fatal disease," and "destroys the nervous system of conscience and wrecks the power of right thinking." The speaker's clarity of thought defines the power of sin as "rebellion against God," and moreover its paralyzing hold of the nation. Taylor notes that "I do not think that any of us, who were back there dealing with the movement took due cognizance of the depth of sin in the creation."[449] The sentences illustrating the symptoms of sin are sharp, concise, and direct, and filled with grief for Israel and America too. James Earl Massey, in his book, *Designing the Sermon*, offers constructive insights into the intentions of Gardner Taylor's style. He writes:

> Gardner Taylor's own pulpit gifts are unusual and highly instructive. Few preachers can handle his penchant for long sentences so well, showing lights and shadows by such ready adjectives, pictorial phrases, and the traditional grand manner of euphony and resonance. One can learn so much about preaching through the exemplary work of this contemporary.[450]

The use of the simple style creates a common, elementary approach to the description of the healing medicine. The basic ideas of Taylor and his father inform the reader of the balm's purpose, origin, physical traits, and extraction process. The parallelism between the balm and Jesus draws suitable metaphors of explaining the power to heal sin diseases, the import concept, the unattractiveness of both, and finally the epigram of cutting each to bleed their healing fluid. Taylor adds a cogent perspective on this issue in his preaching:

> All of my preaching, I think people in my congregation use to say that it was the kind of preaching that a child could get. I hope that is so, I think it is, certainly the ideas. I have held the opinion, the notion, if you are clear on something, anybody could get it, if they listen.[451]

Taylor uses more metaphorical language and imagery to conclude the message by personifying the balm as Jesus, citing the Isaiah 53:5 passage, as humanity's cure for sin. Gardner Taylor, as a serious practicer of preaching, employs in his style of preaching a sense of "being there" which "brings the sermon home" in the hearing of his audience.

"The Scarlet Thread."[452] This Lenten sermon shares the title of Dr. Taylor's second publication of sermons. It was preached in the late seventies using Joshua 2:18–19 as the text. The form of the sermon is narrative and allows for the preacher to draw vivid views of the basic theme, life and death. The style canon, from a narrative folklore perspective, is described by Roger D. Abrahams. He states:

> Ultimately style is not definable as the form of expression which a writer will fall into when he finds his 'true voice.' It is rather the recurrence of linguistic entities which provide an objectively describable pattern in terms of sounds, words, rhythms, syntactical construc-tions, and even perhaps units of meanings.[453]

The sermon is a blend of Taylor's contemporary view of the world and word as a prescription for a redemptive lifestyle. The language of the sermon opens with an alliteration, "sharply aware of the sorrow and sacrifice of the great Savior." The phrase, "our loyalties change and our enthusiasms shift directions," employs the choice of words that moves the sermon towards the next illustration of forgettery.

The sermon's style combines the expression of the Lenten Season with the narrative of the Old Testament. The God of biblical history and the Christ of Calvary become the natural resemblance of "like father, like son." The narrative craft of Taylor tells the story of Joshua's pursuit of "the land of promise." In ordered harmony, the narrator, speaking from the third person, outlines the events of the story. Throughout the narrative, Taylor weaves contemporary applications of Rahab being "of a different race and culture" and a "Canaanite prostitute."

The story is presented using only those details that aide in the speaker's aim of determining how life overcomes death. Even though she lied, Taylor states that "a lie in a cause of goodness, on behalf of the future, may well not be as damnable as others." The point of the story centers upon the fact that "the spies gave their promise" and protection would be rendered "where the scarlet thread hung in the window." These sentences keep the idea of the story centered upon a salvation of Jesus. Rahab and her family are spared as "Joshua fit the battle of Jericho."

The clarity of the story highlights the application of all "under the siege of life and the siege of death." The contrast and comparison of how each deals with humanity brings Taylor to the conviction that "There is but one hope." Using portraits of what Christ had done for humanity within the Pauline epistles, Taylor declares to his readers that "ye are no more strangers and foreigners, but fellow citizens with the saints, and of the household of God." His classic conclusion parallels Christ as "that scarlet thread" through a series of repetitive convictions. Richard John Neuhaus ably describes Taylor's style of explanation. He writes:

> Gardner Taylor begins by picking up a word, such as reconciliation. First he just says it, but then you can see him warming up to it. He tries just rolling it out of his mouth; then, staccato-like, he bounces it around a bit; then he starts to take it apart, piece by piece, and then put it together in different ways. And pretty soon you have a whole lot of people engaged in wondering and puzzling with Dr. Taylor, trying to figure out what this word and this idea of reconciliation is all about.

> They walk around the word, looking at it from different angles. Taylor gets on top of it and looks down, then he lifts up a corner and peeks underneath; you can see that this is going to be a difficult word to get to know. He whispers it and then he shouts it; he pats, pinches, and probes it; and then he pronounces himself unsatisfied, and all the people agree. "It's time to look at what the great Apostle Paul has to say about this here word, reconciliation." And all the people agree.

> There is a playfulness in all this, but the purpose is impressively serious. It may seem like taking the long way to get to the text, but along the way the preacher has tried out a number of convention definitions and explanations of reconciliation and has, in fact, already covered a good deal of what he intends to say on the subject. It is one form of excellent rhetoric.[454]

The style of Taylor brings proclamation to its zenith, from the opening statement to the victorious conclusion. "Christ our Scarlet Thread!"

"A Dedication of the Benjamin E. Mays Hall and the Howard Thurman Chapel."[455] Dr. Gardner Taylor was the featured speaker for the alumni service of thanksgiving on April 24, 1987. This worship service follows two previous days of celebration, at the newly purchased Howard Divinity School, where Andrew Young and Lerone Bennett delivered the messages. The sermon text is Ezekiel 43:1–6, entitled "The Glory of the Lord," and will be critiqued and evaluated from the memory canon.

Gardner Taylor has been naturally blessed with the gift of memory. He carefully draws from a wealth of reading, experience, and biblical images, thus guiding the listener along the sermonic journey. The sermon speaks of a "saving remnant in the land." Those, who have been blessed with training and knowledge through the seminary, must move beyond the bewitching "standards of the culture." He reminds the alumni/ae group of falling into "the escapism of conspicuous consumption" and those who are left behind into the "nirvana of drug-induced stupor."

Taylor recalls the suffering and agony of people who endure heart break in America. He speaks of the church as the "precinct of the holy," and not a "cauldron of undirected emotions," nor a "mausoleum of pointless ceremony." He encourages ministers not to turn the biblical spelling of the word "prophet" into the Wall Street spelling of the word "profit." An aside is made concerning a certain church (Concord) that has a million dollar endowment for communal institutions to encourage every church of the billion dollar potentials for the Black community.

A stern plea from Taylor summons Howard graduates to assist its institution which endured "the long night of slavery and came into the morning of our hopes." The national election speech by former President Ronald Reagan referring to an excerpt from "A City on a Hill" is recounted by Taylor as a cruel, dishonest, pseudo-manipulation of John Winthrop's sermon. From memory, Taylor recites a portion of the sermon and reestablishes the full context of its original intent.

The conclusion draws upon the musical imagery of Handel's "Messiah." Taylor reveals the magnificent oratorio within the vivid imagery of a consecrated imagination. The risen Lord, a detachment of angels, another coterie of angels from the chorus of heaven describe the call and response of Psalm twenty-four. This picture of heaven, painted scene by scene with a spiritual brush, brings the crowd to shouts of jubilation and applause. "For He Shall Reign Forever, and ever, and ever, Amen."

"The Preacher's Reply to the Human Cry."[456] The sermon marked the third anniversary of Dr. Frank M. Reid, III as pastor of the Bethel African Methodist Episcopal Church, located in Baltimore, Maryland. The date of the celebration was October 10, 1991. The sermon will be critiqued and evaluated from the delivery canon perspective. Dr. Taylor was a former seminary instructor of Pastor Reid's at Harvard. The vocal quality of the mentor pastor-professor has a clear distinct tone. Taylor, dressed in a double breasted, dark gray suit, white shirt, gray tie, burgundy handkerchief, possesses a natural, deep baritone voice that resonates with charm and compassion. The speaker's eloquence has been refined by both seasoning and stature as a gospel preacher. Kathleen McClain, a writer for *The Charlotte Observer*, reported on Taylor's delivery style. She writes:

At 72, his rich, deep voice still rolls through the cadences of his Louisiana childhood. He speaks without notes, moving effortlessly from historical anecdotes to quotes from such diverse sources as evangelist Dwight Moody, poet Elizabeth Browning and former Charlotte pastor, Carlyle Marney. Taylor is aware that not all of today's audiences respond to his blending of literature, theology, history, and philosophy.[457]

The text, Psalm 61:1–2, is read very slowly. The preacher pronounces each word distinctively and accurately. Taylor has a pleasing voice as he speaks in a conversational expression. The pauses are well timed. Words roll forth with an accent of an English gentleman. The speaker's style flows with a graceful elegance as can only be delivered by a true orator. Eye contact establishes *ethos* with the listener and soon the audience becomes attentive to every word. The pace is about one hundred and eighty-five words a minute.

Gestures are used by Taylor, but the hands are always kept within reasonable length of the body and always seem to help make the point. Limited body action is displayed. Occasionally, Taylor turns from side to side, but nothing beyond flat-footed, hind leg preaching. Taylor knows how to bring inflection to certain sentences within the text, asking a repetitive question, "Where is the end of the earth?" over, and over again. The question has an answer with a winsomeness of assurance that Taylor leads the audience in answering.

At the conclusion, the voice pitch is raised about three decibels, the word pace moves in rapid, rhythmic patterns. Taylor has total command of the sermon, no manuscript, just pure mind, heart, and soul. The audience gains a greater pathos not just for the rhythms and cadences, but also the wording and vividness of each expression of the voice. Modulations within each set of phrases, "in God's own time, every knee shall bow and tongue shall confess that Jesus is Lord" brings the church to resounding cheers of joy and thanksgiving.

"Inaugural Interfaith Prayer Service."[458] Dr. Gardner C. Taylor was selected as the preacher for the 1993 Presidential Inaugural Interfaith Prayer Service. The worship service was held at the Metropolitan African Methodist Episcopal Church, January 20, 1993, in Washington, D.C. Both President Clinton and Vice President Gore, along with their wives, children, guests, and hundreds of friends attended the 7:30 A.M. gathering. This sermon will be evaluated for both the memory and delivery canons.

He deliberately reflected upon the Metropolitan Church as a "shrine of African Methodism" as a testament of determination through a recollection of Richard Allen's freedom movement. The introduction exhibits Taylor's sense of humor with a fitting joke on practically every denomination represented. There is much laughter by all. He concludes the introduction with reflections particularly from his father and other former slaves of Booker T. Washington's meeting with President Theodore Roosevelt at the White House in the early 1900s.

The text comes from Luke, chapter ten, verse 27. It is read with passionate emphasis on "love, Lord, heart, mind, soul, strength, and neighbor." There are always sufficient pauses, followed by precise language for the moment of "Camelot in the Ozarks." The voice is strong, clear, and full of authority. Taylor holds the packed audience in suspense as the words fulfill their hearing. He recalls the lament of a choreographer of the national recent epidemic over the relationship of life, death, and creativity. The challenge immediately turns toward America.

The body of the sermon states the contract of America's values among its constituents. Without script or notes, Taylor's eyes peer deep into the soul of America sensing a purposefulness from God. He chooses each word, connects every phrase by attacking the issues of the day. The sentences are long, but well structured and articulated. The message is pleasing to the ear and soul by the smooth oratorical powers of the speaker.

Taylor delivers memorized excerpts from the Declaration of Independence and Constitution. With one hand in his pocket and the other gesturing freely as he speaks, Dr. Taylor makes every word count. His open black robe authenticates a style of the black Baptist preaching tradition. The deliberative speech is extempore delivered while arms are folded, head is rubbed, and hands are lifted. Taylor, a master of facial expressions, looks the President and Vice President directly in their eyes stating "people can govern themselves."

At the close of the sermon Taylor gestures a triangle with his hands illustrating the connection of God, humanity, and neighbor. His voice begins to weaken slightly, but it regains the necessary power to drive the sermon home with the famous quote, "Mine Eyes Have Seen the Glory of the Lord . . ." Taylor received a standing ovation from President Clinton, and those in attendance.

CHAPTER SIX

Conclusion

This book has analyzed the historical perspective of the African American preaching tradition and the life, ministry, and preaching methodology of Gardner C. Taylor. An overview of African American preaching and some stellar personalities were presented in chapters two and three. A study of Taylor's ministry and preaching theory was given in chapters four and five. The purpose of this final chapter is to present key contributions of Gardner Taylor's preaching within the historical tradition of African American preaching. Suggestions for further study and research are also provided.

The primary motivation for writing this publication centered upon the author's desire to study the preaching practice of the ingenious Gardner C. Taylor. In addition, the historical development of African American preaching and celebrated preachers is an area which became an attractive option. There has been a concentrated effort to provide historical data and a personalized study of one who is recognized as a master of the art of preaching. The task of the African American preacher became a vital concern for this study.

Social Conditions for Applying the Gospel

The preaching ministry of Gardner Taylor stretches over sixty years. He has preached in many of the most celebrated pulpits around the world. The Black church rightfully claimed ownership of this descriptive and imaginative preacher. The preaching traditions of the Western world have respectfully appreciated his approach to the preaching event. Because of the racial climate of segregation and injustice in America during the pastoral ministries of Taylor and his father, Gardner consciously experienced the redemptive love of God for an oppressed people. Those drained, weary, faithful pilgrims who came to hear his declarations of the gospel were spiritually strengthened and morally motivated to trust in the power of God.

As Taylor's reputation spread throughout both the American and Southern Baptist Conventions, the Baptist World Alliance, and the white seminary community, opportunities were afforded him to challenge the American democratic society with the gospel truth. Moreover, the attitude of the old Negro Church assumed a different posture following World War II. Black people came to realize that American democracy had failed in granting them their God given rights of freedom and equality.

During the early years of Taylor's pastoral ministry, he came to the conclusion that the gospel was intended for every race, creed, and color. The situations in society required a prophetic voice for change and commitment. Taylor had first hand experience of second class citizenship and the tragedies of the American way of life.

The hope of the Black Church took flight on the energetic wings and trained minds of ministers and laypersons of Taylor's caliber. It was necessary for Gardner Taylor to become a spokesperson against the social conditions of Black people and their situation in America. Taylor was equiped and trained to articulate the needs and concern of black people. Alterations within the social and religious fabric of American democracy did not come easily. It was during the preceding years to the Civil Rights Movement that blatant neglect in the social, political, and economic conditions of Black people demanded immediate attention.

The preaching ministry of the Concord Baptist Church of Christ pastor gained tremendous support from his constituents around the country. There was something special in Taylor's spirit which easily attracted people to him. Through his preaching, parishioners began to believe that the God of creation would make a better life for all people in general and black people, in particular. Gardner Taylor's sermons were consumed with an urgency to advance the cause of human dignity and personhood. One of the key characteristics in Taylor's preaching is that after fifty years of preaching, the general themes of his preaching have not deviated nor veered from the redemption and liberation matters of the gospel message.

It could also be said that Taylor's preaching ministry focused heavily upon the entire revelation of the Scriptures. He visualized the God of Israel as the Almighty deliverer who remained forever faithful to humanity. Regardless of how dark the night, those who shared the preaching moment of Gardner Taylor left with a greater appreciation of God's love. Even though the living conditions of African American people improved, Taylor was still at the forefront of proclaiming liberty and justice for all. Through the leadership of the Concord Church, Taylor's preaching advanced similar challenges to initiate self-support ministries as a vital link in the community. He taught Concord members that there was no failure in God.

Evaluation of Taylor's Theory of Preaching

In the African American worship experience, the preaching event has long maintained the dominant position within the church service. The Bible is viewed as God's holy word and the most effective preaching centers upon the scriptures in the biblical narrative. Gardner Taylor is a master of combining the revellent story with the relevant issues of the day. There is a reverent appreciation of the Scriptures deeply embedded in the preaching ministry of Taylor. His preaching style makes specific use of God's word and how the message directly relates to contemporary issues in society. Here lies another key characteristic of Taylor's methodology for preaching. The gist of Taylor's sermons were readily identified by what African American people identified with mostly, the Bible.

The artistic canon of preaching seems to automatically identify with the persona and talents of Gardner Taylor. As a child, he learned from his mother's knee how to train a God-given photogenic mind. The memory canon is a key component for the African American preaching tradition from its inception of early slave churches. Slaves heard and recorded the messages of white preachers and quoted them line for line. Also, the ability to retain quotable materials after the first reading provides an enormous reservoir of information for Taylor to recall naturally. He frequently quotes from literary references, historical documents and facts, and poetry at will. The memory canon enables Gardner Taylor to draw upon his reading habits and preach extemporaneously.

Taylor is an avid reader. He constantly studies the biblical record, always discovering some gripping text to spur his spiritual energies. Taylor also possesses a great appreciation for history and the men and women who have pioneered the pathways of life and freedom. He uses the invention canon as a means of being current, convincing, and knowledgeable. Being a person of moral integrity, Taylor's character has contributed to the success of a dynamic preaching ministry. Moreover, he has the capacity to identify with an audience and move them to levels of cerebral awareness and spiritual celebration.

The ability to arrange sermon content in an orderly fashion is another attribute of Taylor's preaching that resembles the early slave preacher. The arrangement canon in Taylor's theory develops within the textual outline of the Scriptures. For example, the sermon in *Preaching Biblically* by Taylor details a perfect example of how he uses the text to shape the form of his sermon, "A Sad Memorial." Taylor's sermons are basically easy to follow using the rhetorical outline of classical rhetoric. The key to Taylor's effectiveness in this category is how he provides the pictorial imagery and illustrations to support the movement in a sermon.

The style canon of Gardner Taylor's preaching was also learned from parents who had excellent command of the English language. It was very uncommon during Taylor's childhood to have parents who were skilled in the correct uses of diction and grammar. Taylor knew how to speak in a transforming tongue that would say for his audience what they could not say for themselves. He became a translator of the African American plight through symbols, syntax, and songs that captured the spiritual imaginations of the old and young. One might even go forth to write that much of Taylor's success as a preacher resulted in his unique and captivating style. His eloquence is indeed a sight to behold.

The factor which determines the effectiveness of the invention, arrangement, style, and memory canons is the delivery canon of the preaching event. Without a convincing delivery, preaching lives or dies. In this category, Taylor stands second to none. His presence and voice command both attention and respect. The ability to captivate the attention of an audience is the threshold of the preaching event. Taylor is a prime example of how to incorporate gestures, pauses, projections, inflections, and intonations in the delivery. Gardner Taylor's preaching is always an unforgettable experience because he puts every ounce of mind, heart, soul, and strength into the message.

Suggestions for Further Research

The African American preaching tradition is a spiritual phenomenon which has been a validation of God's reliability to sustain an oppressed people. There are numerous books and dissertations written on African American history and the Black Church experience. There are limited works, however, that give strict attention to the art of preaching from the artistic canon perspective. This type of ongoing study is necessary in order to analyze the preaching theories, methods, and practices of Black men and women who were geniuses in their own right.

The implications for future research on the art of African American preaching and preachers provides a number of possibilities. The methodology for this edition could be applied to other cultures and persons. I would strongly suggest that since more African American ministers are involved in Doctor of Ministry programs that this kind of study become a model for the future. It is also important for the student to examine the life and ministry of a life-long practitioner who may have never conceptualized his own style. Gardner Taylor would never write about himself because of his modest personality. Yet his six decades of preaching and pastoral ministries, along with lectures on preaching, now make his preaching ministry available to future generations. May the efforts of this book offer some minister guidance toward the art and craft of preaching the gospel.

APPENDIX A

A Sermon by Dr. Washington M. Taylor

Memorial Program
In Honor of
Rev. Elias Camp Morris, D. D.
of
Helena, Ark.

Who for 27 years was
President of the National Baptist Convention
(Incorporated)
And who departed this life
September 5, 1922

1855-1922

Requiescat in Pace

In grateful memory of Three Million Baptists
who followed and loved him

National Baptist Convention (Inc.)

MEMORIAL PROGRAM

Should ask how is the work
You left behind,
If church and convention
Are both in line?

Will the Baptist family
Be watched with care?
Will any dissension
Destroy them there?

Just say we are coming,
our faith is in God;
Our hope is his promise
Our trust his word.

You fought like a hero
Your victory is won,
Your labor is ended
Your work is done.

———————

"FUNERAL ORATION ON DR. E. C. MORRIS."

———————

Delivered by the Rev. W. M. Taylor, D. D., Pastor of
Mt. Zion Baptist Church, Baton Rouge, La.; and
President Louisiana State Baptist Convention.

[Big of body, brain and bigger of heart, and more eloquent than many, Dr. W. M. Taylor delivered this eulogy with a carefulness, exactness, faithfulness to the truth and the man, that endeared himself and the subject to the hearts of all who were fortunate enough to have heard it. It was a model and classic in the department which it represents and is printed for the meditation of the millions to digest who could not hear it.—Editor-in-chief.]

Dr. E. C. Morris has gone to heaven. He left this world for glory at the rising of the sun on September 5, 1922. And from the known tendency of his soul heavenward and his joyous haste to be gone there can be little doubt but his chariot of fire reached its destination speedily, and the triumphant saint, has, ere this, taken his seat with the heavenly company.

And since he is gone, I register my affectionate remembrance of a man whom I both loved and admired, and at the report of whose death, my heart has been made sick. I loved him for his was an affectionate heart and he was my friend.

But the servant of God, the servant of the church, the servant of the Baptists, and my friend, is dead. I admired him, not for his learning, but the more for the greatness of his soul.

Nature had done much for him. She had fashioned his soul after an enlarged model and had given it an original cast and an independent bearing. She had instilled the sweetening influence of a tender sympathy and infused into the soul the fire of a spirit stirring zeal sustained by a vigorous and untiring energy; but to finish the character, grace came in and renewed the whole man, and the Spirit anointed him to preach the gospel, and the church and God consecrated him to be our leader.

The servant of God superintended with dignity and faithfulness; he preached the gospel with the Holy Ghost sent down from heaven. The unction that attended his word was not merely like the oil that ran down Aaron's beard, but it was like the anointing of the Spirit that penetrates the heart. He preached with his soul full of glory. No wonder, then, that he has fought a good fight, kept the faith and will receive his reward according to his labors here.

Sleep on Dr. Morris, for however mysterious the path, it must be trodden by every member of the human family. Desperate indeed is any attempt on earth to meet correspondently this great dispensation of heaven. For while with pious resignation we submit to an all-gracious Providence, we can not cease lamenting the death of this noble man, whose voice is forever silenced. His footsteps will be heard among us no more. He was pious, just, humane and sincere; faithful to this nation, kind-hearted, and always ready and willing to do anything to promote the cause of Christ and the Baptists. He is now standing in the ranks of the General Assembly and the church of the first-born. It seems I can see his image and hear those deep sinking words from his lips, saying "Cease lamenting, brethren, our separation will not continue always, work on, reverence religion, diffuse knowledge, and let justice and free speech be inseparable companions, and cultivate peace with all nations."

Sleep on, Dr. Morris, until the long roll beats and we will meet you at the inauguration of King Immanuel. Let us all prepare to meet our much beloved and departed leader, for we can not tell the time of our departure from our borrowed home to go to that eternal home not made with hands.

Sleep on, soldier of the cross, I know you are tired. Take your rest, for many years you have led our innumerable host. I wish I had power to withstay every tear and ease the burdened hearts of the bereaved family. For the names of the Morrises will be reverenced as long as there is one Baptist left to worship at the altar of intelligence and sublime Christian service.

Now, comrades, and brother ministers, in the regular order of things the procession must be kept up until every member of the human family has crossed the narrow Divide, when we shall live in the dawning of a new day and evening shadows never fall, where there is no weariness in doing the will of God and offering praises to his name for his redeeming love.

We shall never feel the freshness of the morning, and still farther from the close, no light of the sun or moon. The light of the sun will be superseded by a radiance which is not painfully dazzling, which immeasurably surpasses the brightness of our noontide. The glory of God and the Lamb floods the city with unfading light. The redeemed walk in the sunless glory of perpetual day. There the people of God are privileged to hold open communion with the Father and the son. We shall stand in his presence and behold his glory, the pure communion with holy beings, the harmonious social life with the faithful of all ages who have washed their robes in the blood of the Lamb. The sacred ties that bind us together, the whole family in heaven, these constitute the happiness of the redeemed. These immortal minds will contemplate with never failing delight the wonders of Creative power, the mysteries of redeeming love. Every faculty will be developed, every capacity increased in the Beautiful City, where all the treasures of the sky will be opened to the blood-bought army unfettered by immortality. We shall wing our tireless flight to worlds afar, and the years of eternity shall roll by with richer and still more glorious revelation of God in Christ. And Jesus will open before us the riches of redemption and the amazing achievements in the great controversy with Satan, and the heart of the redeemed shall thrill with more fervent devotion as the sweep of the harps of gold and ten thousand times ten thousand and thousands of thousands and millions of billions and quadrillions of voices unite in the chorus of praise to Him that has redeemed us with His blood. And then we shall see our own Morris robed in heavenly regalia, accompanying Jehovah's only Son back to Calvary's stained mountain.

Appendix B

Sermons by Dr. Gardner C. Taylor

"They Shall Ask the Way"

There is a question on the lips of our times, a poignant, desperate, haunting question. A question which arises because our old confidence is gone. We were sure yesterday that we had the future neatly folded, wrapped and ready for delivery. Utopia was in our hands our chromium-plated, push-button conveniences told us so. A swaggering age was ready to wave a jaunty "Farewell" to God, for we had outgrown him—our streamlined gadgets were the credentials of our adulthood, our bypass of the old verities. We were quite certain that any further truck with God would be on our own terms—all in the frame of our new Science.

"Glory to man in the highest. For man is the master of all things." We granted, with a bit of impatience, that everything was not completely perfected: here and there could be seen man's brutality to man. Education was the answer to such brutality, and since we were not the victims, the length of time it would take was not so crucial a matter. In the meantime, those who were suffering the indignities ought to be patient. However, we forgot that history and history's God would not wait on our disposition. Education was the answer, until along came the Nazi horror, established in the best-educated land on earth. Along it came, breathing its threatening, opening its gas chambers, multiplying the horrors of its concentration camps, venting demonic violence on the basis of race, which was but the elaboration of what other parts of the world had done—some not too far from this pleasant lakefront. An uncertainty leapt to the countenance of our generation.

With a shrug of our shoulder, in the days of our self-confidence, our age confessed that in a world of plenty there were millions who went to bed each night without sufficient food, shivered in the blasts of winter without sufficient clothing, crowded in hovels and ghettos without sufficient shelter. Such conditions men dismissed with catchphrases—the enlightened self-interest of free enterprise would take care of all that. Only it didn't.

With an arrogant twist of the head, a confident age agreed that there were sections of the world where people were denied access to public places, equal wages and self-government islands where their fathers had lived for centuries. After all, they were backward peoples who probably did want anything better. They were the "White man's burden." The mutterings have mounted to thunder in Asia and Africa, and storm clouds hang over lands long smoldering in virtual bondage. The thunders from the East have put a question on the lips of our generation. Our streamlined gadgets, graphs, charts, and scientific knowledge before which we genuflected in worship as to a new god somehow lack the answer to our haunting uncertainties.

We knew that churches divided along the lines of race, class and section were mockeries—but were sure that a more feverish campaign for numbers, a new educational building, larger budgets and well-worded resolution when we sat in solemn conclave, would more than atone for what we lacked of the inclusive spirit of Christ. The only trouble is that the world scorns our preaching of Christ, in whom is neither east nor west, when we give such poor witness to him our actions. There is a question on the lips of our generation!

Our gadgets have turned now into threats, our push buttons now contain cosmic death. The voice of judgement is raised to tones of thunder in our day. Over us the clouds of war hang low: our confidence is shattered. Men ask a repentant church to show the way to the world's great dreams of peace and harmony.

In their question is our opportunity. Our situation calls to mind the words set in the fiftieth chapter of the Book of Jeremiah at the fifth verse. "They shall inquire the way to Zion with their faces thitherward." These words come at the close of a bewildering experience of slavery, hard by the low canals and willow trees in Babylon. For years Zion, City of God set on a hill, beautiful for situation, has been to these poor exiles but a dream, a hope long deferred. But now the long night of captivity is past; the purling dawn of a people's hope brightens the horizon. The children of captivity are free to go home. History's God has given to them a new national opportunity. Alas! the road across the desert is unknown to them; there are no waymakers on their journey, but their journey, but their hopes and hearts are turned toward the city of their dreams. If they can find their way, they will come to its heights, walk its ways which have been hallowed by prophets' tread, and build again on Mt. Zion a sanctuary for their dearest hopes. Thus the word, "They shall inquire the way to Zion with their faces turned thitherward." From the New Testament, as though the question were raised to cosmic proportions, there is bold answer in the fourteenth chapter of John and the sixth verse, "I am the Way."

On the lips of our generation, weary and sick, overtaken by uncertainty, desperate, afraid, lonely and sick, there is the same question. Our age is asking the way: everywhere there is recognition that we are lost.

War after war has been fought with the hope that it was the last one. Alas! the crimson harvest of each succeeding conflict has seemed to bear the seed of the next. Some deep awareness tells us that human life is too precious in the gaze of God to be wasted in the sudden destruction of battlefields, and as targets for bombsights. War is immoral, some deep instinct makes us know. It is not our destined way. We inquire the way to that height where they shall not hurt or kill in all his holy hill. Our faces are turned in the direction of peace; our hearts yearn for it. We ask the way to Zion.

Our question is made the more desperate because we are faced with the old mandate of God underscored with atomic power. "This do and thou shalt live. This do and thou shalt surely die." Holding in our hands the cosmic flame, we inquire for the cosmic wisdom to use it right. But how? Larger armies have not protected us against war, greater navies are no guarantee against bloodshed. The centuries speak with one voice at that point. From sea to shining sea men inquire the way to Zion.

We who name the name of Jesus as Lord proclaim that in his spirit is the way to the world's long-hoped-for Zion of peace. He has plumbed the depths of our universe and come aloft bearing in his spirit the way to peace, the only way honored by the very structure of our universe. It was his faith that a band of committed men and women, partakers of his spirit and consecrated to his will, would be a saving leaven in the world loaf. At a certain point in his ministry, he waited for the return of his disciples he had sent out. When they reported to him their success, his word was "I saw Satan fall from heaven like lightning"—as if their experiences ratified a deep conviction of his. Men aflame with his purposes can storm the ramparts of this world's disharmonies, can bring a new earth wherein dwelleth righteousness and peace. Our world's greatest need is men and women in every land, of every kindred and of greatest need is men and women in every language committed to our oneness in Christ, that is deeper than any national difference—our common faith leaping iron curtains, bridging oceans, uniting continents, abolishing borders, bringing to pass that anguished prayer fashioned in his spirit "Holy Father, keep through thine own name those whom thou hast given me, that they may be one, even as we are." Enough men and women committed to a oneness in Christ can break the evil spell of our recurring slaughters, pull down flags of national pride and raise the blood-stained banner of Calvary's Kingdom in their stead. "I am the way" is his unequivocal word flung back to our desperate questioning. Deeper than all differences of nation or language or culture is our oneness in Christ who hath broken down the middle wall of partition. Committed Christians of every language, of every kindred, of every tribe shall make the earth hear echo of heaven's theme:

"Jesus shall reign where'er the sun
Does His successive journeys run,
His Kingdom stretch from shore to shore
Till moons shall wax and wane no more.
People and realms of every tongue
Dwell on His love with sweetest song
And infant voices shall proclaim
Their early blessings on His name."

We are beginning to recognize that the problem of race sorely vexes our Christian witness as it does our world's peace. There was a day when men boldly proclaimed the superiority of race, even supported it by spurious interpretation of Scripture, a reflection on the integrity of God and the Justice of the Eternal. The day is far spent when men can believe that souls can be evangelized with a Bible in one hand an a whip in the other. Brave voices in Christ are standing up everywhere to declare such doctrines contrary to the spirit of him who made a mercy seat on the ledge of a well in Samaria, and who gave his pronouncement on the oneness of humanity in a parable about a dangerous curve on the road that led from Jerusalem to Jericho. There was a time when men sought to bypass the ultimatum of the gospel for one humanity by a frenzied emphasis on individual salvation, thus bringing a shadow on that fundamental truth. Surely, the claim of God is laid in sovereign demand at each human heart. A man and his God are the crucial figures in the drama of redemption—but the stage for that tender drama is history, a social contact. Surely, the brave shepherd goes aquesting through the night for one sheep—but goes that he may lay it across his shoulder and come home—to put it back in the fold. No doctrine of race can be made to fit the frame of the gospel of Christ. We shall be Christian at the point of race, or forced to confess we are not Christian at all. We cannot be strong on faith and weak on work without being contradictory. How tragic that within the body of Christ there is such mutual enmity and suspicion. Churches all black are no less racial sin than churches all white. I blush still at memory of the words of a friend who a few days ago said in my hearing, "There is more segregation at eleven o'clock on Sunday morning when we stand to sing, 'In Christ There Is No East nor West,' than at any time in the week in the market place, sports arena, or stadium or gaming casino."

We are realizing that ill will begets ill will. Antipathy is not one-sided. Majorities and minorities share the same hatred which is death to both. The same poison is discovered at the bottom of the heap which so evident at the top.

Thank God for courageous voices in the most difficult places inquiring the way to Zion from this captivity of racial hatred. Thank God for a growing awareness that we are all one race—the human race. In the midst of our asking the way, we hear a voice, stronger than the iron mountains, more winsome than the sound of many waters, "I am the way."

The glory of the early church, feeling the fresh breezes of his spirit, was in the abolition of the problem of race. Here men of diverse backgrounds, proud friends and kinsmen of the Caesars, and humble denizens of the black alleys of the cities of the empire, found in Christ a common, gathering place which raised them to the level of a new, blessed, releasing relationship. Perhaps some poor slave the disinherited of the city.

By the flickering light of a humble room he came to the close of the letter, sealed in an affection of brotherhood. These were the words that humble assembly heard, "All the saints salute you, chiefly they that are of Caesar's household." They found their answer to the problem of race in him who says, "I am the way." In the beleaguered catacombs, in a humble upper room, during the treasured hour around a table of the Lord, the early Christians wiped away their early differences of race, awed a world with their devotion to all men, snapped the fascination which old Rome held over them, drew gasps of wonder from their generation, raised the banner of a new kingdom and made the name of Christ a household word in homes around the Mediterranean.

The world looked at them, as it can look at us, asking the way. "What makes you so happy?" said a cynical age to them. They answered saying, "We have come unto life. There is a new dimension to our existence. We were dead behind our crisis-event. Our signal that we have passed from death unto life is, 'We love the brethren' Love has given us new life, immune to even the harvest of death."

His way of a new brotherhood deeper than race is the only way. In a daring parable he sketched the conditions of admission to see the King Eternal. The lines we make he abolishes, the conditions we raise, he wiped out. How shall we see the King? Deeds of kindness, thoughtless incidents of brotherhood are our passports, so said Jesus. A cup of cold water to a thirsting friend, never mind who he is; did it unto one of the least of these—"come ye blessed of my Father, inherit the kingdom prepared for you."

Do we ask the way to Zion? We hear the question framed in the crash of empires, the deep uncertainty which has gripped our times. Agonized, the years of our days seem to wait for some answer. Around us is a world desperate for a new world wherein dwelleth righteousness and peace. "They shall ask the way to Zion with their faces turned thitherward."

Do we ask the way to Zion? Across the centuries his clear voice declares "I am the way"—family in God, a brotherhood originating in me, a comradeship beginning at Calvary, a community in love, a colony of heaven in earth, a blessed fellowship, closed ranks of a marching army moving to the music of God's stirring act in Christ—"I am the way."

Are we sure our universe will support our way? Are the tides of eternity on our side? Is there some sovereign who guarantees our way is right? In other words, is our gospel underwritten by the ultimate nature of our universe? Can we be sure?

Quickly we move to an event insert by God's love in the centuries. God has set authentic evidence for the validity of our way in history. He has given sign and token that he will at all hazards stand fast by our way, will not forsake our way, will not abandon it, though the iniquities of hell spill over the earth. At the place of a skull he left the signature of his power on the side of our way. Dramatic words accompany the event. The sun, as hell and earth do their worst, fades in mourning folds of embarrassment as our Way is tested before the blasphemous eyes of irreverent men. The earth quivers on its axis, as if shocked by the severity of the test to which our Way is subjected. There is a hint that the music of the spheres is suddenly silent in the strain of the test to which our Way is put. For a brief, blinding moment our Way seems abandoned. A black, bleak cry shudders up from the hill, "My God, My God, Why?" Thanks be to God! the last cry is that heaven will not forsake our Way. Up through the pain a cry of tender vindication shatters the darkness. As He reaches for the scepter, we hear a cry that God is holding on, validating our Way. Hands, he says, strong like the fashioners of creations, reach down to vindicate Him by holding Him fast! Hands, great like those that have measured the waters in their hollows, firm like those that give power to the faint, reach down—the cry of validation of our Way is like some anthem as the morning breaks, "Into thy hands, I give my spirit."

"The Christian Drama"

Sitting in a telephone booth in New York City, I heard a man's voice in the next booth. The drift of his conversation indicated that he was talking to his girl friend. Finally, this graphic sentence came through the thin walls of the adjoining booth, "Honey, the merry-go-round done broke down."

Is that a description of our Western civilization? Has the bright dream of human dignity for all men now been dissipated by the rapacity and sinfulness of our society's standards? Are we in the twilight of a day that dawned bright and hopeful for the sons of men—a day whose glistening sunrise brought promise of liberty and equality, the brotherhood of man? Has the old Western ideal of integrity and honor now been laid by the acids of modernity, the brittle creed that a man does not matter in terms of what he is, but in terms of what he has, or what the color his skin is?

Ills of Western Society

Walter Lippmann says that our society here in the Western world is not wounded, not battered under the assault of its enemies from without. He says our society is sick, suffering with internal diseases. Instead of recognizing the Old Testament assertion that all of life is "bound in the bundle of the living," we have separated humanity according to crass human standards, for the satisfaction of our pride and prejudice. Bereft of a Master-sense of God in our lives, we have forgotten who we are because we have forgotten whose we are.

Our society—sore, stricken, separated—needs the infusion of a new sense of spirituality, of the authentic word and will and way of God. We are far-country prodigals, starving beside pigsties and destined never to be whole again until we are back at Father's house, remembering that the Lord has been "our dwelling place in all generations," setting ourselves to his will and his way, obedient to his impulses, thinking his thoughts after him, dreaming of a fairer, more just world as our rightful heritage and our obvious birthright.

The New Testament, face to face with a hardbitten, metallic cultures such as ours, confronted the world with an almost unbelievable, radiant faith. If Rome was the society of the crown, the early Christians were the society of the cross. It was the meeting of two mutually contradictory ways of life. One, Rome's, was haughty; the other, Christ's was humble. Rome's society was founded on success, Christ's way was built on service. The followers of Rome believed in the power of arms and sword, the followers of Christ believed in the power of the spirit of righteousness. One was power-centered, the other was personality-centered.

Commitment to Moral Integrity

The writer of Romans set down in brief compass the faith of true Christians in the way which Christ chose. In one startling sentence that reverses the verdict of the world, this believer declared, "If we have been united with him in a death like his, we shall certainly be united with him in a resurrection like his." The "death like his" describes the way of his life, the nature of his earthly end. It is a summation of the central commitment of the life of Jesus which thrilled and haunted twenty centuries.

The "death like his" represents, surely, his refusal to rely on any earthly weapon; the apparent shame and disgrace with which his career ended. That unknown lycrist whom we call the Second Isaiah was true to the spirit of Christ.

Who has believed what we have heard?
And to whom has the arm of the Lord been revealed?
For he grew up before him like a young plant,
and like a root out of dry ground,
he had no form or comeliness that we should look at him
and no beauty that we should desire him.
He was despised and rejected by men;
a man of sorrows, and acquainted with grief;
and as one from whom men hide their faces
he was despised, and we esteemed him not.

Surely he has borne our griefs
and carried our sorrows;
yet we esteemed him stricken,
smitten by God, and afflicted . . .

He was oppressed, and he was afflicted,
yet he opened not his mouth;
like a lamb that is led to the slaughter,
and like a sheep that before its shearers is dumb,
so he opened not his mouth.
By oppression and judgement he was taken away;
and as for his generation, who considered
that he was cut off out of the land of the living,
stricken for the transgression of my people?

Thus the poetry of Calvary's stark shame and fatal bruise. The likeness of his death represents the way of commitment of a life to faith in the moral integrity of the universe. Jesus went to his Calvary believing that his way would be certified and guaranteed by God.

The Cry Heard in the Land

Such must be the faith of Christians! The moment we stop believing that there is a power not our own which makes for righteousness we have suspended our participation in the life of Christ. What else has kept us firm against overwhelming odds? Far back in the slave quarters our fathers hummed softly in the twilight the words, "I'm so glad trouble don't last always. O my Lord, what shall I do?" The wail of Israel's ancient cry was on their hearts, "Let my people go." The cry is still heard in the land.

We are committed in Montgomery to the faith that righteousness finds its way to resurrection by facing its Calvary. Here some people, "Not many mighty, not many noble," have entrusted their lives and their fortunes and their honor not to the arms of men but to the sword of the spirit. Here a man and men with giant souls in youthful bodies have led some people toward the way of Calvary, for the justification of many. Here some people of humble origin, but with a sense of high destiny, have challenged the conscience of the world.

The likeness of his death, the way of commitment to the moral sanity of the universe, the way of reliance upon God's word and God's promises is never a way of particularism for the special benefits of anyone segment of the society. Jesus did not go to his Calvary for disciples alone. He died as surely for Pilate as he died for Peter. He died as surely for the centurion who plunged the spear in his side as he did for Mary Magdalene who poured her gratitude at his feet. Jesus died as surely for Rome as he died for Galilee and Judea. Jesus died as surely for those who jammed the reed in mockery of a scepter in his hand, as surely for those who threw an old barracks blanket around his shoulder to mock a regal robe, as he did for those simple souls who filled the air with their hosannas and his path with their palms. The word is writ as large as the gospel, "God so loved the world that he gave his only Son, that whoever believes in him should not perish but have eternal life."

Seedtime and Harvest

It behooved some gallant souls to take a cross for the redemption of our republic and this southland to its true dignity, destiny and decency. We would read wrong the Christian way were we to believe or so to bear ourselves as to give the impression that we sorrow and suffer for ourselves alone. Someone must save the nation, someone or some people of vision whose hearts are open to the winds of God's will, whose eyes are open to the beckonings of God's hand, must suffer for the nation's salvation. All the people of this city and section and nation are God's people. Who else could travel the steep, red way of Calvary but those who by bitter plight of circumstance have not known the sins which are nigh inevitable in any majority people?

> And they made his grave with the wicked
> and with a rich man in his death,
> although he had done no violence,
> and there was no deceit in his mouth.

Yet it was the will of the Lord to bruise him;
he has put him to grief; . . .
and was numbered with the transgressors;
yet he bore the sin of many,
and made intercession for the transgressors.

There is in the Christian drama the downward plunge to apparent defeat, and the pained period of waiting to see the result of it all. We must never forget that our Lord Christ did not on Friday die and find victory on the same day. At least the victory was not placarded before the world, or for even the eyes of faith to see. The church rightly shrouds its altar in black during the period between the Black Friday of crucifixion and the Bright Sunday of resurrection. There is a spiritual which runs, "You can't hurry God. Why don't you wait, my brother." The commitment must be made, and we must leave the rest to God. The seed must be planted, and though we till the soil, we must wait in that agony of suspense between seedtime and harvest.

Redemption Is Costly

I do not know why truth and righteousness are not immediately vindicated and justified. It may well be that the "powers of darkness" are not routed with the snapping of a finger. Jesus gave full allowance for the strength of wrong, the power of entrenched evil, as soldiers laid their hands on his innocent person, to lead him away. Said he, "This is your hour, and the power of darkness." I do not know why redemption costs so much—in blood and sweat and shame and suspense—unless it be that evil is a mighty foe, "a strong man armed who keepeth his goods." I only know that when God got ready, as Gossip says, to turn a world free from sin's awful bondage, it took God giving all of God's all. I do not know why the way of men's social redemption must be lined in blood and sorrow. I only know there is no other way. No cross, no crown. No pain, no birth. No suffering, no salvation. No pain, no peace. Such is the law of our universe, or Christ would not have died.

Those across this land who have made their commitment to the Christian way of sacrifice and hazard for the saving of the nation are going through a dark and fearful night of waiting and uncertainty and horror—here and yonder. To some it must appear unbearable, the burden insuperable. And yet, peering through the tortured night waiting for the morning to come, searching the skies for some sign of approaching dawn, we are confident that God makes his universe to turn on axles of justice.

But it were vain to imagine, even in the period of waiting and suspense, that the tides of the universe ceased to flow, that God was absent, silent or inactive.

Even though the Scriptures pull a veil over much of Calvary and the interval of our Lord's time in the grave and shut it from human gaze, as if it were too reverent for human view, still the Scriptures suggest that the Father was at work. Judas flinging his silver and his life away bore tragic testimony in his death to the power of God to work in human situations. Simon, whose base denial had added to the weight of Calvary, was likewise plastic to the workings of God's Grace. His bitter tears dropped as testimony that the Father who worked hitherto works still. The valiant commitment of Jesus' life wrung from unbelieving lips, even while he died, the blurted cry of the centurion: "Truly, this was the Son of God."

The World's Conscience

If no other words of committal were uttered over the Lord's lifeless body, then let the centurion's words be his well-earned eulogy. Many that day, we can safely believe, saw and believed; and, while they were afraid to speak, their hearts were turned toward God's throne. Surely as Friday's lights go out, humble men and plain women standing near the silent hill searched their souls and were touched by this deed of sacrifice.

Make no mistake! Beyond your ken of understanding, even while you wait for the resurrection faith to be reasserted, things are happening. By what has happened here the world's conscience is a little more sensitive to the whispers of God. Here in Montgomery, behind shutters and in rooms of which you know not, and in houses you would not dream, and among people you would not imagine, soul-searching has doubtless taken place. Men and women who want to love the Lord must have asked themselves if they are among those who in your crucifixion help crucify the Lord afresh. Your gallantry and your faith and God's goodness have staved off violence. In distant lands and on lonely islands men have prayed and pray for you. By your Calvary, Montgomery has become a central item on the prayer agenda of the world. Take heart then; even now things of which you and I do not dream are taking place through God's Providence and by your commitment.

There is a faith—it is founded in God—that he will bring to pass what he has begun. It is the faith that no life committed to him can fall beyond his grasp. The central drama of the Christian faith is the death of our Lord, the anguished waiting, the glorious denoument on Easter Sunday, the forth of the conquering Lord. Christians believe that the resurrection of the Lord Christ was the reversal of all the world's verdicts, the annulment of all claims of evil, the repudiation of the supposed power of expediency and sin. The coming forth of the reigning Lord represents for Christians the denial of all the charges of injustice, the disavowal of all the libels that wickedness can impose, the vindication of the sanity of the universe. The trumpets at the end of the drama are no longer muted; they blare the coronation; the banners are lifted to full mast. He leads captivity captive and puts to rout the armies of the aliens.

Here we stake our faith. As surely as God lives, his way must triumph. He will not leave our souls in hell. "He who began a good work in you will bring it to completion at the day of Jesus Christ." Galling may be our cross, steep may be our way, long may be our journey, dark may be our night, cold may be our way, hard may be our lot, heavy may be our hearts, sore may be our spirits, slow may be our down, but if we are "united with him in a death like his, we shall certainly be united with him in a resurrection like his."

One of our forefathers has written, in years now gone, the heart of our faith as we struggle for a free America and for our citizenship:

> Harder yet may be the fight,
> Right may often yield to might.
> Wickedness awhile may reign,
> Satan's cause may seem to gain.
>
> There is a God who rules above,
> With hand of power and heart of love.
> If I am right, he'll fight my battle.
> I shall have peace some day.

"Hearts Waiting for What?"

In "Tintern Abbey," William Wordsworth, in words among the sweetest in the English language, speaks of the haunting sense of high destiny which belongs to us. He speaks for all of us when he describes an inward yearning toward something worthy which he has yet reached, a persisting, poignant compulsion toward a fulfillment not yet achieved. In heart-breakingly touching language, Wordsworth says:

> And I have
> A presence the disturbs me with the joy
> Of elevated thoughts; a sense sublime
> Of something far more deeply interfused,
> Whose dwelling is the light of setting suns,
> And the round ocean and the living air,
> And the blue sky, and in the mind of man . . .

There hangs over each of us the awareness of moving toward something, of becoming something far finer than we have ever been. Ah, we may wince, but we are never for long of that yearning to become better, that instinctive squirming to be let loose from some imprisoning and crippling web in which we are caught. This sense of inward struggle toward something, of awareness of some huge, approaching wonder forms the basis for the earth's finest literature, informs and indwells the world's worthiest crusades and fashions the splendor, the most glorious splendor of our humanity. We speak of this characteristic in us in many ways, as "getting ahead," or "bettering our condition," or "our ship coming in," or "the pot of gold at the end of the rainbow." Whatever the term, we are aware of something about to happen—big, wonderful.

In all the sweep of the Bible there is this constantly recurring note. Hearts waiting—for what? The Bible pulls the tinsel from around this awareness and says quite honestly that we are waiting for God. This is our contract with life. For the coming of the Lord God into our arena of action, into our theater of operations, the righting of wrong by the aid of the Divine arm—for these things our world waits.

So it was with the ancient prophet, this strangely haunting poet whom we call Isaiah. In a day of darkness for his people, as black as midnight, the man speaks of the coming of God in power. Hungry masses will have set before them God's feast, pride and arrogance shall fall and the fortresses of evil shall be leveled with the dust. Beneath the events that fill the Bible there is this continuing theme of God in the act of bringing something unspeakably wonderful to pass. This is the evangel.

"And it shall be said in that day, Lo, this is our God, we have waited for him, and he will save: this is the Lord; we have waited for him, we will be glad and rejoice in his salvation." We need a God Who can get in it with us and we need a God Whose power and might are set against evil. In that day shall we say, "Lo! This is our God."

It has been repeatedly pointed out that a fatal flaw in Greek religious faith as it is represented in Greek mythology is the distance of the gods on Olympus from the heat and fray of life in Athens and the other Greek city-states. Almost all of the Greek tragedies end in the death and disgrace of all of the principals. No one survives, the good die with the bad and there is no vindication for either right or wrong. The gods of Greece were too far from the needs of men, and so the cause of righteousness never known a certain and worthy end.

Any man who would bless the lives of people must somehow "sit where they sit." Wilfred Grenfell became the angel of Labrador because he went and lived with the people of that needy place. If Christians are going to bless their community, it must be because they have entered the same sorrows, felt the same temptations, known the same heartbreaks as those to whom they would speak. As you know more about life you speak less easily about it, but what you have to say carries more weight. Arthur Gossip, so long the prince of the Scottish pulpit, said that shortly after his wife's bewildering and sudden death, when he had finished preaching in a church of a certain Sunday, he heard a woman say to another as he passed, "If I could only believe that man knows what he is talking about, I would start all over again." Another replied to her, "He does. His wife died but the other day." The world does wait for men and women who speak with spiritual authority because they have walked slippery ways and have found and can report that "underneath are the everlasting arms, and the eternal God is our refuge."

God Himself to be our God must enter the arena of our troubles, the theater of our operations. This is at the heart of the Good News we call the Gospel: We have a God Who comes where we are. I hear in the distance the cry of a man who has stood over a fallen and wounded race, and has watched the God of all the earth feel their loneliness, participate in their heartbreak. He cries, "In all their affliction he was afflicted." We have no less a Gospel than that God is kin to us. One hears the words of the brave old Book and takes hope, for our hearts wait for a God Who can feel our sorrow and share our heart's desires.

Dare we hope that God throws His strength in on the side of truth and justice? Or is raw power forever on the throne and the heartbroken disinherited forever on the scaffold? Are we to fight these battles for peace, for a land of equal opportunity by ourselves? Granted the brilliant dedication of those who labor in the cause of true freedom in this land, is this all the strength we have? Is our last court of appeal our own Supreme Court, or is God going it with us? Is He near enough to know the hard fight of downtrodden people? Can He hear the groan of the slave?

A man in the South, a Negro handy man, was asked by his white employer, a bank president, "John, why are the colored people spending all of their money going to court to get equal rights? All of the money and power and government in the South are on our side. How do you hope to get the things you want if we fight you?" The Negro thought a moment and answered, "S'pose God say so?" Does He?

There is great sorrow these days in the hearts of many Americans who love this land and who believe that God has for it some course, we must in sorrow and shame confess that we are reaping the bitter harvest after a long season of sowing expediency and sub-American ideas and attitudes. For the foreseeable future we shall doubtless find ourselves in a painful period of being purged and cleansed of our great national sins.

We can all take comfort and courage in the awareness that there is Another who throws in His strength on the side of justice and a fairer, juster world. Our problems are huge, the road we must travel in this nation and in our world toward peace and harmony may be a long and arduous one, but God travels it with us, or better still, leads us along the road we must journey. Our land, America, has a better day on ahead. We shall yet stand together in this land with all races and regions united in liberty's holy cause to the Glory of God and in the vindication of our democratic assumptions. For God is in it with us.

There are signs almost beyond number of His presence in the struggle of our nation toward its democratic fulfillment. Our history seems to say that God has presented all of us in this nation with the holy possibility of bringing to pass on these shores a society of unity and mutuality in the midst of all our diversities of color and creed and national origin. Step by step, sometimes in a way that we could not comprehend, we have been led to the fulfillment of that destiny. To the glory of this nation, no matter how dim the vision of the better society has become betimes, it has never died in the hearts of millions of Americans. And at times, once in the great national sorrow of civil conflict, the vision has been the paramount concern of our American people.

Take our lives one by one and there is a long chronicle of failure and mediocre living. Is He close enough to sense our broken dreams and our blasted hopes, our failures and our yearnings? How does He look upon our cemeteries of wasted years? The old Book puts it bravely: "Like as a Father pitieth his children, so the Lord pitieth his children." In this we can take hope.

James Stewart reminds us of a poem of Coventry Patmore. "The Boy," it is called, and tells of how one day Patmore's little son, having been disobedient, was sent to bed without supper and unkissed. The poem goes on to tell how the father, his anger cooling, crept up later that night into the room where the child lay asleep, his face still damp with tears, and around him to comfort his sad little heart, the sleeping child had gathered some of his favorite toys. The father leaned over and kissed those childish tears away, and left some of his own. As he did it occurred to him that God might feel the same toward His children. He wrote:

> When Thou rememberest of what toys
> We made our joys
> How weakly understood
> Thy great commanded good
> Then, Father not less
> Than I whom thou hast molded from the clay,
> Thou't leave thy wrath, and say
> I will be sorry for their childishness.

"Like as a father pitieth the Lord his children."

Always the Gospel proclaims God's nearness to our need. Always in our poor stained humanity there is an anguished cry from broken generations, "Is there no balm in Gilead, is there no physician there? Why then is not the health of the daughter of my people!" And there is the answer of God, the tramp of His foot far off-thundering down the road of the centuries toward our relief and redemption, the cry on His lips, "O Israel, Fear not: for I have redeemed thee, I have called thee by thy name; thou art mine. When thou passest through the waters, I will be with thee; and through the rivers, they shall not over flow thee: when thou walkest through the fire, thou shalt not be burned, neither shall the flame kindle upon thee. For I am the Lord thy God . . ."

God close to my crying heart, God close to our broken society!—that is the Gospel of the New Testament.

"Some Comments on Race Hate"

Race hate is an old and persistent disease in the bloodstream of society. It has divided Jew and Samaritan, Greek and barbarian, black American and white American. Race hate is not a one-way street. It infects the hater and the hated, since the hated learns to hate the hater. Prejudice and bigotry produce prejudice and bigotry. The church's supreme consideration must be that such hatred of people, for whatever reason, and most especially on the basis that they are physically different from us, offends heaven and shuts so many out from God. This is the ultimate danger in any sin and makes race hate eligible for consideration and concern by the church. It may, rather it does, shut men from God.

This nearly happened in the well-known meeting of Jesus with the Samaritan Woman. A long and bitter enmity had existed between Jews and Samaritans who, in truth, had a common ancestry. The basis of the ancient rift had been religious, but was also compounded with difference of race. When Jesus appeared at Jacob's well with Mount Gerizen in the background the woman of Samaria of whom he asked water was blinded by her prejudice. Now, let's leave out of the matter the divinity of our Lord. Even then we must say that there was force and thrust in his words of wisdom and insight. He was full of compassion, and an infinite sympathy for people rested like a holy light upon his countenance. Again and again it is said in the New Testament by those who watched as he dealt with the people, "He was moved with compassion." Bigotry blinded this Samaritan woman to the sight of that deep and pervasive sympathy which beamed forth from his face. There were in his voice the accents of conviction and tones of authority, so that people hearing him went away saying, "No man ever spoke like this man." Race hatred deafened this woman's ears to those notes of blessed assurance that sounded forth when he spoke. She said to him, "How is it that thou, being a Jew, asketh drink of me which am a woman of Samaria?" Bias of race blinded this woman's eyes and deafened her ears. Such prejudice can prove fatal.

The pulpits of this land must point out that this hatred—this deep, angry, bitter animosity which we call racial prejudice—warps our thinking in this country and is a cancer eating at this nation's vitals and dooming it to failure. In addition to the acts of hatred aimed at black men, there are depths of hatred and bitterness in the Negro community toward white America which would shock and shake this land if they could be plumbed and beheld.

The Church of Jesus Christ might well bow its head in America, for it, North and South, led in promoting the ceremonies and rituals which institutionalized and shaped the contours of this evil. Kyle Haselden in The Racial Problem in Christian Perspective has pointed out that segregation in pubic facilities in this country goes back only to the 1870s and in many places only to the early 1900s, even in the South. This is true as far as the secular institutions are concerned, but in 1795 in New York City, in the John Street Methodist Church, free black men found so much embarrassment because of race that Peter Williams, a former slave who had purchased his freedom, led the Negro members of that church forth to form the African Methodist Episcopal Zion Church. In Philadelphia at the turn of the century, Richard Allen who started the A.M.E. Church was pulled from his knees while praying in old St. George's Church. In reality the church set the pace, established the pattern, and provided for segregation in this country. For this the church must bow its head in shame.

At the same time, the gospel of Jesus Christ agitated and prodded and disturbed and distressed some Christians so much that they, black and white, made their protest, some in their own blood, against the evils of racism that existed and still exist in this country. John Brown whose raid on Harper's Ferry helped light the fires of civil conflict was religiously motivated. On the side of the slaves, the gospel of Christ helped to motivate the uprisings of Denmark Vesey in Charleston, South Carolina, in 1822 and Nat Turner in Southhampton County, Virginia, in 1831. It is to the credit of the gospel and its releasing power for freedom that these incidents led the Virginia legislature to decree that "No slave, free Negro, or mulatto shall preach, or hold any meeting for religious purposes day or night." The prohibition is a badge of honor for the gospel. For where Christ truly is, man must and will be free.

There are those who constantly assert that morality cannot be legislated, and that people's acceptance of one another must be a matter of religion and not of law. This is palmed off as religious insight. But this is only a half truth. Our Christian faith recognizes the place which law must hold if man will not obey grace. Paul Tillich, the theologian, has put it aright: "If law is not internalized in conscience, then conscience must externalize in law." Christians must press for laws that restrain the wild, primitive, savage lunges of race hatred and bigotry. Paul speaks of the law as a schoolmaster who brings men along, trains them, and restrains them until the power of Christ can go to work.

We must dismiss the idea of a Christian faith that is all sweetness and light and patience and niceness. There is judgement with God, swift and awful. A cry is heard in the midnight chill, "Behold, the bridegroom cometh," and the wise are by that sudden summons divided in judgement from the foolish. Every man's work is judged. Every nation's work is judged. We mourn in this country the necessity for the long bitter campaign that goes forward to make the deeds of the land fit its words. We lament the traumas and shocks and pains and deaths suffered in the cause of liberating the nation. But we would have reason to wonder and doubt God if this season of trouble and tension, hatred and violence had not come upon the nation. This country could have solved this problem with double ease a hundred years ago. It is doubly hard a hundred years later. It will continue to be hard because hatred and suspicion and bitterness are all through the land. This is the judgment of one who has said, "Whatsoever a man soweth, that shall he also reap." In our lifetime we shall not know peace between the blacks and whites in this country. It is because there are not enough blacks are so dedicated to liberty that they are ready to confront the nation in love with every resource at their command, including their own death. It is because not enough whites sufficiently in the Christian religion, the Jewish faith, or the Constitution to make them living reality.

This matter of men disliking each other because of color is basically, like everything else in life, a religious problem. False gods cannot finally save us for they cannot solve our problems. Elijah Muhammed, the Black Muslim, and his followers are understandably angry, and it must be said that he has given to his disciples a sense of identity and dignity. But the doctrine of separation has already failed when sponsored in the white community. It is doomed to the same failure when sponsored by the black community. We, black and white, have irrevocably and indelibly influenced each other and cannot be separated in this land, as James Baldwin has pointed out with classic eloquence.

List the cures and they are all partial. Nonviolence is an attractive, but only a partial answer to the problem of race, since it must be attended by the force of boycott in a situation where boycott will hurt. In addition, it presupposes a goodness in man which may be alien to our true nature. Many speak of amalgamation as the full and sufficient answer to the problem of race in this country. This is to think in terms of centuries rather than years, since the rate of amalgamation in this country is perhaps slower today than ever before. The new status of personhood makes Negro women less vulnerable to the clandestine trespasses of the white male, and the Negro male is better equipped to defend his hearth against the sexual adventures of the white man. In addition, interracial marriages face the severe strains of a society grievously sick at this point of race. In my own fifteen years in Brooklyn, I have performed more than a thousand weddings. Fewer than fifty of them have been interracial.

No, the problem of people accepting one another is religious. James Baldwin, honest, bitter spokesman of the current American scene, has stated the religious consideration, though he doubtless would not admit the religious nature of his thesis. "It is not a question," he said, "of whether the white man can love me, it is a question of whether he can love himself." The same may be said of the black man as he faces the white man. I can accept other people only as I have accepted myself. I must first be delivered from self-loathing before I can regard you with reverence and respect. I must first have my own center of loyalty established before I am eligible to offer loyalty to you.

The reason I owe respect and reverence for every human person is ultimately religious, and roots in my faith about my origin, status, and destiny and, in turn, about every man's. What is it that gives preciousness to every human soul, never mind the color, the creed, the previous condition of servitude, as we like to say? It is our origin, our worth, and our destiny that we find the price tag which belongs upon every man. There is no satisfying word about when and how we started other than that contained in the Hebrew-Christian Bible. God! Our beginnings are not meaner, no more parochial than that! The psalmist, looking back upon the high, brave assumptions of his fathers, exclaimed with a gasp in his voice, "It is he that hath made us, and not we ourselves; we are people, and the sheep of his pasture." There lies our origin, in the words "It is he that hath made us." So! Every man is kin to God. However much we may differ from him there is something in us of him. However defaced the likeness, there is in every man the image of God himself. This is every man's origin, and the nature of his beginning marks every man as authentic nobility.

There is in every man a worth attested by God. Again, the psalmist looks at man and remembers admiringly that God is mindful of him in the face of the vast stretches of his creation and his divine prerogatives and responsibilities. Never was a more extravagant paean of praise sung to man under God than by this ancient Theist, "What is man that thou art mindful of him? and the son of man, that thou visitest him? For thou hast made him a little lower than the angels, and hast crowned him with glory and honor." This is the biography of every human soul.

The New Testament contains a still sublimed proof of worth. There is the act at Calvary and the vast mysterious transaction which occurred there involving us men. All that God means by that hill and that Cross and that man on it we cannot pretend to know. But this one thing we do know: There God placed his price tag, his estimate of value on every human soul who walks the face of the earth. And if God so assesses, so gages worth, then I have an obligation to every man who means as much to God as Calvary.

There is a third element in the constitution of the human spirit which mandates my respect and enlists my regard. There is some august destiny within and beyond this time sphere which belongs to every human being. I sense that awareness in myself and in other men. Wordsworth was spokesmen for all men, black and white, when he wrote:

> Though inland far we be,
> Our Souls have sight of that immortal sea
> Which brought us hither.

I hear that same cadence of destiny in the mysteriously compelling words of the music of my fathers. Black backs glisten with sweat in the moonlight after a long and cruel day of unrequited toil. If ever there was a dead-end street, this is it. They have been snatched from Mother Africa and planted in a cold and hostile land. Their customs have been wrenched from their lives by the alien culture with which they are surrounded. Maybe 30,000,000 of their people died in the iniquitous Middle Passage. They were "motherless children a long ways from home," and yet there is in their music that theme of a high and lofty destiny.

> Before I'd be a slave
> I'd be buried in my grave
> And go home to my Lord
> And be free.
>
> I looked over Jordan
> And what did I see?
> . . . .
> A band of angels coming after me.

That sense of destiny in every man, given body and substance by the New Testament, demands in me respect and regard for every man. It is in this sense that religion, alone, is the answer to our deep chasms of tension and mutual hate which afflict white and black people in this land. God grant us his grace that we may be equal to this issue with which our lives are met.

"The President's Message to the
Progressive National Baptist Convention, Inc.,
September 1968"

Comrades in the Cause of Christ, assembled here in Washington, D.C., a number of considerations impress themselves indelibly upon our minds and clamor insistently for our attention. One feels here in Washington that he stands close to the nerve-center of the political arrangement of the whole earth. The ancients once said that all roads lead to Rome; so today all roads seem to lead to Washington as the governmental leaders of the world shuttle in and out of this Capital of the mightiest land since Rome spread her Pax Romana over almost all of the known earth.

One feels immediately here in Washington the memories and influences of the men of our nation's founding who so conceived and so dedicated this land to freedom's purposes, though like all mortals, they were themselves infected with the foibles and failures which belong to our common humanity. What names out of other eras this city summons to memory—Washington, Jefferson, Lincoln and Douglass to name but a few.

Those of us who see the nation as yet unfulfilled in this historic purpose are moved by other memories and thoughts when we come to this city. We think of that historic day in August, 1963 when a number which it seemed no man could number gathered beneath the likeness of Lincoln and heard our communal leaders issue to the nation in its very Capital the anguished cry of the disinherited, the pained pleading of Democracy's forgotten people: Who can ever forget the ringing words of the only authentic spiritual genius America has produced, Martin King, as he thundered a paean of hope in his immortal "I Have a Dream" address? Who can forget the deafening crescendos of assent as they rose up out of the innumerable host of Americans of all races and classes and colors and creeds gathered here.

As we come back to Washington, we of the Progressive National Baptist Convention are poignantly and painfully aware that our brave, young standard bearer is no longer among us. His gallant heart, his gifted mind, his eloquent voice are denied to us at a time of greatest need. Looking out upon the fulfilled dream, the wasted years, the broken promises, the moral ambiguity, the puzzled uncertainty of the nation, a memorable apostrophe from Literature floods the mind. One thinks of Wordsworth lamenting the passing of the author of "Paradise Lost" from English society at a time of great national crisis:

> Milton, thou should'st be living at this hour
> England hath need of thee.

Ah, Martin King, we mourn for you, but even more
we long for your leadership.

As we remember Dr. Martin King's trials and triumphs, we remember our part
in them. Progressive Baptists may take justifiable pride in the unassailable fact
which must now forever be true, that, when he had no spiritual home among black
Baptists, cast out from the house of his Fathers, Progressive Baptists gave him a
black Baptist residence. You provided him with an address in the community of
black Baptists. Let angels record that truth and let succeeding generations bring
their gratitude to your tent door.

True to Martin King's labors and hopes, we must face forward. Here in
Washington we see more than the shrines of a Nation's shame in its callous
disregard of the cries of hunger and deprivation rising from millions of black,
brown, Puerto Rican and white throats. America, what madness is upon you that
hearing the anguished cries of hunger from your own children you could be so
unmoved, so insolent, so hard-hearted! You do not remember that Jesus said,
"Even evil souls know . . . how to give good to your own children." The cry of the
poor must not be stifled. The indictment by the disinherited must not be silenced
or else the God of history will act with summary judgment upon a Nation which
had so much and would do so little.

How long will we persist in our madness in Viet Nam? Can you not hear our
gallant young leader pleading in that mournful eloquence of his, last year, in
Cincinnati, asking the leaders of the nation to confess and repent of our wrong in
Viet Nam and so to save the nation the judgment of history and history's God?
What an amalgam of destructive results has flowed from our futile commitment in
that land so far away. Our boys die; our nation is divided; our young people despise
us; our poor are unfed; our postal service must be curtailed; the world condemns
us; our police are made the suppressers of legitimate protest and all our instrumen-
talities of Law are made the ugly tools of an evil National policy, thus rendering
them enemies of peace foes of Christian idealism and servants of sin and wrong.
Ah, Brash Young Republic, hear from their graves the pleading of Robert Kennedy
and Martin King and thousands of our slain young men begging for the end of war
and carnage!

Progressive Baptists, we must ask ourselves where we are going and why. It
would be improper for me, as I pass on the standard of this host of the Lord to
other hands, to command the direction in which we are to move. However, I make
bold to throw out some hints of what it seems to me God is saying to us.

The division of Baptists into so many factions along racial and other lines must
shame and pain us all. I know that we Progressive Baptists represent a new aspect
of that division. I believe that God has called us out for a purpose. We have already

extended a hand to other Baptists. Conversation has begun with American Baptists looking to closer cooperation. National Baptists of America have extended a hand of Christian friendliness to us. I preached for them in February. Through a delay in correspondence, we did not receive their acceptance in time to have one of their preachers open to us here the things of God. I hope that you will see to this another year. Likewise, our outstretched hand must be offered to others. We are sufficiently fluid, sufficiently fresh, sufficiently unencumbered and, I trust, sufficiently inspired of God to initiate the work of reconciliation which at last will make of our Baptist witness in this land one grand, united fellowship, to the glory of God and to the honor of Christ and to the healing of the nation.

I rejoice that our Christian Education Congress goes forward under the leadership of Dr. William Upshaw of Akron. We all take enormous pleasure in the progress of Progressive Women's President, Mrs. Uvee Arbouin. I plead for support of our Laymen now headed by Mr. Roy Riser. Likewise, our Ushers Convention merits our interest and encouragement as they move under the Presidency of Mrs. Annie M. Serrano. Dr. R. A. Cromwell continues to guide our Foreign Mission Bureau with dedication and discernment. We must enlarge our support of our Foreign Mission enterprise. We must likewise continue our interest in Christian Education.

I shall not dwell on our desire to secure property. The issue is very much alive, and it may be that God is even now opening before us a fresh possibility. Better to take our time and buy wisely than to rush and purchase blindly and foolishly. We still must secure land and we will.

I have recently attended the Baptist World Alliance Executive Committee as your representative, along with Dr. L. V. Booth, our Executive Secretary. You will be gratified to know that Progressive Baptists enjoy a very great regard and confidence in World Baptist family. Also we have assisted some of our young people in their trip to the World Baptist Youth Conference at Berne, Switzerland.

I do not know how to assess the contribution and consecration of L. V. Booth to our Progressive Baptist Work. I have found in him thorough and thoughtful, filled with vision and vigor. Indeed, I count the friendship which has grown between us one of the rich rewards of my tenure. He has put aside personal preference and opportunity more than once, as you know, in order to serve our Convention. I pray and hope that the Convention will remain aware of his spirit of devotion to our cause.

Progressive Baptists cannot live apart from the heady ferment now occurring in the land among our own people. The winds of change are blowing in the thinking of many people about our present stance and future direction in this land. We who minister to people must listen carefully to hear what is being said, to catch the words of truth being uttered in the excessive rhetoric of violence of so many of our best young minds. Those of us who are thirty-five and over came forward in an integrationist generation. We are startled and sometimes angered by younger people as they talk about separatism. Much of this talk is angry, petulant, pointless. We need not abandon the dream of an integrated society, but we need to hear what is real in much current comment.

To the amazement of some and the anger of others young black people have evolved a whole new thing about integration and separatism. At a memorial service at Oberlin College (whose child I proudly am) following Dr. King's martyrdom, white people were shocked to see the first rows of venerable old Finney Chapel reserved for blacks. Preaching in Chicago this past year, I was astonished to learn that black students had demanded segregated housing. At Colgate Rochester Divinity School, I was steered to a separate section of the cafeteria by black students who wanted to be among themselves. In Dearborn, Michigan, a minister announced that he would leave that community where he is the only black family, to return, he said, "to be with my own people."

I find it illuminating that Jesus called his disciples apart as it is recorded in the ninth Chapter of Luke. Jesus must have seen that every group must at some time or the other get with itself, find itself.

I have come to see that a Church needs to separate from the world every so often. It must carry on its own ceremonies of identification, its own acts of worship and praise when and where there are people of the same conversion, who love the same Lord and march under the same banner.

The Scriptures suggest that the "Apartness" into which Jesus led his disciples was redemptive, cleansing creative, restoring, preparatory. He called them apart that they might be empowered. "He gave them power and authority." Is this the valid word in the pained shrieks and the angry screams of the young "black-power" men? He gave them power. Something must stir inside of us if we are going to be adequate. That theme of power recurs like a symphonic theme through Holy Writ. I count one hundred fifty-five times it is used. The stranger who certified Jacob's new relationship spoke of power, "Thy name shall be called no more Jacob, but Israel, for as a Prince hast thou power with God and with men." In the magnificent, singing Fortieth of Isaiah the promise about enablement is clear, "He giveth power to the faint. Even the youth shall faint and be weary, and the young men shall utterly fall, but they that wait upon the Lord shall renew their power. They shall mount up with wings as eagles, they shall run and not be weary and they shall walk and not faint." Of Jesus it was said, "As many as received him, to them gave he power to become the Sons of God."

There is a power growing out of our experience of blackness in this land. There is much that is wrong, distorted, disfigured, crippled about us, but there are gifts and powers in the very limp which is our history here. There is a quality of rapture among black people which is authentically Christian. There is a sense of optimism which sees the threatening clouds of life but sees them shot through with the light of God. "Over my head I see trouble in the air, there must be a God somewhere." Black people have been forced to be "three-world people," inhabitants of white America, inhabitants of Black America, inhabitants of that strange land of the amalgam of their racial dreams and what was beheld in the haunting report: "Looked over Jordan, and what did I see? A band of angels coming after me." There is the gift and power of black people as members of the "disestablishment" to see the society in its splendor and in its shame. There is the power of a rhythmic beat orchestrated by trouble and mourning and hope and which one hears in the strange, sad music of the black preacher when he moves honestly within the cultic setting. There is an apocalypticism, a Christian anticipation in vivid imagery of new structures produced out of cutting moral judgment, a beholding of stillborn societal aspirations and aided by the bitter midwifery of rejection and scorn.

When Jesus had empowered his disciples, he sent them back into the world. So finding ourselves as black Christians with a peculiar experience in this nation, we must return to the nation bearing in Christ's Name the gifts of our blackness.

We must take our stand in this ugly, sorrowing, sinning world. We must lift the hope of life in the colony of death even as Moses lifted the serpent in the wilderness. We must tell men that God loves this world—this angry, ailing world—unto Calvary. We must bear the tidings of redemption to earth's darkest places.

As we serve we must ever tell men who sent us. We are not among men of ourselves, of or by our own choice. We must tell men who sent us. We are not placed among men as a gimmick or a gesture. We must ever remind men to whom we bring a cup of cold water, a visit in sickness, a concern in nakedness and imprisonment as to who sent us.

We bear the Crown Seal of Jesus Christ. We are sent by One who loved the world so intensely that hate could not remold his love into its own likeness. We are sent by One who confronted evil with a character so clear and a purpose so pure that the hitherto unconquerable powers of wickedness were powerless before him. We are sent by a God who actually came where we are in Jesus of Nazareth in order that we might get where He is. He came here, being born in Bethlehem, reared in Nazareth, tempted in the wilderness, preached in Galilee, arrested in Gethsemane, tried in Caesar's court, died on Calvary's Cross and rose from

Joseph's tomb. We must tell the world such a God has credentials of identification with us and certificates of care.

And now as I prepare to pass the standard of leadership on to others and more capable hands and turn to take my place loyally again in the ranks among Progressive Baptists "To Jesus Christ be glory and honor and thanksgiving and power and might forever and ever."

"Balm in Gilead"

The title of this chapter stands as I first heard it more than fifty years ago. The yellowed page on which the main points of the sermon were written is still in my possession and will in time go to the Boston University library where my papers will one day be housed. In my earliest days as a preacher, I copied the main points of the sermon and tried to preach it. It has now been forty and more years since that sermon was heard by a young woman, a recent graduate with highest honor from Oberlin College, who said upon hearing the sermon that she thought she detected promise in the young preacher. It is not for me to say how sound was her judgment on that day long ago as to that young preacher's future. I do know that she has been hearing that preacher ever since. I felt no shame in taking the points of the sermon, since the sermon was by a preacher born in 1870 and he was my father. The points of the sermon are still his; the amplification and application of those points belong to my own spiritual pilgrimage through the years.

Jeremiah spoke out of a deep ache caused by the extreme difficulty in which he saw his own people in Israel trapped and suffering. If we know nothing else about the prophet Jeremiah than these words, we would mark him as a person of the most sensitive makeup and as belonging to that rare and wonderful breed of human beings who feel the sorrows and heartbreaks of their fellows and associates as their very own. Few of us are sufficiently tender of soul to actually enter into sufferings other than our own, to feel truly what another feels or are able, as our American Indians say, to really walk in another's moccasins. For instance, do you ever feel a pain because someone you know does not know the Lord or will not obey Him? Across all these centuries and struggling up out of the entombment of print, the prophet's words drip with inexpressible grief. Do you hear the pain in the two questions with which the prophet concluded the eighth chapter of the Book of Jeremiah, "Is there no balm in Gilead; is there no physician there? why then is not the health of the daughter of my people recovered?"

What the prophet saw in the old Israel sent him into the deepest mourning and wrung from his heart sorrow and from his eyes copious tears of sympathy. He saw his people trying to play the game of international politics between Egypt and

Babylonia. Israel was not called into nationhood to play the old game of power but to be God's people. How sad to see the people of the Lord trying to be something else. Jeremiah saw that the Babylonian king, Nebuchadnezzar, was an instrument in the divine hand, the wicked pagan means by which God's people would be brought to judgment for their sins. The profound insight of Jeremiah was that in all the give and take the thrust and counter thrust of human struggle and international politics, there is a sickness, a malady, a sinful disease. The affairs of state and the procedures of government prey more times than not on the sins of the people. The persons who would be leaders say, "I will give you more and a way to get ahead of the other fellow." We are subjected again and again to an "us-against-them" mentality. We are manipulated and victimized again and again by appeals which shrewd people make to something sinful in us—our pride, race, class, section, type of work, neighborhood, or education—anything which will drive a wedge between people and divide us into "outs" and the "ins." Jeremiah saw this in the parties and cliques and schemes of his own time.

There is a disease in our humanity, and the correct name for it is sin. Dress it up if you wish. Call it by some polite name if this will make you feel better. Say that what is wrong with us is "cultural lag," if you choose. Say that all we need to do is to catch up with what is best in the human experience. Say that what is wrong with us is "ignorance," that when we know what is right, we will do what is right. Jeremiah would tell us that this is trifling with a terrible and fatal disease—sin—which destroys the nervous system of conscience and wrecks the power of right thinking. Sad it is that a polite hypocrisy has censored that word sin out of decent speech, so it has almost disappeared from our preaching and has dropped out of our religious vocabulary. No wonder Dr. Karl Menninger, the psychiatrist, wrote a book and entitled it: Whatever Became of Sin? What other word can describe the sickness which brings us to rebellion against God and our best selves, to estrangement, to unfriendly distance from our Source of being, from God to error, missing the mark in life?

Jeremiah saw in his people the awful symptoms of this dread disease of sin. In the eighth chapter, the prophet listed some of the effects of this fatal malady. The bonds of kings, princes, priests, prophets, and citizens shall become as dung, as fertilizer on the face of the earth. Death shall be chosen in preference to life. The people had slidden back with a "perpetual backsliding." They held fast and firmly to lies and deceit. No one repented. People said that they were wise and needed no guidance (vv. 8–9). Some had introduced false cures which, as Jeremiah said, healed the hurt of the people only slightly (v. 11a). Many confused and deceived by crying, "Peace, peace; when there is no peace" (v. 11b). People did the worst things and were not ashamed, neither did they "blush" at the most terrible outrages (v. 12).

Then near the end of this most mournful of chapters and at the beginning of the next, all of Jeremiah's pent-up sorrow burst the bounds of self-restraint like a river in flood time. The prophet's cry sends a chill through us:

> The harvest is past, the summer is ended, and we are not safe. For the hurt of my people am I hurt; I am black [or I mourn in sackcloth and ashes]; astonishment hath taken hold on me. Is there no balm in Gilead; is there no physician there? why then is not the health of the daughter of my people recovered? O that my head were waters, and mine eyes a fountain of tears, that I might weep day and night for the slain of the daughter of my people! (8:20–22 to 9:1).

"Is there no balm in Gilead?" Now, we are told that Jeremiah was referring to a balsam which the ancient physicians found to have almost unbelievable healing power. The Ishmaelites, the Arabian merchants, brought among their cargo in the camel caravans this powerful, aromatic preparation to Israel. It was credited with marvelous cures. This balm from Gilead reached diseases otherwise beyond the power of the ancient doctors. The worst, the most painful, the most dread sickness seemed not beyond its reach. So the prophet cried for some spiritual balm in Gilead which would get down to the awful disease at the center of the soul of the people.

There are several qualities we read about this balm from Gilead which suggest to us our Christ Jesus who is healing for all of our spiritual sickness and distress.

The first thing we notice about the balm from Gilead is that it did not grow in Palestine. It came from a land east of Jordan, from Gilead. It had to be brought into the land from elsewhere. No plant grew naturally in Palestine which was as effective as balm from Gilead for the worst and ugliest diseases of its inhabitants.

In the sickness of the soul, there is no earthly balm, no human cure which will get the seat of the disease. Sin has no mortal cure. Education makes the sickness of sin more resourceful, more adroit. Culture makes this sickness more polished, more sophisticated. Prisons make this disease more virulent, more vicious. Recreation makes this sickness of sin more vigorous, and more supple. Nothing grown here on earth can take away this disease.

We have a balm that will cure a sin-sick soul, and it was imported from another land. No one on earth could save us. For such a one to come, prophets longed and priests ministered in hope at countless altars. Generations sighed for some such cure. In the fullness of time, when all things were ready, God sent His Son. In Bethlehem of Judea, there arrived on earth One who heals all our diseases and takes away the awful sickness of sin. No wonder the angel said, "Thou shalt call his name Jesus: for he shall save his people from their sins" (Matt. 1:21). Christ came here from a great distance that we might be healed. No mere person could save us, but the One who could and does heal us came as a stranger from a long distance; He was born as a stranger in a stable, lived as a stranger without a place to lay His head, and died as a stranger outside the city's gates.

> Hail the heav'n-born Prince of Peace!
> Hail the Sun of righteousness!
> Light and life to all he brings,
> Ris'n with healing in his wings.
> Mild he lays his glory by,
> Born that man no more may die,
> Born to raise the sons of earth,
> Born to give them second birth.

There was another quality of the balm in Gilead which resembles our Savior Jesus who is healing for the sickness of our souls. We read that the balm tree was not a tree of beauty and attractiveness. It was not a stately tree, nor did it grow great limbs which would grant to it great beauty. The tree in Gilead from which the healing balm was extracted was a kind of shrub. It would not compare favorably with our huge oaks or fir trees or the mighty and legendary redwoods of California. Its wood was light and gummy, and it was quite incapable of being polished as mahogany can be polished.

The Healer of our soul's hurts was not attractive when He came here and is not now attractive to so many. All of you who are hurting with sin right now want to be healed, but you keep looking for pretty, attractive healers. The government cannot heal you, nor itself, with its new deals, fair deals, new frontiers, or new federalisms. Schools cannot heal your soul, churches cannot heal your soul, priests cannot heal your soul, and preachers cannot heal your soul. For those of us who live under the signs of Bethlehem and Calvary, "There is none other name under heaven given among men, whereby we must be saved" (Acts 4:12b). Christ has never been attractive by the world's standards, and the prophet spoke well when he said, "He shall grow up before him as a tender plant, and as a root out of a dry ground: he hath no form nor comeliness; and when we shall see him, there is no beauty that we should desire him" (Isa. 53:2). The world's warped view cannot see beauty in Jesus, but seen by faith He is altogether lovely, the Lily of the Valley, the Rose of Sharon, the bright and Morning Star, and the "Sun of righteousness [risen] with healing in his wings" (Mal. 4:2).

There is one other quality about the no-so-attractive balm tree which made it a far-famed agent in the healing of disease. The medicine of the tree was not in its leaves as in Madeira leaves with which some of our old people wrapped us in order to cool fever. The healing medicine of the balm tree was not in the root bark as some of us were given in sassafras tea. The healing power in the balm tree was in the thick liquid which flowed out of the tree. There was but one way to release that fluid, and that was by cutting and piercing the tree until it bled its healing fluid.

That child born in Bethlehem came from a long distance and was a stranger to the earth He came to save. That child born in Bethlehem was not attractive and still is not glamorous to those bewitched by this world's fading splendors. And that baby born in Bethlehem had to be bruised, like the balm tree, before healing power could pour forth to save a sin-cursed world and sin-sick souls. The little Christ child came from a long ways to be born at Bethlehem; that same baby at Calvary was wounded that the healing of His crimson flow might make us clean forevermore. That baby born in Bethlehem had to be pierced at Calvary. Our Balm of Gilead was bruised for our iniquities, wounded for our transgressions, and "with his stripes we are healed" (Isa. 53:5). There is no one doctrine of Christ's sacrifice for us which fully covers the subject, but standing—or better kneeling—at Calvary we know that His broken body in some way beyond telling has opened the way to wholeness for our brokenness. We know at levels deeper than reason that by His wounds we are healed, and in His abandonment the way is open for us to be won forever to God. Christ heals our soul's disease, and He is our Balm in Gilead. All the ends of the world, hear! Christ heals, heals all, heals sweetly, and heals completely.

"The Scarlet Thread"

We come again to the season of the Lent. Christian people everywhere become more sharply aware of the sorrow and sacrifice of our great Saviour. It is generally acknowledged that most public events become less and less focused in the memory of people as time passes. Our heroes and our benefactors are not remembered long. Once Vice-President Alben W. Barkley said he found that the chief question among his Kentucky constituents was, "What have you done for me lately?" It is but another way of saying that in most cases our memories are short. Many men and women who render service have their hearts broken later on because they feel that the rest of us will go on remembering and being grateful. As a matter of fact, our loyalties change and our enthusiasms shift directions.

I remember having dinner with a cultured group of Southern people in the home of a faculty member of the Southern Baptist Seminary. Talk turned to the work of some of the greatest of our black leaders in Civil Rights during the sixties. Some of the women in the company who teach in public schools in Louisville shocked me by saying that some children, some black children even, now hardly know the names of men and women who purchased the nation's chance for freedom with their own lives in the Civil Rights uprising.

Our Lord stands solitary in this regard in all of the history of the world. This Lenten Season proves once again that succeeding generations cannot forget Him. His name has not dimmed one bit in brightness though nearly two thousand years have passed since He walked the earth. Someone will say that people still flock to see things associated with other figures who lived even before Jesus. Tutankhamen, the boy Pharoah, is a case in point. The answer must be made that these others owe their popularity to curiosity. Our blessed Saviour owes His popularity, if I may call it that, to love and reverence. To these others, men and women come to stand and stare; to the person of Jesus we come rather to kneel and worship. And so the world enters again and again into the season of Lent.

Those of us whose work it is to try to make a little plainer to people what Jesus meant and what He did are forever finding examples and illustrations of how the Lord stands in relationship to our salvation. Thoughtful Biblical understanding will not claim that every incident in the Old Testament is a prophecy of Jesus. Some of us will say, and must go on saying, that Old Testament people were looking at God, and looking at God, were, therefore, indeed often describing conditions and acts which would fit the life of Jesus. Looking at the Father, they spoke of things which resemble the Son, also—and naturally, since "like father, like son."

I find in the story of Rahab incidents which might well be applied to Jesus. Let me set the story. The Book of Joshua opens with a transfer of leadership of God's people from Moses to Joshua. It had been the long and honored responsibility of Moses to get Israel in a position to become a free people and to enter the land of promise, Canaan. It fell to Joshua's responsibility actually to lead the people into their new home. The first thing which Joshua did was to send two spies to survey that portion of the land in which the city of Jericho was located. The spies arrived in Jericho and made their way to the home of a prostitute named Rahab. Perhaps they knew that in such a house anyone who decided to enter would be welcome and not too many questions would be asked.

Rahab was touched by word she had heard of the followers of Jehovah whose representatives now were in her house as spies. This woman was of a different race and culture. She was not a part of the Israelite nation. Still, Rahab hides the spies from the searches of the citizens of Jericho because of what she had heard of these people as being truly the people of God. She threw in on the side of the purposes of God.

I find that this is what we are called on to do in our relationship to Jesus Christ. There are two communities in any city. There is the community of death and there is the community of life. I say that any and all who organize their lives with no thought of God are turned toward night and death. This has nothing to do with their prosperity, since prosperity can be unto death, as well as poverty. This has nothing to do with decency and uprightness and being good citizens. The life that is organized without taking God into consideration is lying on what we are all about as human beings who were made by God and made for God.

There is a community of life. It is most clearly made visible in the Church of Jesus Christ, though I would never claim that all of the church's members are partakers in the life of God, nor would it be right to say that everybody outside of the fellowship of the church is excluded from the community of life. There are "other sheep" who are, also, the Lord's. God has not left Himself without witnesses among any community or life style. I do say that the community of life is marked by several things. One is a strong desire to be a Christian in one's heart and in one's life. Another is a relish for the worship of Almighty God, for the old lessons of Scripture read in the great congregation, for the hymns which have spoken healing and blessing to those who sing their way through Jordan and for all of those who serve without honor, sometimes in spite of it. The community of love is turned toward God and they find themselves blessed because they walk "not in the counsel of the ungodly, nor stand in the way of sinners, nor sitteth in the seat of the scornful. But his delight is in the law of the Lord; and in His law doth he meditate day and night." Yes, they are like trees "planted by the rivers of water."

So Rahab, Canaanite prostitute threw in on the side of the people of God. First, she protected the two spies by telling the people who had detected their entrance into the city and who were searching for them that they had, indeed, been in her house but were gone, when in fact they continued to hide beneath Rahab's roof. A lie? To be sure. Lies are wrong. Still, one is tempted to say that a lie in the cause of goodness, on behalf of the future, may well not be as damnable as others. Surely, truth need not always be spoken. A person fighting for life and appearing to be losing the battle is not encouraged by the truth from a visitor, who says, "You look as if you are dying." And as we get older we really do not need to be told how old we are looking, true though it might be. Rahab protected the spies from the men of Jericho . . . she let them out by a rope from a window in her house which was built on the city wall. Before the spies sent by Joshua had left, Rahab made them give to her one promise. She asked in return that in the attack of the children of Israel upon Jericho, which she believed would be successfully concluded, because of God, that she and her family would be protected.

The men who were the spies gave their promise that Rahab and all of her family who would be together in her house would be spared when the siege of Jericho had been made and the city captured and in Israel's hands. They took a scarlet thread and gave it to Rahab, telling her to put that bright red cord in the window of her house and when the armies of the Lord passed through they would protect the house where the scarlet thread hung in the window.

Events moved on their way. The armies of Israel cross the Jordan and face Jericho. In the strangest military operation in all of history, Jericho falls on the seventh day of the siege. The great shout of the people, joined to the trumpet blasts as the priests blow upon the trumpets and the rams' horns, the city fell. Our forefathers were captivated in imagination by this peculiar military attack and sang, "Joshua fit the battle of Jericho, of Jericho, and the walls came tumbling down."

The sixth chapter tells us that the walls of Jericho indeed came tumbling down and the victors swept through the city in what we would call an orgy of destruction. Joshua told the invaders to watch out for the house of Rahab. They were commanded to find that one house, go in, get the occupants, every one of them, and the possessions which were theirs and bring all of them safely out from the path of destruction and death. How would the soldiers know the house of Rahab? Why, they would find a scarlet thread hung in the window. That house where the scarlet thread hung in the window was the house protected by a promise and was to be saved. And so it happened. We read no more of this woman through all of the Old Testament. You ask me as to what happened to her. Oh, she turns up in the New Testament. Where, you ask? As an ancestress of Jesus Christ. And all because of a scarlet thread hung in a window!

Rahab and her scarlet thread are not a prophecy of Jesus. The scarlet thread perhaps looks back more consciously to the night of Israel's departure from Egypt than it does to our Lord's death for us on Calvary. And yet, a sanctified Christian imagination cannot help seeing in Rahab's story something of our own redemption and salvation in Jesus Christ.

All of us are under the siege of life and the siege of death. These two mighty warriors come roaring through where we live. They spare no man; they turn away from no woman. They bring down to dust the fairest and noblest sons of men. They crush the stoutest hearts and they defeat the shrewdest minds. These warriors, life and death, ride through the land bringing down the highest, spoiling the beauty of the youngest and prettiest. Life wears us down by skirmish after skirmish. Death cuts us down with swift, devastating strokes.

There is but one hope. The New Testament trumpets again and again what that hope is. Listen to Romans saying that Christ Jesus "was delivered up for our offenses; and was raised again for our justification." Listen to I Corinthians: "we preach Christ crucified, unto the Jews a stumbling block, and unto the Greeks foolishness; But unto them that are called, both Jews and Greek, Christ the power of God, and the wisdom of God." Hear II Corinthians: "God was in Christ reconciling the world unto himself." Hear Galatians: "Christ has redeemed us from the curse of the law." Listen to Ephesians say that once we "were without Christ, being aliens from the commonwealth of Israel, and strangers from the covenants of promise, having no hope, and without God in the world: but now in Christ Jesus" we "who sometimes were far off are made nigh by the blood of Christ. For he is our peace, who hath made both one, and hath broken down the middle wall of partition between us . . . Now, therefore, ye are no more strangers and foreigners, but fellow citizens with the saints, and of the household of God."

Christ is that scarlet thread behind which our souls are safe when the enemy comes and the storm of battle rages. Christ is that scarlet thread behind which we who trust Him may have the blessed assurance that it is well with our souls. Christ is that scarlet thread, the sinner's perfect plea, the seeker's end of the search, the saint's everlasting rest, a hiding place when the storms are raging. I speak of Christ as the scarlet thread of safety and security when enemies besiege our souls, when friends fail us and forsake us, as bread in a starving land and rivers of water in a dry and barren place. Christ, our Passover, Christ, the firstfruits of them that sleep. Christ, the end of the law and the first of many brethren. Christ, Mary's baby and older than Abraham. Christ, our great High Priest. Christ, our Scarlet Thread!

NOTES

1. Henry H. Mitchell, *Black Preaching: The Recovery of a Powerful Art* (Nashville: Abingdon, 1990), p. 54. Dr. Mitchell acclaims Gardner C. Taylor as the greatest preacher of his lifetime.

2. "Religion," *Time Magazine*, 125 (December 31, 1979), p. 67.

3. "Fifteen Greatest Preachers in America," *Ebony Magazine*, 39 (September, 1984) p. 25.

4. See Henry H. Mitchell, *Black Preaching* (San Francisco: Harper & Row, Publishers, Inc., 1970); Mitchell, *Black Preaching: The Recovery of a Powerful Art*; Kelly Miller Smith, *Social Crisis Preaching* (Macon: Mercer University Press, 1984); Bruce A. Rosenberg, *Can These Bones Live?* (Chicago: University of Illinois Press, 1988).

5. Statement by Fred Craddock, E. Y. Mullins Lecturer at The Southern Baptist Theological Seminary, Louisville, Kentucky, during a luncheon with professors, pastors, and students, March 7, 1991. See also David Albert Farmer, "The New Moves in Preaching: An Interview with David G. Buttrick," *Pulpit Digest*, 67 (May/June).

6. J. Randall Nichols, "Is Homiletics a Field for Doctoral Research?" *Homiletic*, 8, No. 1 (1983), p. 2.

7. Dan Francis, "Carlyle Marney's Hermeneutic and Methodology for Preaching" (Ph.D. dissertation, The Southern Baptist Theological Seminary, 1985).

8. Mitchell, *Black Preaching*; Henry H. Mitchell, *Recovery of Preaching* (San Francisco: Harper & Row Publishers, Inc., 1977).

9. These terms were used by William Pipes and Gerald Davis in their summation of the African American preaching tradition.

10. William H. Pipes, *Say Amen, Brother!* (Westport: Negro University Press, 1950) and Gerald L. Davis, *I Got the Word in Me and I Can Sing It, You Know* (Philadelphia: University of Pennsylvania, 1970).

11. See books by Gardner C. Taylor: *How Shall They Preach* (Elgin: Progressive Baptist Publishing House, 1977); *The Scarlet Thread* (Elgin: Progressive Baptist Publishing House, 1981); and *Chariots Aflame* (Nashville: Broadman Press, 1988).

12. Aristotle, *The Rhetoric*, ed. Lane Cooper (Englewood Cliffs: Prentice Hall, 1932), p. 10. See also Cicero, *De Oratore*, trans. H. Rackham (Cambridge: Harvard University Press, 1948); *Rhetorica ad Herennium*, trans. Harry Caplan (Cambridge: Harvard University Press, 1954); and Quintillion, *Institutes of Oratory I & II*, trans. John Shelby Watson (London: George

Bell & Sons, 1892 & 1895). These references will serve as standard texts for the artistic canon perspective in this work.

13. Lester Thonssen, A. Craig Baird, and Waldo W. Braden, *Speech Criticism* (Malabar: Krieger Publishing Co., 1981). See William H. Roen, *The Inward Ear* (Washington, D.C.: Alban Institute Publication, 1989).

14. Bower Aly and Lucile Folse Aly, *A Rhetoric of Public Speaking* (New York: McGraw-Hill Co., 1973) and Marie Hochmuth Nichols, *Rhetoric and Criticism* (Baton Rouge: Louisiana State University Press, 1963), pp. 49–78.

15. Terry Muck and Paul Robbins, "The Sweet Torture of Sunday Morning, An Interview with Gardner C. Taylor," *Leadership*, 2 (Summer 1981), pp. 17–29.

16. Robert Hughes, "The Fraying of America," *Time*, 139 (February 3, 1992), p. 44.

17. Henry H. Mitchell, *Black Belief* (New York: Harper & Row Publishers, Inc. 1975), p. xii.

18. John S. Mbiti, *African Religions and Philosophy* (New York: F. A. Praeger, 1969), pp. 6–7.

19. See Bronislaw Malinowski, *The Dynamics of Cultural Change* (New Haven: Yale, 1945) pp. 24, 153–161. See also E. B. Taylor's quote cited in Stephen S. Farrow, *Faith, Fancies and Fetich or Yoruba Paganism* (New York: Negro Universities Press, 1969), p. 2, originally published in 1926 by Society for Promoting Christian Knowledge.

20. Charles B. Copher, "African Roots of Christianity: Our First Ancestors and the Biblical World," *The A.M.E. Zion Quarterly Review*, 101 (1989), pp. 2–8.

21. Stephen S. Farrow, *Faith, Fancies and Fetich or Yoruba Paganism*, p. 4.

22. J. D. Y. Peel, *Aladura: A Religious Movement Among the Yoruba* (London: Oxford University Press, 1968), p. 2.

23. M. E. Spiro, "Religion: Problems of Definition and Explanation," in *Anthropological Approaches to the Study of Religion*, ed. M. Banton (London: Oxford Press, 1966), p. 97.

24. Merrick Posnansky, "Archaeology, Ritual, and Religion," in *The Historical Study of African Religion*, ed. T. O. Ranger and I. N. Kimambo (Los Angeles: University of California Press, 1972), p. 30.

25. Patrick Kalilombe, "The Salvific Value of African Religions," in *Missions Trends No. 5*, eds. Gerald H. Anderson and Thomas F. Stansky (Grand Rapids: Eerdmans Publishing Co., 1981), p. 51.

26. Ibid., p. 66.

27. Ibid., p. 67.

28. Mitchell, *Black Belief*, pp. 61–62.

29. Robert H. Milligan, *The Jungle Folk of Africa* (New York: Revell Co., 1908), p. 249.

30. Mbiti, *African Religions and Philosophy*, p. 39.

31. Ibid., p. 39.

32. Charles Shelby Rooks, "The Black Experience in America: A Union of Two Worlds," in *The American Experiment: Piety and Practicality*, ed. Clyde L Manschreck and Barbara Brown Zikmund (Chicago: Exploration Press, 1977), p. 17.

33. Chukwenyere Kamalu, *Foundations of African Thought* (London: Karnak House, 1990), p. 40.

34. E. A. Wallis Budge, *Egyptian Book of the Dead*, 1911 rpt. (Dover: University Books, 1967), pp. 92–93.

35. Chukwenyere Kamalu, *Foundations of African Thought*, p. 41.

36. Godfrey Lienhardt, *Divinity and Experience: The Religion of the Dinka* (Oxford: Clarendon Press, 1961), p. 56.

37. Ibid., p. 56.

38. Ibid., p. 105.

39. Stephen S. Farrow, *Faith, Fancies, and Fetich or Yoruba Paganism*, p. 24.

40. Ibid., pp. 30–31.

41. C. Eric Lincoln, "The Black Heritage in Religion in the South," in *Religion in the South*, ed. Charles Reagan Wilson (Jackson: University Press of Mississippi, 1985), p. 35.

42. Edward D. Smith, *Climbing Jacob's Ladder: The Rise of Black Churches in Eastern American Cities, 1749–1877* (Washington: Smithsonian Institute Press, 1988), pp. 25–26.

43. John B. Boles, *Religion in Antebellum Kentucky* (Lexington: University of Kentucky Press, 1976), p. 80.

44. Ibid., p. 85.

45. C. Eric Lincoln, "The Black Heritage in Religion in the South," in *Religion in the South*, p. 38.

46. Smith, *Climbing Jacob's Ladder: The Rise of Black Churches in Eastern American Cities, 1740-1877*, p. 26.

47. Richard C. Wade, *Slavery in the Cities: The South 1820–1860* (New York: Oxford University Press, 1964), p. 160.

48. Arnold A. Dallimore, *George Whitefield: The Life and Times of the Great Evangelist of the Eighteenth-Century Revival* (London: Billing & Sons, Ltd., 1970) p. 495.

49. Ibid., p. 500. See also William H. Pipes, *Say Amen, Brother!* (New York: William-Frederick Press, 1951), pp. 60–62 and Henry H. Mitchell, *The Recovery of Preaching* (San Francisco: Harper & Row Publishers, Inc., 1977), pp. 22–24.

50. Ibid., p. 508.

51. Ibid.

52. L. V. Stennis, *Why Sit Here Until We Die?* (Seattle: Chi-Mik Publishing Company, 1981), p. 17.

53. Smith, *Climbing Jacob's Ladder: The Rise of Black Churches in Eastern American Cities, 1740–1877*, p. 30. See also Albert J. Raboteau, *Slave Religion* (New York: Oxford University Press, 1978), pp. 65–69.

54. Lincoln, "The Black Heritage in Religion in the South," in *Religion in the South*, p. 40.

55. Ibid., p. 46.

56. Ibid., p. 39. Cited in Lorenzo J. Greene, *The Negro in Colonial New England* (New York: Atheneum, 1968), p. 186.

57. Ibid., p. 54.

58. Ibid., p. 53.

59. John W. Blassingame, *The Slave Community* (New York: Oxford University Press, 1979), p. 92.

60. Ibid. See also Patrick C. Kennicott, "Negro Anti-Slavery Speakers in America" (Ph.D. dissertation, Florida State University, 1967), pp. 21–26.

61. Richard C. Wade, *Slavery in the Cities: The South 1820–1860*, p. 163.

62. Boles, *Religion in Antebellum Kentucky*, p. 93.

63. Smith, *Climbing Jacob's Ladder: The Rise of Black Churches in Eastern American Cities, 1740–1877*, p. 40.

64. Henry H. Mitchell, *The Recovery of Preaching* (San Francisco: Harper & Row Publishers, Inc., 1977), p. 75. See also Henry H. Mitchell, Celebration & Experience in Preaching (Nashville: Abingdon Press, 1990), pp. 87–100.

65. G. A. Theodorson and A. G. Theodorson, *Modern Dictionary of Sociology* (New York: J. Y. Crowell, 1969), p. 285.

66. John S. Pobee, "Oral Theology and Christian Oral Tradition: Challenge to Our Traditional Archival Concept," *Mission Studies*, 6 (1989), 87–93.

67. Sonja H. Stone, "Oral Tradition and Spiritual Drama: The Cultural Mosaic for Black Preaching," *The Journal of the I.T.C.*, 8 (1980), 17–27.

68. Lawrence W. Levine, *Black Culture and Black Consciousness* (New York: Oxford University Press, 1977), p. 134.

69. Ella P. Mitchell, "Oral Tradition: Legacy of Faith for the Black Church," *Religious Education*, 8 (1986), 93–112.

70. Herbert V. Klem, *Oral Communication of the Scripture: Insights from African Oral Art* (Pasadena: William Carey Library, 1982), p. xv.

71. Levine, *Black Culture and Black Consciousness*, pp. 88–89.

72. Albert J. Raboteau, *Slave Religion* (New York: Oxford University Press, 1978), p. 232.

73. W. E. B. DuBois, *The Negro Church* (Atlanta: Atlanta University Press, 1898), p. 5. See also Charles V. Hamilton, *The Black Preacher in America* (New York: William Morrow & Company, Inc., 1972), pp. 37–69.

74. Raboteau, *Slave Religion*, p. 233.

75. Milton C. Sernett, *Black Religion and American Evangelicalism: White Protestants, Plantation Missions, and the Flowering of Negro Christianity, 1787–1865* (Metuchen: The Scarecrow Press, Inc., 1975), p. 93. See also Harry V. Richardson, "The Negro in American Religious Life," in *The American Negro Reference Book*, ed. John P. Davis (Englewood Cliffs: Prentice-Hall, Inc., 1966), pp. 296–413.

76. John W. Blassingame, *The Slave Community*, p. 131. See also Nancy B. Woolridge, "The Slave Preacher—Portrait of a Leader" *Journal of Negro Education* 16 (1945) 28–37; Lewis V. Baldwin, "Deliverance to the Captives: Images of Jesus Christ in the Minds of Afro-American Slaves" *Journal of Religious Studies* 12 (1985) 27–45; Frances L. Hunter, "Slave Society on the Southern Plantation" *The Journal of Negro History* 7 (1922) 1–10.

77. Rabateau, *Slave Religion*, p. 236.

78. Ibid. Cited from *American Missionary*, 8 (1864), 165–68.

79. Ibid. Cited from A. M. French, *Slavery in South Carolina and the Ex-Slaves;or The Port Royal Mission* (New York, 1862), p. 131.

80. Blassingame, *The Slave Community*, p. 131.

81. Mitchell, *The Recovery of Preaching*, p. 101.

82. Newbell N. Puckett, "Religious Folk-Beliefs of Whites and Negroes," *Journal of Negro History* 16 (1931) 9–35. For a more thorough investigation of this type of sermon construction see David T. Shannon, "An Ante-bellum Sermon: A Resource for an African American Hermeneutic," in *Stony the Road We Trod*, ed. Cain Hope Felder (Minneapolis: Fortress Press, 1991), pp. 98–123.

83. Bruce A. Rosenberg, *The Art of the American Folk Preacher* (New York: Oxford Press, 1970), pp. 46–47.

84. Rabateau, *Slave Religion*, p. 236.

85. Ibid., p. 237. Two of the best examples of this Black folk sermonic method are represented by H. Dean Trulear and Russell E. Richey, ed., "Two Sermons by Brother Carper: The Eloquent Preacher," *American Baptist Quarterly*, 6 (1987) 3–16. Carper's preaching was based upon a theory of language and a single, Biblical, topographical theme which compellingly combines a sustained image with the experience, present or past, of his hearers; and lading it with a theology of grace.

86. Pipes, *Say Amen, Brother!* p. 66.

87. Lincoln, "The Black Heritage in Religion in the South," in *Religion in the South*, p. 55. See also Carter G. Woodson, *The History of the Negro Church* (Washington, D.C.: Associated Publishers, 1925), p. 56; Henry H. Mitchell, *Black Preaching* (San Francisco: Harper and Row, Publishers, 1979), p. 69; Warren Thomas Smith, "Harry Hoosier: Black Preacher Extraordinary," *The Journal of the I.T.C.* 7 (1980), 111–128. The latter articulates thoroughly the preaching ministry of Hoosier via an extensive biographical summary.

88. G. A. Raybold, *Reminiscences of Methodism in West Jersey* (New York: Lane & Scott, 1849), pp. 166–167.

89. Sondra O'Neale, "Jupiter Hammon and His Works: A Discussion of the First Black Preacher to Publish Poems, Sermons and Essays in America," *The Journal of the I.T.C.* 9 (1982) 99–113.

90. Lincoln, "The Black Heritage in Religion in the South," in *Religion in the South*, p. 54. For a complete analysis on the study of slave preachers see David Charles Dennard, "Religion in the Quarters: A Study of Slave Preachers in the Antebellum South, 1800–1860" (Ph.D. dissertation, Northwestern University,1983), pp. 199–255.

91. Ruby F. Johnston, *The Development Negro Religion* (New York: Philosophical Library, 1954), p. 36.

92. Joseph R. Washington, Jr., *Black Religion* (Boston: Beacon Press, 1964), p. 31.

93. Richardson, "The Negro in American Religious Life" in *The American Negro Reference Book*, ed. John P. Davis (Englewood Cliffs: Prentice-Hall, Inc., 1966), p. 401.

94. Smith, *Climbing Jacob's Ladder: The Rise of Black Churches in Eastern American Cities, 1740–1877*, p. 44.

95. John W. Cromwell, *The Negro in American History,* 1914 rpt. (New York: Johnson Reprint Corporation, 1968), p. 67.

96. Ibid.

97. Lincoln, "The Black Heritage in Religion in the South," in *Religion in the South*, p. 56.

98. Ibid., p. 51.

99. Ibid., p. 57.

100. Wade, *Slavery in the Cities*, p. 172. See also Lewis V. Baldwin, "Deliverance to the Captives: Images of Jesus Christ in the Minds of Afro-American Slaves" *Journal of Religious Studies*, 12 (1985), 27–45. Here, the image of Christ as "liberator" becomes the primary recognition of the slave community which results in a marginalized freedom from the slavemasters.

101. Smith, *Climbing Jacob's Ladder: The Rise of Black Churches in Eastern American Cities, 1740–1877*, p. 88.

102. Stennis, *Why Sit We Here Until We Die?*, p. 18.

103. Gayraud S. Wilmore, *Black Religion and Black Radicalism*, 2nd ed. (Maryknoll: Orbis Books, 1983) p. 55.

104. Smith, *Climbing Jacob's Ladder: The Rise of Black Churches in Eastern American Cities, 1740–1877*, p. 88.

105. Benjamin Quarles, *Black Abolitionists* (New York: Oxford University Press, 1969), p. 81.

106. Monroe Fordham, *Major Themes in Northern Black Religious Thought, 1800–1860* (New York: Exposition Press, 1975), pp. 34–35.

107. Ibid., p. 48.

108. Martin Burt Pasternak, "Rise Now and Fly to Arms: The Life of Henry Highland Garnet" (Ph.D. dissertation, The Graduate School of the University of Massachusetts, 1981), pp. 33–34. Cited from *National Anti-Slavery Standard*, June 11, 1840; *Liberator*, May 22, 1840; *Colored American*, May 30, 1840. For other discussions on the life of Henry Highland Garnet see the following: Gayraud S. Wilmore, *Black Religion and Black Radicalism* 2nd ed. (Maryknoll: Orbis Books, 1983), pp. 93–95; Derek Q. Reeves, "Beyond the River Jordon: An Essay on the Continuity of the Black Prophetic Tradition," *The Journal of Religious Thought*, 47 (1990–1991), 42–54.

109. Smith, *Climbing Jacob's Ladder: The Rise of Black Churches in Eastern American Cities 1740–1877*, p. 119.

110. Fordham, *Major Themes in Northern Black Religious Thought, 1800–1860*, p. 43. Cited from Daniel A. Payne, *History of the African Methodist Episcopal Church*, rpt. ed. (New York: 1968), p. 195.

111. Ibid., p. 44. Cited from Alexander Crummell, "The Necessities and Advantages of Education Considered in Relation to Colored Men." The Anniversary Address before the Hamilton Lyceum of the city of New York delivered July 4, 1844. (Copy in the Schomberg collection, New York Public Library)

112. Ibid., pp. 43–44.

113. Ibid., p. 37. For a comprehensive description of this genre in the African American preaching experience see James Henry Harris, "Preaching Liberation: The Afro-American Sermon and the Quest for Social Change," *The Journal of Religious Thought*, 46 (1989–90) 72–89; and James L. Golden and Richard D. Rieke, *The Rhetoric of Black Americans* (Columbus: Charles E. Merrill Publishing Co., 1971).

114. Frederick Douglass, *Life and Times of Frederick Douglass*, 1892 rpt. (New York: Collier Publishing Company, 1962), p. 83.

115. Ibid., p. 84.

116. Ibid., p. 85. Much to my amazement, this book was in the restricted area of the James P. Boyce Library, The Southern Baptist Theological Seminary, Louisville, Kentucky.

117. Caleb Bingham, *The Columbian Orator* (Troy: William S. Parker, 1821), pp. 7–29.

118. Quarles, *Black Abolitionists*, p. 70. The most outstanding scholarly biography of Douglass is still Benjamin Quarles, *Frederick Douglass* (Washington, D. C.: Associated Publishers, 1948); The best recent study of Douglass' thought is Waldo E. Martin, *The Mind of Frederick Douglass* (Chapel Hill: University of North Carolina Press, 1984). See also Lenwood G. Davis, "Frederick Douglass as a Preacher, and One of His Last Most Significant Letters," *The Journal of Negro History*, 66 (1981), 140–143; and Riggins R. Earl, Jr., "The Genesis of Douglass' Moral Understanding While a Slave: A Methodological Approach to Freedom," *The Journal of the I.T.C.*, 9 (1981), 19–29.

119. Wilson Jeremiah Moses, *Black Messiahs and Uncle Toms: Social and Literary Manipulations of a Religious Myth* (University Park: The Pennsylvania State University Press, 1982), pp. 30–33.

120. Sacvan Bercovitch, *The American Jeremiad* (Madison: University of Wisconsin Press, 1978), pp. 6–7.

121. Ibid., p. 18.

122. David Howard-Pitney, "The Enduring Black Jeremiad: The American Jeremiad and Black Protest Rhetoric, From Frederick Douglass to W. E. B. DuBois, 1841–1919," *American Quarterly*, 38 (1986), 481–492. The quotations were cited from Frederick Douglass, "The War With Mexico," *The North Star*, January 21, 1848. See also David Howard-Pitney,

"Afro-American Jeremiads: Black Thought and Leadership and Civil Religion, 1880–1968" (Ph.D. dissertation, The University of Minnesota, 1984). Another article informing Douglass' rhetorical jeremiad is Derek Q. Reeves, "Beyond the River Jordon: An Essay on the Continuity of the Black Prophetic Tradition," *The Journal of Religious Thought*, 47 (1990–1991), 42–54.

123. Ibid., p. 484. For a more in-depth investigation of the writings of Frederick Douglass, see Philip S. Foner, ed. *The Life and Writings of Frederick Douglass* (New York: International Publishers, 1950–54).

124. Floyd T. Cunningham, "Wandering in the Wilderness: Black Baptist Thought After Emancipation," *American Baptist Quarterly*, 4 (1985), 268–281.

125. Ibid., p. 270.

126. Levine, *Black Culture and Black Consciousness*, p. 122.

127. William E. Hatcher, *John Jasper: The Unmatched Negro Philosopher and Preacher* (New York: Fleming H. Revell Company, 1908), pp. 36–38.

128. Ibid., p. 65.

129. Richard Ellsworth Day, *Rhapsody in Black* (Philadelphia: The Judson Press, 1953), p. 114. For further insights into the preaching of John Jasper see H. H. Smith, "John Jasper: The Unmatched Negro Philosopher and Preacher," *The Methodist Quarterly Review*, 72 (1923), 466–480; and Robert B. Johnson, "From Slavery to Servanthood: John Jasper Sang the Praises of Jews," *Fundamentalist Journal* 5 (1986), 32–36.

130. Ibid., p. 117.

131. Smith, *Climbing Jacob's Ladder: The Rise of Black Churches in Eastern American Cities, 1740–1877*, p. 110.

132. Day, *Rhapsody in Black*, p. 133.

133. W. E. B. DuBois, *The Philadelphia Negro*, 1899 rpt. (New York: Schocken Books, 1967), p. 206.

134. Washington, *Black Religion*, p. 35.

135. Ibid.

136. Levine, *Black Culture and Black Consciousness*, p. 90.

137. Benjamin E. Mays, "The Black Experience and Perspective," in *American Religious Values and the Future of America*, ed. Rodger Van Allen (Philadelphia: Fortress Press, 1978), p. 123.

138. Rev. Washington M. Taylor, father of Dr. Gardner C. Taylor, preached the eulogy of Morris in 1923. A printed copy of the sermon is located in Appendix I to illustrate the similarities of their rhetorical styles.

139. Robert T. Handy, *A Christian America* (New York: Oxford University Press, 1971), pp. 179–80.

140. August Meir, *Negro Thought in America 1880–1915* (Ann Arbor: University of Michigan Press, 1966), p. 131.

141. E. C. Morris, *AME Review*, 13 (January 1887), as quoted in August Meir, *Negro Thought in America 1880–1915*, p. 132.

142. Meir, *Negro Thought in America 1880–1915*, p. 131.

143. Ibid., p. 133. See also C. James Trotman, "Matthew Anderson: Black Pastor, Churchman, and Social Reformer," *American Presbyterians: Journal of Presbyterian History*, 66 (1968), 10–21. In 1880, Anderson established the Berean Presbyterian Church as one of the leading churches of its day by liquidating a $34,000 mortgage ten years later, starting a bank (Berean Savings and Loan) in 1884 which has never closed and still operates today, and a vocational training school in 1899, the Berean Institute.

144. J. Carleton Hayden, "Black Episcopal Preaching in the Nineteenth Century: Intellect and Will," *Journal of Religious Thought*, 39 (1982), 12–20.

145. Cornish R. Rogers, "Black Ministry," in *Creating an Intentional Ministry*, ed. John E. Biersdorf (Nashville: Abingdon Press, 1976), p. 176.

146. W. E. B. DuBois, *The Souls of Black Folk* (New York: McClure & Company, 1903), p. 146.

147. Washington, *Black Religion*, p. 35.

148. Gayraud S. Wilmore, *Black Religion and Black Radicalism*, p. 143.

149. Ibid., pp. 143–144.

150. Rogers, "Black Ministry," in *Creating an Intentional Ministry*, p. 176.

151. Washington, *Black Religion*, pp. vii, 30–33.

152. Marion Joseph Franklin, "The Relationship of Black Preaching to Black Gospel Music" (D.Min. dissertation, Drew University, 1982), p. 11–12.

153. Ralph H. Jones, *Charles Albert Tindley* (Nashville: Abingdon, 1982), p. 13.

154. Ibid., p. 38.

155. Ibid., p. 41. This was an edited interview recorded at the Philadelphia Cobbs Creek home of John Summers by Ralph H. Jones.

156. Lee Heinze, "Charles A. Tindley—Preacher, Pastor, Hymnwriter," *Fundamentalist Journal* 4 (1985) pp. 40–41.

157. Horace Clarence Boyer, "Charles Albert Tindley: Progenitor of Black-American Gospel Music," *The Black Perspective in Music*, 11 (1983), 103–129.

158. Ibid., p. 113.

159. Ibid., pp. 103–104.

160. Ibid., p. 103. Quoted in Arna Bontemps, "Rock, Church, Rock," *Common Ground* (Autumn 1942). Reprint in *The Negro in Music and Art*, ed. Lindsey Patterson (New York: Publishers Company, 1967), p. 78.

161. James Weldon Johnson, *God's Trombone*, 1927 rpt. (New York: Penguin Books, 1976), pp. 5–7.

162. Geneva Southall, "Black Composers and Religious Music," *The Black Perspective in Music* 1 (1974), 45–50.

163. Johnson, *God's Trombone*, pp. 8–9.

164. Gardner C. Taylor, "The Mitchell Lectures" (speech delivered at The Eastern Baptist Theological Seminary, Philadelphia, PA, February 18, 1986).

165. William C. Turner, Jr., "The Musicality of Black Preaching: A Phenomenology," *The Journal of Black Sacred Music* 2 (1988), 21–33. See also Elizabeth Achtemeier, "The Use of Hymnic Elements in Preaching," *Interpretation* 34 (1985), 46–59; Michael A. Battle, "The Kerygmatic Ministry of Black Song and Sermon," *The Journal of Black Sacred Music* 1 (1987), 17–20; Francis Bebey, "The Vibrant Intensity of Traditional African Music," *The Black Perspective in Music* 2 (1974), 117–121; Calvin E. Bruce, "Black Spirituality, Language and Faith," *Religious Education* 71 (1976), 363–376; B. Lee Cooper, "The Image of the Black Man: Contemporary Lyrics as Oral History" *The Journal of the I.T.C.* 5 (1977–78), 105–117; Lazarus E. N. Ekwueme "African-Music Retentions in the New World," *The Black Perspective in Music* 2 (1974), 128–139; Willis Laurence James, "The Romance of the Negro Folk Cry in America," *Phylon* 16 (1955), 15–20; Don Jackson, "The Function of Feedback in Preaching," *The Journal of Communication and Religion* 14 (1991), 40–47; Emanuel McCall, "Singing in a Strange Land: The Religious Contributions of Blacks to America," *Southwestern Journal of Theology* 18 (1976), 62–70; S. Margaret W. McCarthy, "The Afro-American Sermon and the Blues: Some Parallels," *The Black Perspective in Music* 4 (1976), 269–277; Henry H. Mitchell, "Black Improvisation! Real and Imitation," *Freeing the Spirit* 2 (1973), 36–40; Walter Pitts, "Keep the Fire Burnin': Language and Ritual in the Afro-Baptist Church," *Journal of the American Academy of Religion* 61 (1988), 77–97; Clarence Joseph Rivers, "To Train a Preacher—Train a Performer" *Freeing the Spirit* 2 (1973), 49–51; Jon Michael Spencer, "Rhythm in Black Religion of the African Diaspora," *The Journal of Religious Thought* 44 (1988), 67–82; Jon Michael Spencer, *Protest and Praise: Sacred Music of Black Religion* (Minneapolis: Fortress Press, 1990), pp. 225–243; Jon Michael

Spencer, *Sacred Symphony: The Chanted Sermon of the Black Preacher* (Westport: Greenwood Press, 1987); Brett Sutton, "Speech, Chant, and Song: Patterns of Language and Action in a Southern Church," in *Diversities of Gifts*, eds. Daniel W. Patterson, James L. Peacock, and Ruel W. Tyson, Jr. (Chicago: University of Illinois Press, 1988); Harold Dean Trulear, "The Sacramentality of Preaching," *Liturgy* 7 (1988), 15–21.

166. James Weldon Johnson, *Along the Way* (New York: The Viking Press, 1933), quoted in Marcus H. Boulware, *The Oratory of Negro Leaders: 1900–1968* (Westport: Negro Universities Press, 1969), p. 3.

167. Jon Michael Spencer, *Sacred Symphony: The Chanted Sermon of the Black Preacher* (Westport: Greenwood Press, 1987), p. x. The forward is written by William C. Turner, Jr. ("The Musicality of Black Preaching") who reinvented the term as was used in Mercea Eliade, *The Myth of the Eternal Return* (New York: Harper & Row Publishers, Inc., 1959) p. 139.

168. Cornel West, *Prophesy Deliverance: An Afro-American Revolutionary Christianity* (Philadelphia: Westminster Press, 1982), p. 19.

169. Lillian B. Horace, *Crowned with Glory and Honor*, ed. L. Venchael Booth (Hicksville: Exposition Press, 1978), p. 179.

170. Ibid., pp. 195–96.

171. Ibid., p 205.

172. Ibid., pp. 205–206.

173. Luther E. Smith, Jr., *Howard Thurman: The Mystic as Prophet* (Washington, D.C.: University Press of America, 1981) pp. 3–4. This was a personal interview by the author with Howard Thurman at the Howard Thurman Educational Trust Office, San Francisco, California, June 13, 1977.

174. Benjamin E. Mays, "Introduction," in *God and Human Freedom*, ed. Henry James Young (Richmond: Friends United Press, 1983), p. xv.

175. Ibid., p. xv.

176. Ibid., p. xvi.

177. "Great Preachers," *Life Magazine*, April 6, 1953, p.127; and "Great Preachers," *Ebony*, July 1954, p. 26.

178. Smith, *Howard Thurman: The Mystic as Prophet*, p. 157. Quoted from a paper presented in a worship service for the 1977 Earl Lectures at the Pacific School of Religion, February 1977, p. 5.

179. Ibid., p. 158.

180. Marcus H. Boulware, *The Oratory of Negro Leaders: 1900–1968* (Westport: Negro Universities Press, 1969), pp. 185–186.

181. Smith, *Howard Thurman: The Mystic as Prophet*, p. 158.

182. James Earl Massey, "Thurman's Preaching: Substance and Style" in *God and Human Freedom*, ed. Henry James Young (Richmond: Friends United Press, 1983), pp. 110–121.

183. Howard Thurman, *With Head and Heart* (New York: Harcourt Brace Jovanovich, Publishers, 1979), p. 176.

184. Quoted in Stephen D. Johnson, "The Role of the Black Church in Black Civil Rights Movements," in *The Political Role of Religion in the United States*, eds. Stephen D. Johnson and Joseph B. Tamney (Boulder: Westview Press, 1986), p. 320. See also Gunnar Myrdal, *An American Dilemma: The Negro Problem and Modern Democracy* (New York: Harper and Row, 1944).

185. Albert J. Raboteau, "The Black Church: Continuity within Change," in *Altered Landscapes: Christianity in America, 1935–1985*, ed. David W. Lotz (Grand Rapids: William B. Eerdmans Publishing Company, 1985), p. 86.

186. Ibid.

187. Ralph A. Felton, "Untrained Negro Clergy," *The Christian Century*, 72 (February 2, 1955), 141–142.

188. Johnston, *The Development of Negro Religion*, pp. 91–94.

189. Raboteau, "The Black Church: Continuity within Change" in *Altered Landscapes: Christianity in America, 1935–1985*, p. 87.

190. Frederick L. Downing, *To See the Promised Land* (Macon: Mercer University Press, 1986), p. 49.

191. Reverend Martin Luther King, Sr., *Daddy King: An Autobiography* (New York: William Morrow, 1980), pp. 108–109.

192. Stephen B. Oates, *Let the Trumpets Sound* (New York: Harper and Row, 1982), p. 15.

193. Lerone Bennett, *What Manner of Man: A Biography of Martin Luther King, Jr.* (Chicago: Johnson Publishing Co., 1964), p. 96.

194. Martin Luther King, Jr., *Stride Toward Freedom*, 1958 rpt. (New York: Harper and Row, Publishers, 1986), p. 17.

195. Washington, *Black Religion*, pp. 3–4, 12.

196. Lewis V. Baldwin, *There is a Balm in Gilead* (Minneapolis: Fortress Press, 1991), p. 289.

197. Ibid., p. 290. See also, James H. Cone, "Martin Luther King, Jr.: Black Theology—Black Church," *Theology Today*, 40 (January 1984), 409–420.

198. Ibid., p. 295.

199. Mervyn A. Warren, "A Rhetorical Study of the Preaching of Doctor Martin Luther King, Jr., Pastor and Pulpit Orator" (Ph.D. dissertation, Michigan State University, 1966), pp. 69–73. See also Donald Hugh Smith, "Martin Luther King, Jr.: Rhetorician of Revolt" (Ph.D. dissertation, University of Wisconsin, 1964), pp. 233–354. For a detailed presentation on the rhetorical analysis of the verbal and non-verbal responses of King's speeches, see Keith D. Miller, *Voice of Deliverance* (New York: The Free Press, 1992), pp. 112-141. Chapter Six, "He Wanted to be an Outstanding Preacher" is a devastating discredit to the homiletical genius of King and the folk art of the black preaching tradition.

200. Hortense J. Spillers, "Martin Luther King and the Style of the Black Sermon," *The Black Scholar*, 3 (September 1971), 14–27. See also, Carl H. Marbury, "An Excursus on the Biblical and Theological Rhetoric of Martin Luther King," in *Essays in Honor of MLK, Jr.*, ed. John H. Cartwright (Evanston: Leiffer Bureau of Social and Religious Research, 1971), pp. 14–28.

201. Ronald L. Johnstone, "Negro Preachers Take Sides", *Review of Religious Research*, 11 (Fall 1969), 81–89.

202. Leon H. Sullivan, *Build Brother Build* (Philadelphia: Macrae Smith Company, 1969), p. 70.

203. Leon H. Sullivan, *Alternatives to Despair* (Valley Forge: Judson Press, 1972), p. 92.

204. Church Stone, "The National Conference on Black Power," in *The Black Power Revolt*, ed. Floyd B. Barbour (Boston: Porter Sargent, 1968), p. 189.

205. James H. Cone, *Black Theology and Black Power* (New York: The Seabury Press, 1969), p. 6.

206. Ibid., p. 117. See also James H. Cone, *A Black Theology of Liberation* (Philadelphia: J. B. Lippincott Company, 1970).

207. James H. Cone, *God of the Oppressed* (New York: The Seabury Press, 1975), p. 138.

208. Olin P. Moyd, *Redemption in Black Theology* (Valley Forge: Judson Press, 1979), pp. 23 & 35.

209. J. DeOtis Roberts, *Liberation and Reconciliation. A Black Theology* (Philadelphia: Westminster Press, 1974), p.10.

210. J. DeOtis Roberts, *Black Theology Today: Liberation and Contextualization* (New York: The Edwin Mellen Press, 1983), pp. 91–92.

211. Statement by the National Committee of Black Churchmen, "Black Theology," in *Black Theology: A Documentary History, 1966–1979*, ed. Gayraud S. Wilmore and James H. Cone (Maryknoll: Orbis Books, 1979), pp. 100–101. For a chronological reading on the subject of works not mentioned in this chapter, see also Albert Cleage, *Black Messiah* (New York: Sheed and Ward, 1966); Robert W. Duke, "Black Theology—and the Experience of Blackness," *The Journal of Religious Thought*, 29 (Spring/Summer 1972), 28–42; James H. Cone, *The Spirituals and the Blues: An Interpretation* (New York: Seabury Press, 1972); William R. Jones, "Theodicy: The Controlling Category for Black Theology," *The Journal of Religious Thought*, 30 (Spring/Summer 1973) 28–38; J. DeOtis Roberts, *A Black Political Theology* (Philadelphia: Westminster Press, 1974); James H. Cone, "A Critique of J. DeOtis Roberts, Sr. A Black Political Theology," *The Journal of the I.T.C.*, 3 (Fall 1975), 55–57; J. DeOtis Roberts, "A Critique of James H. Cone's God of the Oppressed," *The Journal of the I.T.C.*, 3 (Fall 1975), 58–63; James H. Cone, "The Content and Method of Black Theology," *The Journal of Religious Thought*, 32 (Fall/Winter 1975), 90–103; Luther E. Smith, Jr., "Black Theology and Religious Experience," *The Journal of the I.T.C.*, 8 (Fall 1980), 59–72; Louis Charles Harvey, "Black Theology and the Expanding Concept of Oppression," *The Journal of Religious Thought*, 38 (Fall/Winter 1981–82), 5–15; Cornel West, "Black Theology of Liberation as Critique of Capitalist Civilization," *The Journal of the I.T.C.*, 10 (Fall 1982), 67–83; James H. Evans, Jr., "Towards an Afro-American Theology," *The Journal of Religious Thought*, 40 (Fall/Winter 1983–84), 39–54.

212. Mitchell, *Black Preaching*, pp. 196–208. See also Henry H. Mitchell, *Black Preaching: The Recovery of a Powerful Art* (Nashville. Abingdon Press, 1990), Chapter 9.

213. Mervyn A. Warren, *Black Preaching: Truth and Soul* (Washington, D.C.: University Press of America, 1977), pp. 9–12.

214. Hycel B. Taylor, "The Language of the Black Church," *Katallagete* 6 (Summer 1976), 34–41.

215. Lawrence E. Carter, "Black Preaching Poetry and a Text," *Nexus* 16 (Spring 1972–73), 13–20. See also Wyatt Tee Walker, "The Sermon as Literature," *Sagala*, 3 (Summer 1980), 12–20; Olin P. Moyd, "Elements in Black Preaching," *The Journal of Religious Thought*, 30 (Spring/Summer 1973). 52–62; Olin P. Moyd, "The Word in the Black Church," *Freeing the Spirit*, 2 (Spring 1973), 23–29; Warren H. Stewart, Sr., *Interpreting God's Word in Black Preaching* (Valley Forge: Judson Press, 1984). The latter three give signal recognition to the distinct preaching style of Dr. Sandy F. Ray, former pastor of the Cornerstone Baptist Church, Brooklyn, New York and Vice-President of the National Baptist Convention, USA, Inc.

216. John A. Blackwell, "Black Preaching," *The Princeton Seminary Bulletin*, 65 (July 1972), 37–42. See also James S. Tinney, "The Miracle of Black Preaching," *Christianity Today*, 20 (January 30, 1976), 14–16; Anthony Frazier Lloyd, "The Black Preacher: Divine Pathos vs. Divine Apathy," *The A.M.E. Zion Quarterly Review*, 94 (January 1983) 18–33; Thomas Kilgore, Jr., "Preaching in the Black Church," *The Christian Ministry*, 19 (March/April 1988), 19–20; Oneal Claven Sandidge, "The Uniqueness of Black Preaching," *The Journal of Religious Thought*, 49 (Summer/Fall 1992), 91–97.

217. See Molefi Kete Asante, *Afrocentricity* (Trenton: Africa World Press, Inc., 1988), p. viii. Afrocentricity is defined as pro-African; African genius and African values created, reconstructed, and derived from our history and experiences in our best interests.

218. For further comments see James S. Tinney, "Black Religion is Black Politics," *The Christian Century*, 95 (June 7–14, 1978), 622; John Maust, "Black Preaching and Politics: Pastors Bask in their Clout," *Christianity Today*, 23 (December 21, 1979), 32–33; Lynda Wright, "Politics and the Pulpit," *Newsweek*, 111 (February 15, 1988), 28–29; Kirk Byron Jones, "The Activism of Interpretation: Black Pastors and Public Life," *The Christian Century*, 106 (September 13–20, 1989), 817–818.

219. C. Eric Lincoln and Lawrence Mamiya, *The Black Church in the African American Experience* (Durham: Duke University Press, 1990), p. 167. The entire summary of the Black Conscious Profile is located on page 169.

220. Quoted in Johnson, "The Role of the Black Church in the Black Civil Rights Movement," in *The Political Role of Religion in the United States*, pp. 307–336.

221. James Henry Harris, "Preaching Liberation: The Afro-American Sermon and the Quest for Social Change," *The Journal of Religious Thought*, 46 (Winter/Spring 1989–190) 72–89.

222. Bert James Lowenbert and Ruth Bogin, eds., *Black Women of Nineteenth Century American Life, Their Words, Their Thoughts, Their Feelings* (University Park: The Pennsylvania State University Press, 1976), p. 236.

223. Thomas Kilgore, Jr., "Preaching in the Black Church" *The Christian Ministry* 19 (March-April 1988) 19–20.

224. The leading Black Womanist Theologians include Jacquelyn Grant of the Interdenominational Theological Center in Atlanta, Georgia; Delores S. Williams of Union Theological Seminary of New York City, New York; and Kelly Brown Douglass of the Howard University School of Divinity in Washington, D. C. All three women studied extensively under James Cone.

225. Jacquelyn Grant, "Black Theology and The Black Woman," in *Black Theology: A Documentary History, 1966–1979*, eds. Gayraud S. Wilmore and James H. Cone (Maryknoll: Orbis Books, 1979), pp. 418–433. See also Riggins R. Earl, "The Black Church, Black Women and the Call," *Liturgy* 7 (Spring 1989), 87–95; James H. Evans, Jr., "Black Theology and Black Feminism," *The Journal of Religious Thought*, 38 (Spring/Summer 1981), 43–53; Cain H. Felder, "The Bible, Black Women, and Ministry," *The Journal of Religious Thought*, 41 (Fall/Winter 1984–85), 47–58.

226. Delores S. Williams, "The Color of Feminism: Or Speaking the Black Woman's Tongue," *The Journal of Religious Thought*, 43 (Spring/Summer, 1986), 42–58.

227. Alice Walker, *In Search of Our Mother's Garden* (New York: Harcourt Brace Jovanovich, 1983), pp. xi–xii.

228. Katie G. Canon, "The Emergence of Black Feminist Consciousness" in *Feminist Interpretations of the Bible* (Philadelphia: Westminster Press, 1985), p. 35. For further reference see Kelly Delaine Brown, "God Is as Christ Does: Toward a Womanist Theology," *The Journal of Religious Thought*, 46 (Summer/Fall, 1989), 7–16; Jacquelyn Grant, "Womanist Theology; Black Women's Experience as a Source for Doing Theology, with Special Reference to Christology," *The Journal of the Interdenominational Theological Center*, 13 (Spring 1986), 195–212; Delores S. Williams, "Womanist Theology: Black Women's Voices," *Christianity and Crisis*, 47 (March 2, 1987), 66–70.

229. Quoted in William L. Andrews, ed., *Sisters of the Spirit* (Bloomington: Indiana University Press, 1986), p. 35. From the original autobiography Jarena Lee, *The Life and Religious Experience of Jarena Lee* (Philadelphia: Printed and Published for the Author, 1836). See also Milton C. Serpett, ed., *Afro-American Religious History: A Documentary Witness* (Durham: Duke University Press, 1983), pp. 160–179; and Jualynne Dodson, "Nineteenth-Century A.M.E. Preaching Women," in *Women in the New Worlds*, eds. Hilah F. Thomas and Rosemary Skinner Keller (Nashville: Abingdon, 1981), pp. 276–289.

230. Amanda Smith, *An Autobiography: The Story of the Lord's Dealing with Mrs. Amanda Smith the Colored Evangelist* 1893 rpt. (New York: Oxford University Press, 1988), p. xxxii. For a more complete composite of the movement of black women clergy see Delores C. Carpenter, "Black Women in Religious Institutions: A Historical Summary from Slavery to the 1960s," *The Journal of Religious Thought*, 46 (Winter/Spring, 1989–90), 7–27.

231. Richette Haywood, "A Ministry of Equality and Hope," *Ebony*, 47 (November 1991), 103–106.

232. James Melvin Washington, *Frustrated Fellowship: The Black Baptist Quest for Social Power* (Macon: Mercer University Press, 1986), p. 139. Washington states in the footnote that women played a prominent role in these deliberations. Although they were not permitted to preach, they gave lectures on such topics as "Woman's Place in the Work of the Denomination." The new role of inclusion was due primarily to the progressive leadership of William J. Simmons, its founder and President. See Evelyn Brooks, "The Women's Movement in the Black Baptist Church" (Ph.D. dissertation, The University of Rochester, 1984), pp. 71–75.

233. Evelyn Brooks, "The Women's Movement in the Black Baptist Church, 1880–1920" (Ph.D. dissertation, The University of Rochester, 1984), p. 82. See also Virginia W. Broughton, *Twenty Years' Experience of a Missionary* (Chicago: The Pony Press Publishers, 1907), 7–14.

234. Ibid., p. 83.

235. Ibid., p. 100.

236. Leontine T. C. Kelly, "Preaching in the Black Tradition," in *Women Ministers*, ed. Judith L. Weidman (San Francisco: Harper & Row Publishers, Inc., 1981), p. 74.

237. Brooks, "The Women's Movement in the Black Baptist Church, 1880–1920," p. 151.

238. Ibid., p. 191.

239. Ibid., p. 256.

240. Leontine T. C. Kelly, "Preaching in the Black Tradition," in *Women Ministers*, pp. 73–74.

241. Harold Carter, *The Prayer Tradition of Black People* (Valley Forge: Judson Press, 1976), pp. 78–79.

242. Ella Pearson Mitchell ed., *Women: To Preach or Not To Preach* (Valley Forge: Judson Press, 1991), pp. 1–17.

243. Lincoln and Mamiya, *The Black Church in the African American Experience*, pp. 286–287.

244. Cheryl Townsend Gilkes, "The Role of Women in the Sanctified Church," *The Journal of Religious Thought*, 43 (Spring/Summer, 1986), pp. 24–41.

245. Ibid., p. 33.

246. Ibid., pp. 34–35.

247. Joseph R. Washington, *Black Sects and Cults* (Garden City: Doubleday & Company, 1972), pp. 66–67.

248. Arthur H. Fauset, *Black Gods of the Metropolis* (Philadelphia: University of Pennsylvania Press, 1944), pp. 14–17. See also Harold Dean Truelear, "Reshaping Black Pastoral Theology," *The Journal of Religious Thought*, 46 (Summer/Fall 1989), 17–31.

249. This text originated in a special lecture series that Links, Inc. sponsored at Howard University Divinity School in October of 1985, entitled "The Feminine in Religious Traditions." See also Cheryl J. Sanders, "The Woman as Preacher," *The Journal of Religious Thought*, 43 (Summer/Spring, 1986), 5–23.

250. Cheryl J. Sanders, "The Women as Preacher," in *African American Religious Studies*, ed. Gayraud S. Wilmore (Durham: Duke University Press, 1989), pp. 372–391.

251. Catherine Louise Peck, "Your Daughters Shall Prophesy: Women in the Afro-American Preaching Tradition" (M.A. thesis, University of North Carolina, 1983), pp. 51–52. See also Catherine L. Peck, "Your Daughters Shall Prophesy: Women in the Afro-American Preaching Tradition," in *Diversities of Gifts* (Chicago University of Illinois Press, 1988), pp. 143–155.

252. Lincoln and Mamiya, *The Black Church in the African American Experience*, p. 216.

253. Lester Thonssen, A. Craig Baird, and Waldo W. Braden, *Speech Criticism* (Malabar: Krieger Publishing Co., 1981), Chapter 11, "Understanding A Speaker and His Background," serves as a guide for this study by focusing upon seven factors to interpret and analyze a speaking career.

254. Gardner C. Taylor, personal interview, Brooklyn, New York, March 21, 1991, telephone interviews September 19, 1991 and November 19, 1991.

255. Charles R. Darwin, *On the Origin of Species by Means of Natural Selection; or, The Preservation of Favored Races in the Struggle for Life* (New York: D. Appleton & Co., 1872).

256. Herman Stewart, telephone interview, Baton Rouge, Louisiana, October 19, 1991.

257. Dr. C. D. Simmons, telephone interview, Louisville, Kentucky, December 17, 1991.

258. Laura Taylor, telephone interview, Brooklyn, New York, September 20, 1991.

259. Ruby Taylor Harris, telephone interview, Tacoma, Washington, January 9, 1992.

260. Gardner C. Taylor, telephone interview, September 19, 1991.

261. Theresa Noble, telephone interview, Baton Rouge, Louisiana, April 13, 1991.

262. Ibid.

263. Ibid.

264. This information was supplied through telephone interviews with Dr. Henry H. Mitchell, Atlanta, Georgia, former colleague of Milton Froyd's at Colgate Rochester Divinity School, Dr. Samuel McKinney, Seattle, Washington (in whose church Froyd was a former member), and Dr. Bobby Joe Saucer, an executive with the American Baptist Convention, also Atlanta, Georgia. Froyd consisted of the team which monitored the test and determined the IQ scores of the students.

265. Gardner C. Taylor, personal interview.

266. This information was confirmed through telephone interviews with Henry H. Mitchell, former colleague of Froyd's at Colgate Rochester, Atlanta, Georgia, Dr. Samuel McKinney, Seattle, Washington (whose church Dr. Milton Froyd was a former member) and Dr. Bobby Jo Saucer, an executive with the American Baptist Convention.

267. Daniel Haley, telephone interview, Seattle, Washington, January 11, 1992.

268. Robert Green Ingersoll, *Some Mistakes of Moses* (1879; rpt. Buffalo: Prometheus Books, 1986).

269. Gardner Calvin Taylor, interview.

270. Gardner C. Taylor, "Why I Believe There Is a God," in *Why I Believe There Is a God*, ed. Howard Thurman (Chicago: Johnson Publishing Co., 1965), p. 86.

271. Laura Scott Taylor, telephone interview, Brooklyn, New York, September 20, 1991.

272. Ibid.

273. Taylor, "Why I Believe There Is a God," in *Why I Believe There Is a God*, p. 86.

274. Laura Taylor, telephone interview.

275. Laura Taylor, interview.

276. Laura Taylor, interview.

277. Cyprian and Anna Belle, telephone interview, Brooklyn, New York, December 7, 1991.

278. Phyllis Strong Taylor, telephone interview, Brooklyn, New York, March 31, 1999.

279. Ibid.

280. Ibid.

281. Ibid.

282. Mrs. Mary Kendal, telephone interview, Oberlin, Ohio, April 13, 1991.

283. Gardner C. Taylor, interview.

284. Laura Taylor, interview.

285. Carl Stewart, telephone interview, Baton Rouge, Louisiana, March 30, 1991.

286. Herman Stewart, interview.

287. Laura Taylor, interview.

288. Carl Stewart, interview.

289. Carl Stewart, interview.

290. Dr. C. D. Simmons, interview.

291. Theresa Nobles, interview.

292. Cyprian and Anna Belle, telephone interview.

293. Gardner Taylor, "They Shall Ask The Way," *Eighth Baptist World Congress* (Philadelphia: The Judson Press, 1950), pp. 50–55.

294. Laura Scott, interview.

295. Anna Belle, interview.

296. Gardner Taylor and Martin Luther King, Jr. were best of friends. King preached for him at the Concord Baptist Church of Christ, September 1951 before going to Boston University School of Theology as a first semester Ph.D. student. Taylor also held the first Northern fund raising rally for his colleague and the MIA. For other connections with the Civil Rights Movement, see Taylor Branch, *Parting the Waters* (New York: Simon & Schuster, Inc., 1988).

297. Gardner C. Taylor, telephone interview, November 19, 1991.

298. Alex Poinsett, "Suffer the Little Children," *Ebony Magazine* 43 (August 1988) pp. 144–148.

299. Marcus H. Boulware, *The Oratory of Negro Leaders: 1900–1968* (Westport: Negro Universities Press, 1969), p. 194.

300. Taylor Branch, *Parting the Waters*, pp. 335–339 and 502–507.

301. Alfredo Graham, "Election Satisfies Taylor," *The Courier*, September 23, 1961, p. 10. In this article Taylor stated, "I believe it was an honest election. Dr. Jackson received the mandate of the convention to pursue the line for which the people voted. As a good Baptist, I heartily accept the vote of the people. Now that the election is over, I am not the leader of any 'opposition party' within the ranks of the convention."

302. William D. Booth, *The Progressive Story* (1979; rpt. St. Paul: Braun Press, 1981), p. 173.

303. Gardner C. Taylor, "The President's Message To The Progressive National Baptist Convention, Inc., September 1968," in *Black Theology: A Documentary History, 1966–1972*, ed. Gayraud S. Wilmore and James H. Cone (Maryknoll: Orbis Books, 1979), pp. 262–267.

304. Stan Hastey, "Thomas Nomination Riles Progressive Baptist," *The Christian Century*, 108 (September 4–11, 1991), pp. 798–79.

305. Dr. Samuel McKinney, telephone interview, Seattle, Washington, November 17, 1991.

306. Dr. Edward Wheeler, telephone interview, Tuskegee, Alabama, November 15, 1991.

307. Dr. Bobby Joe Saucer, telephone interview, Atlanta, Georgia, January 5, 1992.

308. Dr. Calvin Butts, telephone interview, Harlem, New York, November 14, 1991.

309. Rev. Johnnie Skinner, telephone interview, Knoxville, Tennessee, November 23, 1991.

310. Dr. Calvin Butts, telephone interview.

311. Dr. Frank Reid, telephone interview, Baltimore, Maryland, November 23, 1991.

312. Ibid.

313. Ibid.

314. Gardner Taylor, "Foreword," *Dynamic Preaching* (Nashville: Broadman Press, 1983).

315. Gardner C. Taylor, "Introduction," in *Best Black Sermons*, ed. William M. Philpot (Valley Forge: Judson Press, 1972), p. 6.

316. Gardner Taylor, "The Preacher's Calling" (Lecture delivered at The McCreary Center for African American Religious Studies, Cleveland, OH, October 22, 1990).

317. Gardner C. Taylor, *How Shall They Preach* (Elgin: Progressive Baptist Publishing House, 1977), p. 13.

318. Gerald L. Davis, *I Got the Word in Me and I Can Sing It, You Know* (Philadelphia: University of Pennsylvania. Press, 1985), p. 73.

319. Gardner Taylor, "Shaping Sermons by the Shape of Text and Preacher," in *Preaching Biblically*, ed. Don M. Wardlaw (Philadelphia: Westminster Press, 1983), p. 137.

320. Terry C. Muck and Paul D. Robbins, "The Sweet Torture of Sunday Morning: An Interview with Gardner C. Taylor," *Leadership*, 2 (Summer 1981), 16–29.

321. Gardner Taylor, "The Preacher's Calling."

322. Ibid.

323. Terry C. Muck and Paul D. Robbins, "The Sweet Torture of Sunday Morning: An Interview with Gardner C. Taylor," pp. 16–29.

324. Gardner Taylor, "The Preaching Function" (speech delivered at The Virginia Baptist Pastor's School, Richmond, VA, July 10, 1986).

325. Ibid.

326. Gardner Taylor, "The Personality of the Preacher" (speech delivered at The Southern Baptist Theological Seminary, Louisville, KY, March 2, 1979).

327. Gardner Taylor, "On Recognizing and Removing the Presumptuousness of Preaching" (speech delivered at the Louisville Presbyterian Theological Seminary, Louisville, KY, April 20, 1972. See also Gardner C. Taylor, *How Shall They Preach* (Elgin: Progressive Baptist Publishing House, 1977), pp. 23–39.

328. Gardner Taylor, *How Shall They Preach*, pp. 27–29.

329. Gardner Taylor, "On Recognizing and Removing the Presumptuousness of Preaching."

330. Ibid.

331. Ibid.

332. Gerald L. Davis, *I God the Word in Me and I Can Sing it, You Know*, pp. 39–40.

333. Ibid., pp. 62–64. See also Mitchell, *Black Preaching* (San Francisco: Harper & Row Publishers, Inc., 1979), pp. 23–31.

334. Muck and Robbins, "The Sweet Torture of Sunday Morning: An Interview with Gardner C. Taylor," pp. 16–29.

335. Ibid.

336. Gardner Taylor, "The Shape of the Text and Preacher," pp. 141–142. For a detailed demonstration of how Taylor utilizes this approach to preaching see also O. C. Edward, Jr. and Gardner C. Taylor, *Pentecost 3: Aids for Interpreting the Lessons of the Church Year*, eds. Elizabeth Achtemeier, Gerhard Krodel, and Charles P. Price (Philadelphia: Fortress Press, 1980).

337. Gardner C. Taylor, "A Panel Discussion on the Definition of Preaching" (speech delivered at The Louisville Presbyterian Theological Seminary, Louisville, KY, April 22, 1972).

338. Taylor, *How Shall They Preach*, pp. 57–59.

339. See W. M. Taylor, *The Parables of Our Savior* (London: Hodder and Stoughton, 1887).

340. Muck and Robbins, "The Sweet Torture of Sunday Morning: An Interview with Gardner C. Taylor," p. 19.

341. Taylor, *How Shall They Preach*, p. 62.

342. Taylor, "A Clinical Session on Preaching," (speech delivered at The Louisville Presbyterian Theological Seminary, Louisville, KY, April 21, 1972).

343. Taylor, *How Shall They Preach*, pp. 65–68.

344. Eward P. J. Corbett, *Classical Rhetoric for the Modern Student* (New York: Oxford University Press, 1965), p. vii. Corbett credits Aristotle, Cicero, and Quintillion as the men from whom we inherited the classical system.

345. Sonja K. Foss, *Rhetorical Criticism: Exploration & Practice* (Prospect Heights: Waveland Press, Inc., 1989), pp. 3–4.

346. Raymond Bailey, "Proclamation as a Rhetorical Art," *Review and Expositor* 84 (1987), 7–21.

347. The most resourceful references available for the study of Aristotle's *Rhetoric* see Lane Cooper, trans., *The Rhetoric of Aristotle* (Englewood Cliffs: Prentice-Hall, Inc., 1932); Eward P. J. Corbett, *Classical Rhetoric for the Modern Student*, 3rd ed. (New York: Oxford University

Press, 1990); Keith V. Erickson, ed., *Aristotle: The Classical Heritage of Rhetoric* (Metuchen: Scarecrow Press, Inc., 1974); George A. Kennedy, *Aristotle On Rhetoric* (New York: Oxford University Press, 1991).

348. W. Ross Winterowd, *Rhetoric: A Synthesis* (New York: Holt, Rinehart and Winston, Inc.,1972), p. 18.

349. Thonssen, Baird, and Braden, *Speech Criticism*, p. 150.

350. Aristotle, *The, Rhetoric* 1, 2, trans. Lane Cooper, *The Rhetoric of Aristotle* (Englewood Cliffs: Prentice-Hall, Inc., 1932), p. vii. All subsequent citations refer to this edition.

351. Ibid., 1, 2.

352. Ibid.

353. Ibid., 1, 3.

354. Ibid., 2. 1.

355. Ibid., 2.2–2.17.

356. Bailey, "Proclamation as Rhetorical Art," p. 12.

357. George A. Kennedy, *Classical Rhetoric and Its Christian and Secular Tradition from Ancient to Modern Times* (Chapel Hill: The University of North Carolina Press, 1980), p. 72.

358. Aristotle, *Rhetoric*, 2.22. This set of discussion resumes from the initial presentation in 1.2 on arguments based upon illustrations or thoughts.

359. Ibid.

360. Ibid., 3, 1.

361. Ibid.

362. Ibid.

363. Ibid., 3, 2.

364. Ibid., 3, 3.

365. Alfred North Whitehead, *The Aims of Education and Other Essays* (New York: The Macmillan Co., 1929), p. 19; cited in Marie Hochmuth Nichols, *Rhetoric and Criticism* (Baton Rouge: Louisiana State University Press, 1963), p. 32.

366. Ibid., 3, 13.

367. Ibid.

368. Ibid., 3, 14.

369. Ibid.

370. Ibid., 3, 19.

371. Ibid.

372. Thomas M. Conley, *Rhetoric in the European Tradition* (White Plains: Longman, 1990), p. 33.

373. Cicero, *De Inventione* I. v. 6, trans., H. M. Hubbell, Loeb Classical Library (1949; rpt. Cambridge: Harvard University Press, 1960). All subsequent citations refer to this edition.

374. Ibid., I. vii. 9.

375. Cicero, *De Oratore* I. ii. 5, trans., H. Rackham, Loeb Classical Library (Cambridge: Harvard University Press, 1948). All subsequent citations refer to this edition.

376. Ibid., I. xxxi. 140–143.

377. Ibid., I. xxviii. 128–130.

378. Ibid., I. xxxiii. 148–151.

379. Ibid., I. xxxiv. 154–160.

380. Ibid., II. i. 4–7.

381. Ibid., II. xxvii. 116–118.

382. Ibid., II. lxxvi. 308.

383. Ibid., II. lxxviii. 315.

384. Ibid., II. lxxx. 325.

385. Ibid., II. lxxxvi. 353.

386. Ibid., II. lxxxvii. 357.

387. Ibid.

388. Ibid., II. lxxxviii. 359–360.

389. Ibid., III. vi. 24.

390. Ibid., III. x. 39.

391. Ibid., III. xxiii. 91.

392. Ibid., III. lv. 213.

393. Ibid., III. lx. 224.

394. Thonssen, Baird, and Braden, *Speech Criticism*, p. 169.

395. Conley, *Rhetoric in the European Tradition*, p. 33. For a complete discussion on "status" in rhetorical invention, see pp. 32–33.

396. *Rhetorica ad Herennium*, I. iv. 7., trans., Harry Caplan (Cambridge: Harvard University Press, 1954). All subsequent citations refer to this edition. See also Harry Caplan, *Of Eloquence: Studies in Ancient and Medieval Rhetoric* (Ithaca: Cornell University Press, 1970), pp. 1–25.

397. Ibid., I. iv. 8.

398. Ibid., II. xxx. 47.

399. Ibid., II. xxxi. 50.

400. Ibid., II. i. 1.

401. Ibid., III. ix. 16–17.

402. Ibid., III. xi. 19.

403. Ibid., III. xi–xv. 20–27.

404. Ibid., III. xvi. 28.

405. Ibid.

406. Ibid., III. xvi. 28–29.

407. Ibid., III. xxii. 27.

408. Ibid., Iv. i. 1–2.

409. Ibid., IV. i. 3.

410. Ibid., IV. xii–xiii. 17–18.

411. Conley, *Rhetoric in the European Tradition*, p. 38.

412. Quintillion, *De Institutione Oratoria*, Vols. I & II, trans., John Shelby Watson (London: George Bell & Sons, 1892 & 1895). All subsequent citations refer to these editions.

413. Ibid., I. v. 1.

414. Ibid., I. xiv. 4.

415. Ibid., II. xvii. 23.

416. Ibid., V. x. 109–110.

417. Ibid., VII. x. 15.

418. Ibid., VIII. Introduction, 13–16.

419. Ibid., XI. ii. 1.

420. Ibid., XI, iii. 30–32.

421. Ibid., XI. iii. 87.

422. Ibid., XII. i. 23.

423. Kennedy, *Classical Rhetoric and Its Christian and Secular Tradition from Ancient to Modern Times*, p. 102.

424. Gardner C. Taylor, "They Shall Ask The Way," in *Eighth Baptist World Congress*, ed. Arnold T. Ohrn (Philadelphia: The Judson Press, 1950), pp. 50–55.

425. Aristotle, *The Rhetoric*, 2.1.

426. Gardner Taylor, telephone interview, July 28, 1993, Brooklyn, New York. All subsequent citations refer to this interview.

427. See also Sherrye Henry, "Are These the Smartest People in America?," *Parade* (August 4, 1991), 6. In this informal survey, the name of Rev. Dr. Gardner Taylor is included on the list of the Ford Foundation President, Franklin Thomas.

428. Cicero, *De inventione* I. v. 6.

429. Gardner Taylor, "The Christian Drama," *The Pulpit*, 28 (1957), 10–12.

430. Aristotle, *The Rhetoric*, 2.2-2.17.

431. Cicero, *De oratore* I .ii. 5.

432. *Rhetorica ad herennium*, I. iv. 7.

433. Taylor, telephone interview.

434. Artistotle, *The Rhetoric*, 1. 2.

435. Gardner Taylor, telephone interview.

436. *Rhetorica ad herennium*, II. xxxi. 50.

437. Gardner Taylor, "Hearts Waiting for What?" in *Best Sermons*, ed. G. Paul Butler (New York: Thomas Y. Crowell Company, 1959), pp. 276–281.

438. Gardner Taylor, telephone interview.

439. Aristotle, *The Rhetorica*, 2.22.

440. Quintillian, *De institutione oratoria*, V. x. 109–110.

441. Aristotle, *The Rhetorica*, 3. 13.

442. Gardner Taylor, "Some Comments on Race Hate," in *The Pulpit Speaks*, ed. Alfred T. Davies (New York: Harper & Row Publishers, Inc., 1965), pp. 184–191.

443. Aristotle, *The Rhetorica*, 3. 13.

444. Gardner C. Taylor, "The President's Message to the Progressive National Baptist Convention, Inc." in *Black Theology: A Documentary History, 1966–1979*, eds. Gayraud S. Wilmore and James H. Cone (Maryknoll: Orbis Books, 1979), pp. 262–167.

445. Gardner Taylor, telephone interview.

446. Gardner C. Taylor, *Chariots Aflame* (Nashville: Broadman Press, 1988), pp. 71–80.

447. Gardner Taylor, telephone interview.

448. Gardner Taylor, telephone interview.

449. Ibid.

450. James Earl Massey, *Designing the Sermon* (Nashville: Abingdon Press, 1980), p. 90.

451. Gardner Taylor, telephone interview.

452. Gardner C. Taylor, *The Scarlet Thread* (Elgin: Progressive Baptist Publishing House, 1981), pp. 13–20.

453. Roger D. Abrahams, *Deep Down in the Jungle* . . . (Hatboro: Folklore Associates, 1964), p. 90.

454. Richard John Neuhaus, *Freedom for Ministry* (San Francisco: Harper & Row Publishers, Inc., 1979), pp. 157–58.

455. *A Dedication of the Benjamin E. Mays Hall and the Howard Thurman Chapel*, presented by Dr. Gardner Taylor, produced by Howard University Divinity School (Washington D.C.: Howard University, 1987).

456. *The Preacher's Reply to the Human Cry*, presented by Dr. Gardner C. Taylor, produced by the Bethel African Methodist Church (Baltimore: Bethel AME, 1991).

457. Kathleen McClain, "Preachers Hear Role is to Cut Against Grain," *The Charlotte Observer*, Wednesday, March 20, 1991, sec. A. p. 1. 6.

458. *Inaugural Interfaith Prayer Service*, presented by Dr. Gardner C. Taylor, produced by Purdue University Public Affairs Video Archives (Purdue, IN: C-SPAN, 1993).

BIBLIOGRAPHY

Books

Abrahams, Roger D. *Deep Down in the Jungle* . . .. Hatboro: Folklore Associates, 1964.

Aly, Bower, and Lucile Folse Aly. *Rhetoric of Public Speaking.* New York: McGraw-Hill Co., 1973.

Andrews, William L., ed. *Sisters of the Spirit.* Bloomington: Indiana University Press, 1986.

Aristotle. *The Rhetoric,* Trans. Lane Cooper. *The Rhetoric Of Aristotle.* Englewood Cliffs: Prentice Hall, 1932.

Asante, Molefi Kete. *Afrocentricity.* Trenton: Africa World Press, Inc., 1988.

Baldwin, Lewis V. *There Is a Balm in Gilead.* Minneapolis: Fortress Press, 1991.

Bennett, Lerone. *What Manner of Man: Biography of Martin Luther King, Jr.* Chicago: Johnson Publishing Co., 1964.

Bercovitch, Sacvan. *The American Jeremiad.* Madison: University of Wisconsin Press, 1978.

Bingham, Caleb. *The Columbian Orator.* Troy: William S. Parker, 1821.

Blaikie, William Garden. *The Preachers of Scotland From the Sixteenth to the Nineteenth Century.* Edinburgh: T & T Clark, 1888.

Blassingame, John W. *The Slave Community.* New York: Oxford University Press, 1979.

Boles, John B. *Religion in Antebellum Kentucky.* Lexington: University of Kentucky Press, 1976.

Booth, William D. *The Progressive Story.* 1979; rpt. St. Paul: Braun Press, 1981.

Boulware, Marcus H. *The Oratory of Negro Leaders: 1900–1968.* Westport: Negro Universities Press, 1969.

Branch, Taylor. *Parting the Waters.* New York: Simon & Schuster, Inc., 1988.

Budge, E. A. Wallis. *Egyptian Book of the Dead.* 1911; rpt. Dover: University Books, 1967.

Canon, Katie G. "The Emergence of Black Feminist Consciousness." In *Feminist Interpretations of the Bible.* Philadelphia: Westminster Press, 1985.

Carter, Harold. *The Prayer Tradition of Black People.* Valley Forge: Judson Press, 1976.

Cicero. *De Inventione.* Trans. H. M. Hubbell. Loeb Classical Library. Cambridge: Harvard University Press, 1949.

_____ . *De Oratore.* Trans. H. Rackham. Loeb Classical Library. Cambridge: Harvard University Press, 1949.

Cone, James H. *Black Theology and Black Power.* New York: The Seabury Press, 1969.

_____ . *God of the Oppressed.* New York: The Seabury Press, 1975.

Conley, Thomas M. *Rhetoric in the European Tradition.* White Plains: Longman, 1990.

Corbett, Edward P. J. *Classical Rhetoric for the Modern Student.* New York: Oxford University Press, 1965.

Cromwell, John W. *The Negro in American History.* 1914; rpt. New York: Johnson Reprint Corporation, 1968.

Dallimore, Arnold A. *George Whitefield: The Life and Times of the Great Evangelist of the Eighteenth-Century Revival.* London: Billing & Sons, Ltd., 1970.

Darwin, Charles R. *On the Origin of Species by Means of Natural Selection; or The Preservation of Favored Races in the Struggle for Life.* New York: D. Appleton & Co., 1872.

Davis, Gerald L. *I Got the Word in Me and I Can Sing it, You Know.* Philadelphia: University of Pennsylvania, 1970.

Day, Richard Ellsworth. *Rhapsody in Black.* Philadelphia: The Judson Press, 1953.

Douglass, Frederick. *Life and Times of Frederick Douglass.* 1892; rpt. New York: Collier Publishing Company, 1962.

DuBois, W. E. B. *The Negro Church.* Atlanta: Atlanta University Press, 1898.

_____ . *The Philadelphia Negro.* 1899; rpt. New York: Schocken Books, 1967.

_____ . *The Souls of Black Folk.* New York: McClure & Company, 1903.

Farrow, Stephen S. *Faith, Fancies, and Fetich or Yoruba Paganism.* New York: Negro Universities Press, 1969.

Fauset, Arthur H. *Black Gods of the Metropolis.* Philadelphia: University of Pennsylvania Press, 1944.

Fordham, Monroe. *Major Themes in Northern Black Religious Thought, 1800–1860.* New York: Exposition Press, 1975.

Forsyth, P. T. *Positive Preaching and the Modern Mind.* London: Independent Press LTD, 1949.

Foss, Sonja K. *Rhetorical Criticism: Exploration & Practice.* Prospect Heights: Waveland Press, Inc., 1989.

Gossip, Arthur. *In Christ's Stead.* London: Hodder and Stoughton Limited, 1925.

Grant, Jacquelyn. "Black Theology and The Black Woman." In *Black Theology: A Documentary History, 1966–1979.* Eds. Gayraud S. Wilmore and James H. Cone. Maryknoll: Orbis Books, 1979.

Greene, Lorenzo J. *The Negro in Colonial New England.* New York: Atheneum, 1968.

Hamilton, Charles V. *The Black Preacher in America.* New York: William Morrow & Company, Inc., 1972.

Handy, Robert T. *A Christian America.* New York: Oxford University Press, 1971.

Hatcher, William E. *John Jasper: The Unmatched Negro Philosopher and Preacher.* New York: Fleming H. Revell Company, 1908.

Horace, Lillian B. *Crowned with Glory and Honor.* Ed. L. Venchael Booth. Hicksville: Exposition Press, 1978.

Ingersoll, Robert Green. *Some Mistakes of Moses.* 1879; rpt. Buffalo: Prometheus Books, 1986.

Johnson, James Weldon. *God's Trombone.* 1927; rpt. New York: Penguin Books, 1976.

_____ . *Along the Way.* New York: The Viking Press, 1933.

Johnson, Stephen D. "The Role of the Black Church in Black Civil Rights Movements." In *The Political Role of Religion in the United States.* Eds. Stephen D. Johnson and Joseph B. Tamney. Boulder: Westview Press, 1986.

Johnston, Ruby F. *The Development of Negro Religion.* New York: Philosophical Library, 1954.

Jones, Ralph M. *Charles Albert Tindley.* Nashville: Abingdon, 1982.

Kalilombe, Patrick. "The Salvific Value of African Religions." In *Missions Trends No. 5.* Eds. Gerald H. Anderson and Thomas F. Standsky. Grand Rapids: Eerdmans Publishing Co., 1981.

Kamalu, Chukwenyere. *Foundations of African Thought.* London: Karnak House, 1990.

Kelly, Leontine T. C. "Preaching in the Black Tradition." In *Women Ministers.* Ed. Judith L. Weidman. San Francisco: Harper & Row Publishers, Inc., 1981.

Kennedy, George A. *Classical Rhetoric and Its Christian and Secular Tradition from Ancient to Modern Times.* Chapel Hill: The University of North Carolina Press, 1980.

King, Jr., Martin Luther. *Stride Toward Freedom*. 1958; rpt. New York: Harper and Row, Publishers, 1986.

King, Sr., Reverend Martin Luther. *Daddy King: An Autobiography*. New York: William Morrow, 1980.

Klem, Herbert V. *Oral Communication of the Scripture: Insights from African Oral Art*. Pasadena: William Carey Library, 1982.

Levine, Lawrence W. *Black Culture and Black Consciousness*. New York: Oxford University Press, 1977.

Lienhardt, Godfrey. *Divinity and Experience: The Religion of the Dinka*. Oxford: Clarendon Press, 1961.

Lincoln, C. Eric. "The Black Heritage in Religion in the South." In *Religion in the South*. Ed. Charles Reagan Wilson. Jackson: University Press of Mississippi, 1985.

Lincoln, C. Eric and Lawrence Mamiya. *The Black Church in the African American Experience*. Durham: Duke University Press, 1990.

Lowenbert, Bert James and Ruth Bogin, eds. *Black Women of Nineteenth Century American Life, Their Words, Their Thoughts, Their Feelings*. University Park: The Pennsylvania State University Press, 1976.

Malinowski, Bronislaw. *The Dynamics of Cultural Change*. New Haven: Yale, 1945.

Massey, James Earl. "The Preacher's Rhetoric." In *A Celebration of Ministry*. Ed. Kenneth Cain Kinghorn. Wilmore: Francis Asbury Publishing Co., Inc., 1982.

_____ . *Designing the Sermon*. Nashville: Abingdon Press, 1980.

_____ . "Thurman's Preaching: Substance and Style." *In God and Human Freedom*. Ed. Henry James Young. Richmond: Friends United Press, 1983.

Mays, Benjamin E. "The Black Experience and Perspective." In *American Religion Values and the Future of America*. Ed. Rodger Van Allen. Philadelphia: Fortress Press, 1978.

_____. "Introduction." In *God and Human Freedom*. Ed. Henry James Young. Richmond: Friends United Press, 1983.

Mbiti, John S. *African Religions and Philosophy*. New York: F. A. Praeger, 1969.

Meir, August. *Negro Thought in America, 1880–1915*. Ann Arbor: University of Michigan Press, 1966.

Milligan, Robert H. *The Jungle Folk of Africa*. New York: Revell Co., 1908.

Mitchell, Ella, ed. *Women: To Preach or Not To Preach*. Valley Forge: Judson Press, 1991.

Mitchell, Henry H. *Black Belief*. New York: Harper & Row Publishers, Inc., 1975.

_____. *Black Preaching: The Recovery of a Powerful Art*. Nashville: Abingdon, 1990.

_____. *Celebration and Experience in Preaching*. Nashville: Abingdon Press, 1990.

_____. *The Recovery of Preaching*. San Francisco: Harper & Row Publishers, Inc., 1977.

Moses, Wilson Jeremiah. *Black Messiahs and Uncle Toms: Social and Literary Manipulations of a Religious Myth*. University Park: The Pennsylvania State University Press, 1982.

Moyd, Olin P. *Redemption in Black Theology*. Valley Forge: Judson Press, 1979.

Neuhaus, Richard John. *Freedom for Ministry*. San Francisco: Harper & Row Publishers, Inc., 1979.

Nichols, Marie Hochmuth. *Rhetoric and Criticism*. Baton Rouge: Louisiana State University Press, 1963.

Oates, Stephen B. *Let the Trumpets Sound*. New York: Harper and Row, 1982.

Peel, J. D. Y. *Aladura: Religious Movement Among the Yoruba*. London: Oxford University Press, 1968.

Pipes, William H. *Say Amen, Brother!* Westport: Negro University Press, 1950.

Posnansky, Merrick. "Archaeology, Ritual, and Religion." In *The Historical Study of African Religion*. Ed. T. O. Ranger and I. N. Kimambo. Los Angeles: University of California Press, 1972.

Quarles, Benjamin. *Black Abolitionists*. New York: Oxford University Press, 1969.

Quintillion. *De Institutione Oratoria I & II*. Trans. John Shelby Watson. London: George Bell & Sons, 1892 & 1895.

Raboteau, Albert J. *Slave Religion*. New York: Oxford University Press, 1978.

_____. "The Black Church: Continuity within Change." In *Altered Landscapes: Christianity in America, 1935–1985*. Ed. David W. Lotz. Grand Rapids: William B. Eerdmans Publishing Company, 1985.

Raybold, G. A. *Reminiscences of Methodism in West Jersey*. New York: Lane & Scott, 1849.

Rhetorica, ad Herennium. Trans. Harry Caplan. Cambridge: Harvard University Press, 1954.

Richardson, Harry V. "The Negro in American Religious Life." In *The American Negro Reference Book*. Ed. John P. Davis. Englewood Cliffs: Prentice-Hall, Inc., 1966.

Roberts, J. DeOtis. *Black Theology Today: Liberation and Contextualization*. New York: The Edwin Mellen Press, 1983.

_____. *Liberation and Reconciliation: A. Black Theology*. Philadelphia: Westminster Press, 1974.

Rogers, Cornish R. "Black Ministry." *In Creating an Intentional Ministry*. Ed. John E. Biersdorf. Nashville: Abingdon Press, 1976.

Rooks, Charles Shelby. "The Black Experience in America: A Union of Two Worlds." In *The American Experiment: Piety and Practicality*. Eds. Clyde L. Manschreck and Barbara Brown Zikmund. Chicago: Exploration Press, 1977.

Rosenberg, Bruce A. *The Art of the American Folk Preacher*. New York: Oxford Press, 1970.

Sandres, Cheryl J. "The Woman as Preacher." In *African American Religious Studies.* Ed. Gayraud S. Wilmore. Durham: Duke University Press, 1989.

Sernett, Milton C. *Black Religion and American Evangelicalism: White Protestants, Plantation Missions, and the Flowering of Negro Christianity, 1787–1865.* Metuchen: The Scarecrow Press, Inc., 1975.

Smith, Amanda. *An Autobiography: The Story of the Lord's Dealing with Mrs. Amanda Smith, the Colored Evangelist.* 1893; rpt. New York: Oxford University Press, 1988.

Smith, Edward D. *Climbing Jacob's Ladder: The Rise of Black Churches in Eastern American Cities, 1740–1871.* Washington, D.C.: Smithsonian Institute Press, 1988.

Smith, J. Alfred. *Preach On!* Nashville: Broadman Press, 1984.

Smith, Jr., Luther E. *Howard Thurman, The Mystic as Prophet.* Washington, D. C.: University Press of America, 1981.

Spencer, Jon Michael. *Sacred Symphony: The Chanted Sermon of the Black Preacher.* Westport: Negro Universities Press, 1969.

Spiro, M. E. "Religion: Problems of Definition and Explanation." In *Anthropological Approaches to the Study of Religion.* Ed. M. Banton. London: Oxford Press, 1966.

Statement by the National Committee of Black Churchmen. "Black Theology." In *Black Theology: A Documentary History, 1966–1979.* Ed. Gayraud S. Wilmore and James H. Cone. Maryknoll: Orbis Books, 1979.

Stennis, L. V. *Why Sit Here Until We Die?* Seattle: Chi-Mik Publishing Company, 1981.

Stewart, James S. *Heralds of God.* New York: Scribner's Son, 1946.

Stone, Church. "The National Conference on Black Power." In *The Black Power Revolt.* Ed. Floyd B. Barbour. Boston: Porter Sargent, 1968.

Sullivan, Leon H. *Build Brother Build.* Philadelphia: Macrae Smith Company, 1969.

_____ . *Alternatives to Despair.* Valley Forge: Judson Press, 1972.

Taylor, Gardner C. "Introduction." In *Best Black Sermons.* Ed. William M. Philpot. Valley Forge: Judson Press, 1972.

_____ . "Hearts Waiting for What?" In *Best Sermons.* Ed. G. Paul Butler. New York: Thomas Y. Crowell Company, 1959.

_____ . "The President's Message to the Progressive National Baptist Convention, Inc." In *Black Theology: A Documentary History, 1966–1979.* Eds. Gayraud S. Wilmore and James H. Cone. Maryknoll: Orbis Books, 1979.

_____ . *Chariots Aflame.* Nashville: Broadman Press, 1988.

_____ . "Foreword." *Dynamic Preaching.* Nashville: Broadman Press, 1983.

_____ . "They Shall Ask the Way." In *Eighth Baptist World Congress.* Ed. Arnold T. Ohrn. Philadelphia: The Judson Press, 1950.

_____ . *How Shall They Preach.* Elgin: Progressive Baptist Publishing House, 1977.

_____ . "Shaping Sermons by the Shape of Text and Preacher." In *Preaching Biblically.* Ed. Don M. Wardlaw. Philadelphia: Westminster Press, 1983.

_____ . "Some Comments on Race Hate." In *The Pulpit Speaks.* Ed. Alfred T. Davies. New York: Harper & Row Publishers, Inc., 1965.

_____ . *The Scarlet Thread.* Elgin: Progressive Baptist Publishing House, 1981.

_____ . "Why I Believe There Is a God." In *Why I Believe There Is a God.* Ed. Howard Thurman. Chicago: Johnson Publishing Co., 1965.

Taylor, W. M. *The Parables of Our Savior.* London: Hodder and Stoughton, 1887.

_____ . *The Scottish Pulpit: From the Reformation to the Present Day.* London: Charles Burnet & Co., 1887.

Theodorson, G. A. and A. G. Theodorson. *Modern Dictionary of Sociology.* New York: J. Y. Crowell, 1969.

Thonssen, Lester, A. Craig Baird, and Waldo W. Braden. *Speech Criticism*. Malabar: Krieger Publishing Co., 1981.

Thonssen, Lester. *Selected Readings in Rhetoric and Public Speaking*. New York: The H. W. Wilson Co., 1942.

Thurman, Howard. *With Head and Heart*. New York: Harcourt Brace Jovanovich Publishers, 1979.

Wade, Richard C. *Slavery in the Cities: The South 1820–1860*. New York: Oxford University Press, 1964.

Walker, Alice. *In Search of Our Mother's Garden*. New York: Harcourt Brace Jovanovich, 1983.

Warren, Mervyn A. *Black Preaching: Truth and Soul*. Washington D.C.: University Press of America, 1977.

Washington, James Melvin. *Frustrated Fellowship: The Black Baptist Quest for Social Power*. Macon: Mercer University Press, 1986.

Washington, Jr., Joseph R. *Black Religion*. Boston: Beacon Press, 1964.

_____ . *Black Sects and Cults*. Garden City: Doubleday & Company, 1972.

West, Cornel. *Prophesy Deliverance: An Afro–American Revolutionary Christianity*. Philadelphia: Westminster Press, 1982.

Whitehead, Alfred North. *The Aims of Education and Other Essays*. New York: The Macmillan Co., 1929.

Wilmore, Gayraud S. *Black Religion and Black Radicalism*. Maryknoll: Orbis Books, 1983.

Winterowd, W. Ross. *Rhetoric: A Synthesis*. New York: Holt, Rinehart and Winston, Inc., 1972.

Periodicals

Achtemeier, Elizabeth. "The Use of Hymnic Elements in Preaching." *Interpretation*, 34 (1985), 46–59.

Bailey, Raymond. "Proclamation as a Rhetorical Art." *Review and Expositor*, 84 (1987), 7–21.

Boyer, Horace Clarence. "Charles Albert Tindley: Progenitor of Black-American Gospel Music." *The Black Perspective in Music*, 11 (1983), 103–129.

Blackwell, John A. "Black Preaching." *The Princeton Seminary Bulletin*, 65 (July 1972), 37–42.

Carter, Lawrence E. "Black Preaching Poetry and a Text." In *Nexus*, 16 (Spring 1972–73), 13-20.

Copher, Charles B. "African Roots of Christianity: Our First Ancestors and the Biblical World." *The A.M.E. Zion Ouarterly Review*, 101 (1989), 2–8.

Cunningham, Floyd T. "Wandering in the Wilderness: Black Baptist Thought After Emancipation." *American Baptist Quarterly*, 4 (1985), 268–281.

Ehninger, Douglass. "On Systems of Rhetoric." *Philosophy and Rhetoric*, 1 (1968), 131–144.

Felton, Ralph A. "Untrained Negro Clergy." *The Christian Century*, 72 (February 2, 1955), 141–142.

"Fifteen Greatest Preachers in America." *Ebony Magazine*, 39 (September 1984), 25.

Gilkes, Cheryl Townsend. "The Role of Women in the Sanctified Church." *The Journal of Religious Thought*, 43 (Spring/Summer, 1986), 24–41.

Graham, Alfredo. "Election Satisfies Taylor." *The Courier*, September 23, 1991.

"Great Preachers." *Ebony*, July 1954, 26.

"Great Preachers." *Life Magazine*, April 6, 1953, 127.

Harris, James Henry. "Preaching Liberation: The Afro-American Sermon and the Quest for Social Change." *The Journal of Religious Thought*, 46 (Winter/Spring 1989–90), 72–89.

Hayden, J. Carleton. "Black Episcopal Preaching in the Nineteenth Century: Intellect and Will." *Journal of Religious Thought*, 39 (1982), 12–20.

Hastey, Stan. "Thomas Nomination Riles Progressive Baptist." *The Christian Century*, 108 (September 4–11, 1991, 778–779.

Haywood, Richette. "A Ministry of Equality and Hope." *Ebony*, 47 (November 1991), 103–106.

Heinze, Lee. "Charles A. Tindley—Preacher, Pastor, Hymnwriter." *Fundamentalist Journal*, 4 (1985), 40–41.

Howard-Pitney, David. "The Enduring Black Jeremiad: The American Jeremiad and Black Protest Rhetoric, From Frederick Douglass to W. E. B. DuBois, 1841–1919." *American Quarterly*, 38 (1986), 481–492.

Hughes, Robert. "The Fraying of America." *Time*, 139 (February 3, 1992), 44.

Johnstone, Ronald L. "Negro Preachers Take Sides." *Review of Religious Research*, 11 (Fall 1969), 81–89.

Kilgore, Jr., Thomas. "Preaching in the Black Church." *The Christian Ministry*, 19 (March-April 1988), 19–20.

McClain, Kathleen. "Preachers Her Role is to Cut Against Grain." *The Charlotte Observer*, (March 20, 1991), Sec. A. 1 & 6.

Mitchell, Ella P. "Oral Tradition: Legacy of Faith for the Black Church." *Religious Education*, 8 (1986), 93–112.

Muck, Terry and Paul Robbins. "The Sweet Torture of Sunday Morning, An Interview with Gardner C. Taylor." *Leadership*, 2 (Summer 1981), 17–29.

Nichols, J. Randall. "Is Homiletics a Field for Doctoral Research?" *Homiletic*, 8 (1983), 2.

O'Neale, Sondra. "Jupiter Hammon and His Works: A Discussion of the First Black Preacher to Publish Poems, Sermons, and Essays in America." *The Journal of the I.T.C.*, 9 (1982), 99–113.

Pobee, John S. "Oral Theology and Christian Oral Tradition: Challenge to Our Traditional Archival Concept." *Mission Studies*, 6 (1989), 87–93.

Poinsett, Alex. "Suffer the Little Children." *Ebony*, 43 (August 1988), 144–148.

Puckett, Newbell N. "Religious Folk-Beliefs of Whites and Negroes." *Journal of Negro History*, 16 (1931), 9–35.

Sanders, Cheryl J. "The Woman as Preacher." *The Journal of Religious Thought*, 43 (Summer/Spring, 1986), 5–23.

Southall, Geneva. "Black Composers and Religious Music." *The Black Perspective in Music*, 2 (19740, 45–50.

Spillers, Hortense J. "Martin Luther King and the Style of the Black Sermon." *The Black Scholar*, 3 (September 1971), 14–27.

Stone, Sonja H. "Oral Tradition and Spiritual Drama: The Cultural Mosaic for Black Preaching." *The Journal of the I.T.C.*, 8 (1980), 17–27.

"Religion." *Time Magazine*, 125 (December 31, 1979), 67.

Taylor, Gardner. "The Christian Drama." *The Pulpit*, 28 (1957), 10–12.

Taylor, Hycel B. "The Language of the Black Church." *Katallagete*, 6 (Summer 1976), 34–41.

Turner, Jr., William C. "The Musicality of Black Preaching: A Phenomenology." *The Journal of Black Sacred Music*, 2 (1988), 21–33.

Williams, Delores S. "The Color of Feminism: Or Speaking the Black Woman's Tongue." *The Journal of Religious Thought*, 43 (Spring/ Summer, 1986), 42–58.

Unpublished Materials

Brooks, Evelyn. "The Women's Movement in the Black Baptist Church, 1880–1920." Ph.D. dissertation, The University of Rochester, 1984.

Francis, Dan. "Carlyle Marney's Hermeneutic and Methodology for Preaching." Ph.D. dissertation, The Southern Baptist Theological Seminary, 1985.

Franklin, Marion Joseph. "The Relationship of Black Preaching to Black Gospel Music." D. Min. dissertation, Drew University, 1982.

Kennicott, Patrick C. "Negro Anti-Slavery Speakers in America. Ph.D. dissertation, Florida State University, 1967.

Pasternak, Martin Burt. "Rise Now and Fly to Arms: The Life of Henry Highland Garnet." Ph.D. dissertation, The Graduate School of the University of Massachusetts, 1981.

Peck, Catherine Louise. "Your Daughters Shall Prophesy: Women in the Afro-American Preaching Tradition." M.A. thesis, University of North Carolina, 1983.

Warren, Mervyn A. "A Rhetorical Study of the Preaching of Doctor Martin Luther King, Jr., Pastor and Pulpit Orator." Ph.D. dissertation, Michigan State University, 1966.

Lectures

Taylor, Gardner C. "A Clinical Session on Preaching." Speech delivered at The Louisville Presbyterian Theological Seminary, Louisville, KY, April 21, 1972.

_____. "The Mitchell Lectures." Speech delivered at The Eastern Baptist Theological Seminary, Philadelphia, PA, February 18, 1986.

_____. "On Recognizing and Removing the Presumptuousness of Preaching." Speech delivered at The Louisville Presbyterian Theological Seminary, Louisville, KY, April 20, 1972.

_____. "A Panel Discussion on the Definition of Preaching." Speech delivered at The Louisville Presbyterian Theological Seminary, Louisville, KY, April 22, 1972.

_____. "The Personality of the Preacher." Speech delivered at The Southern Baptist Theological Seminary, Louisville, KY, March 2, 1979.

_____. "The Preacher's Calling." Speech delivered at The McCreary Center for African American Religious Studies, Cleveland, OH, October 22, 1990.

_____. "The Preaching Function." Speech delivered at The Virginia Baptist Pastor's School, Richmond, VA, July 10, 1986.

Nonprint Sources

Belle, Cyprian and Anna. Telephone conversation with author. December 7, 1991.

Butts, Calvin. Telephone conversation with author. November 14, 1991.

Haley, Daniel. Telephone conversation with author. January 11, 1992.

Harris, Ruby Taylor. Telephone conversation with author. January 9, 1992.

Kendal, Mary. Telephone conversation with author. April 13, 1991

McKinney, Samuel. Telephone conversation with author. November 17,1991.

Mitchell, Henry. Telephone conversation with author. August 15, 1991.

Noble, Theresa. Telephone conversation with author. April 13, 1991.

Reid, Frank. Telephone conversation with author. November 23, 1991.

Saucer, Bobby Joe. Telephone conversation with author. January 5, 1992.

Simmons, Dr. C. D. Telephone conversation with author. December 23, 1991.

Skinner, Johnnie. Telephone conversation with author. November 23, 1991.

Stewart, Carl. Telephone conversation with author. March 30, 1991.

Stewart, Herman. Telephone conversation with author. October 19, 1991.

Taylor, Gardner C. Interview with author. Brooklyn, NY. March 21, 1991.

_____. Telephone conversation with author. September 19, 1991.

_____. Telephone conversation with author. November 19, 1991.

_____. Telephone conversation with author. July 28, 1993.

Taylor, Laura Scott. Telephone conversation with author. September 20, 1991.

Taylor, Phyllis S. Telephone conversation with author. March 31, 1999.

Wheeler, Edward. Telephone conversation with author. November 15, 1991.

Videocassettes

A Dedication of the Benjamin E. Mays Hall and The Howard Thurman Chapel. Presented by Dr. Gardner Taylor. Produced by Howard University Divinity School. Washington, D. C.: Howard University, 1987.

Inaugural Interfaith Prayer Service. Presented by Dr. Gardner C. Taylor. Produced by Purdue University Public Affairs Video Archives. Purdue: C–Span, 1993.

The Preacher's Reply to the Human Cry. Presented by Dr. Gardner Taylor. Produced by the Bethel African Methodist Church. Baltimore: Bethel AME, 1991.

Martin Luther King, Jr. Memorial Studies in Religion, Culture, and Social Development

Mozella G. Mitchell, General Editor

This series is named for Martin Luther King Jr., because of his superb scholarship and eminence in religion and society, and is designed to promote excellence in scholarly research and writing in areas that reflect the interrelatedness of religion and social/cultural/political development both in American society and in the world. Examination of and elaboration on religion and sociocultural components such as race relations, economic developments, marital and sexual relations, inter-ethnic cooperation, contemporary political problems, women, Black American, Native America, and Third World issues, and the like are welcomed. Manuscripts must be equal to a 200 to 425 page book and are to be submitted in duplicate.

For additional information about this series or for the submission of manuscripts, please contact:

Peter Lang Publishing, Inc.
Acquisitions Department
275 Seventh Avenue, 28th floor
New York, New York 10001

To order other books in this series, please contact our Customer Service Department:

800-770-LANG (within the U.S.)
(212) 647-7706 (outside the U.S.)
(212) 647-7707 FAX

Or browse online by series at:

www.peterlang.com